The New Comparative Theology

The New Comparative Theology

*Interreligious Insights from
the Next Generation*

Edited by

FRANCIS X. CLOONEY, SJ

t&t clark

Published by T&T Clark International
A Continuum imprint
The Tower Building, 11 York Road, London SE1 7NX
80 Maiden Lane, Suite 704, New York NY 10038

www.continuumbooks.com

First published 2010

British Library Cataloguing-in-Publication Data
A catalogue record for this book is available from the British Library.

ISBN 13: 9780567310484 (hardback)
9780567141378 (paperback)

Designed and typeset by Kenneth Burnley, Wirral, Cheshire
Printed in the United States of America

CONTENTS

PREFACE

James Fredericks has written a very fine Introduction to this volume of essays by younger scholars in the field of the new comparative theology, and I need not add further words of explanation here. But as editor, I would like to express my appreciation and gratitude for all that follows. From the initial 2007 panel at the American Academy of Religion Annual Meeting in San Diego to the gathering of those who would contribute to this volume and the several drafts of each essay, the process has been positive and collegial. In a commendable commitment to collaborative practice, all the contributors read and commented on each other's work, and likewise read and critiqued the Introduction by James Fredericks and the Response by me. My only regret is that the necessary limits of such a volume have meant that other fine younger comparativists could not be invited to contribute their own new and fruitful insights into comparative theology. I would like also to thank in a particular way Lee F. Spriggs, recently graduated from the Harvard Divinity School, for his most capable and painstaking work in taking our disparate efforts, putting them in order, and thus making it possible for this volume to move quickly toward publication.

Francis X. Clooney, SJ
Cambridge, MA

Introduction

JAMES L. FREDERICKS

All journeys have secret destinations of which the traveler is unaware.
(Martin Buber)

Christians now live in a time when looking on the plurality of faiths as a sub-
sidiary problem for their theology and practice is no longer possible. To be sure,
sweeping statements about the present as the dawn of a 'new era' or calls for
'new paradigms' for understanding 'the current crisis' are not only tiresome;
they are usually misleading. The increased proximity of religious communities
to one another and their de-territorialization as cultural systems, however,
cannot be ignored. Christians, and everybody else for that matter, have only
begun to discern the import of the end of the colonial system, the rise of new
forms of trans-national capitalism and the transformations being wrought by
global communication and transportation technologies. Therefore, anyone who
would try to think theologically about the diversity of religions today would
do well to keep Buber's aphorism in mind. This includes those, like Francis
Clooney and me, who would presume to give advice as to how theology should
be done today. Starting in the later 1980s, Frank and I began to suggest a way in
which we might rethink faith by means of a critical reflection on the texts and
practices of other religious paths. Comparative theology, as we have proposed it,
entails the interpretation of the meaning and truth of one's own faith by means
of a critical investigation of other faiths.

The initial impetus for this volume came from a discussion within the Comparative Theology Group at the 2007 meeting of the American Academy of
Religion. Michelle Voss Roberts, Tracy Tiemeier, Kristin Beise Kiblinger and
Hugh Nicholson, all of whom have essays in this volume, presented their
concerns about the problem of hegemony in comparative theology. Frank
Clooney responded. In their presentation, these comparative theologians
showed how what we are calling 'the new comparative theology' needs to be
situated within the past history of Christianity's dealings with other religious

paths, a history that leads to a sobering recognition of Christian theology's willingness to implicate itself with western imperialism and its Orientalist discourses. This history includes traditional forms of Christian apologetics, Christian fulfillment theologies and proposals for 'pluralist' theologies of religions. Comparative theologians should not be sanguine about being immune from the problem of hegemony. After the 2007 AAR meeting, Frank invited Bagus Laksana, David Clairmont, Daniel Joslyn-Semiatkoski, Jeffery Long, and John Sheveland to expand the discussion.

The essays in this volume provide an opportunity to sample the work of scholars who are taking comparative theology in many different directions. I am happy to say that these essays prove that Buber was right – they are furrowed with trails leading to destinations about which Frank and I were unaware when we began our reflections some twenty years ago. No doubt there are more destinations to be discovered that remain a secret to us all. In any event, Frank and I are grateful for these essays and the new destinations to be discovered in them. I want to offer some introductory comments on each of the essays in this volume. Before doing so, a few thoughts about comparative theology as Frank Clooney and I have proposed it may provide a helpful trail-head for the journeys to come.

The vexations and enticements of religious diversity are certainly nothing new to Christianity. Neither is the term 'comparative theology', whose roots go back to the eighteenth and nineteenth centuries.[1] David Tracy notes that 'comparative theology' is used in two different ways today. First, the term refers to the comparison of the doctrinal systems of two or more religious traditions. This is a non-theological (non-confessional) enterprise that is part of the general academic study of religion.[2] Tracy also outlines a use of this term that is both more precise and more widely used today. Comparative theology is a confessional discipline where one religious tradition (usually but not necessarily a 'home tradition') is critically correlated with another religion.[3]

Frank Clooney and I have proposed a procedure for doing theology comparatively that constricts Tracy's second definition somewhat. Comparative theology is not only a revisionist but also a constructive project in which theologians interpret the meaning and truth of one tradition by making critical

---

1 For a discussion of the history of this term, see Francis X. Clooney, SJ, 'Comparative Theology', in John Webster, Kathryn Tanner and Iain Torrence (eds), *The Oxford Handbook to Systematic Theology* (Oxford: Oxford University Press, 2007), 653–69. See also, David Tracy, 'Comparative Theology', in *The Encyclopedia of Religions*, Lindsay Jones (ed.), Vol. 13 (2nd edn) (Detroit: Macmillan Reference USA, 2005), 9125–34; and Tomoko Masuzawa, *The Invention of World Religions* (Chicago: University of Chicago Press, 2005).
2 See for example, Keith Ward, *Religion and Revelation* (Oxford: Oxford University Press, 1994), 40; and Robert Neville and Wesley J. Wildman, 'On Comparing Religious Ideas', in Robert Cummings Neville (ed.), *The Human Condition: A Volume in the Comparative Religious Ideas Project* (Albany: State University of New York Press, 2001), 9–20.
3 Tracy, 'Comparative Theology', 9126; Hugh Nicholson, 'A Correlational Model of Comparative Theology', in *Journal of Religion* (85:2, 2005), 191–213.

correlations with the classics of another religious tradition. Generally, as Tracy noted, comparative theology will be a confessional enterprise.[4] A number of observations can be made about this proposal for comparative theology.

First, comparative theology proceeds dialectically. Comparison begins with the critical study of another religion, sometimes by means of the reading of classic texts, sometimes by means of personal dialogue with the practitioners of the other religious paths, and optimally by taking both routes.[5] The conversation with the other tradition eventually becomes a conversation within the home tradition in which its classic texts, art, rituals, ascetic practices, etc. are reinterpreted in light of the study of the other tradition. The critical correlations established in the work of comparison can be positive or negative – sometimes the correlation will be a recognition of similarity, sometimes of difference. Both similarity and difference are of theological significance to the comparative theologian. I have tended to emphasize the theological interest of difference in my work. This emphasis is warranted by the need to resist theories of religion that marginalize difference and reduce religions to 'more of the same'.[6] Of course, theories of religion which privilege difference by contending that religions are incommensurate need to be resisted as well.

Second, comparative theology highlights the fact that thinking interreligiously is an intrinsic aspect of the theological enterprise itself (at least for Christian theology), not a supplementary reflection that can be consigned to an appendix of systematics. Frank Clooney makes this point as follows: 'Comparison and the appropriation of the new and different now take place *within* Christian theology, *while* it is being formulated, *not* as an appendage or corollary to an already fully formed theology.'[7] Doing theology comparatively, therefore, means that the correlation of Christian doctrines and

---

4 See, inter alia, Francis X. Clooney, SJ, *Hindu God, Christian God: How Reason Helps to Break Down the Boundaries Between Religions* (Oxford: Oxford University Press, 2001), 10–11; and James L. Fredericks, *Buddhists and Christians: Through Comparative Theology to Solidarity* (Maryknoll, NY: Orbis Books, 2004), 96–9.

5 Frank Clooney has emphasized the importance of the 'patient reading' of texts. See Francis X. Clooney, SJ, *Theology after Vedanta: An Experiment in Comparative Theology* (Albany: State University of New York Press, 1993), 153–6, 163–4; and *Hindu God, Christian God*, 10. In my work, I have given more emphasis to inter-personal character of dialogue and what I have called 'interreligious friendships'. See James L. Fredericks, 'Interreligious Friendship: A New Theological Virtue', in *Journal of Ecumenical Studies* (35:2, Spring 1998), 159–74; and 'Abe Masao: A Friendship', in *Spiritus* 3 (2003), 237–48.

6 Perhaps my emphasis is also attributable to the fact that I work with Buddhists who highlight the non-theistic aspects of their tradition, instead of with Muslims or Hindus who emphasize theism. More inquiry into how the choice of a dialogue partner is leading to different emphases in our understanding of comparative theology would be welcome.

7 Francis X. Clooney, SJ, 'The Study of Non-Christian Religions in the Post-Vatican II Church', in *Journal of Ecumenical Studies* (28:3, 1991), 488. Italics in the original. See also Francis X. Clooney, SJ, 'Neither Here Nor There: Crossing Boundaries, Becoming Insiders, Remaining Catholic', in Jose Cabezon and Sheila Davaney (eds), *Identity and Politics of Identity in Scholarship in the Study of Religion* (New York: Routledge, 2004), 99–111.

practices with those of other religious traditions must be located at the center of the Christian theological *querens* itself.

Third, the problems of interpretation raised by comparison cannot be restricted to the soteriological questions that tend to dominate theologies of religions. Comparative theology addresses every aspect of the home tradition's doctrine and practice. Doing theology comparatively, therefore, is theology in the broadest sense of the word: the intellectually rigorous interpretation of the classic texts, doctrines and practices of one tradition in its entirety. Comparative theology certainly does not exclude a robust apologetics. A proper apologetics, however, does not render certain theological affirmations immune from the need to be revised by means of comparison with the affirmations of another tradition.

Fourth, comparative theology relies on limited experiments in comparison instead of theories about 'religious experience' or religion in general that seek to provide a foundation for comparison. In Frank Clooney's view,

> The more specific a comparison, the better; the more particular a Christian effort to understand a non-Christian text or practice, the better; the more we attend to learning about particular things and ideas that were previously 'other' to us, the better; and the more we write from within this expanded realm of knowledge, and not simply about it, the better.[8]

In varying degrees, this preference for specific, limited exercises in comparison is shared by theologians as diverse as John Berthrong, David Burrell, Catherine Cornille, Thomas Cattoi, Peter Feldmeier, John Keenan, Leo Lefebure, Michael Meyers, and Pim Valkenberg.[9]

The correlational character of comparative theology implies that it is a hermeneutical project in addition to being a constructive enterprise. The comparative theologian constructs correlations by maintaining a commitment to a home tradition and to what Frank Clooney has called a 'vulnerability' to the truth of another religious tradition.[10] Comparative theology requires a sophisticated

---

8 Clooney, 'The Study of Non-Christian Religions', 489–90.

9 John Berthrong, *All Under Heaven: Transforming Paradigms in Confucian–Christian Dialogue* (Albany: SUNY Press, 1994); David Burrell, *Freedom and Creation in Three Traditions* (Notre Dame: University of Notre Dame Press, 1993); Catherine Cornille, *The Guru in Indian Catholicism: Ambiguity or Opportunity of Inculturation?* (Louvain: Peeters Press, 1991); Thomas Cattoi, *Divine Contingency: Theologies of Divine Embodiment in Maximos the Confessor and Tsong kha pa* (Piscataway, NJ: Gorgias Press, 2008); Peter Feldmeier, *Christianity Looks East: Comparing the Spiritualities of John of the Cross and Buddhaghosa* (New York: Paulist Press, 2006); John Keenan, *The Meaning of Christ – A Mahayana Christology* (Maryknoll, NY: Orbis Books, 1989); Leo Lefebure, *The Buddha and the Christ: Explorations in Buddhist and Christian Dialogue* (Maryknoll, NY: Orbis Books, 1993); Michael Meyers, *Brahman: Systematic Theology from a Comparative Perspective* (Richmond, UK: Curzon, 2000); John Thatamanil, *The Immanent Divine: God, Creation and the Human Predicament* (Minneapolis: Fortress, 2006); Pim Valkenberg, *Sharing Lights on the Way to God: Muslim–Christian Dialogue and Theology in the Context of Abrahamic Partnership* (New York: Editions Rodopi, 2006).

10 Francis X. Clooney, SJ, *Theology After Vedanta* (Albany, NY: SUNY Press, 1993), 4–6; James L. Fredericks, *Faith among Faiths* (Mahwah, NJ: Paulist Press, 1999), 169–71.

hermeneutics in that both poles of this tension require interpretation. First, there is the need to understand the Other in a way that does not annul the Other's alterity. This problem, enormous in itself, is but a preliminary step leading to the reinterpretation of the home tradition. And since the work of comparison usually leads to a heightened appreciation of the ambiguity and poly-vocality of the home tradition, the comparative theologian's need for hermeneutics cannot be over-emphasized. However daunting these challenges may be, doing theology comparatively requires us to resist the temptation to escape the tension of rooted-ness and vulnerability. Loss of commitment to the home tradition may make the work of comparison no longer theological. This opens up the question of how comparative theology is related to comparative religion and religious studies. By contrast, the loss of the allure of the Other leads us to the question of the relation-ship of comparative theology to the theology of religions. I want to offer brief comments on both of these issues.

No current construal of the relationship between comparative theology and comparative religion is entirely satisfactory. This is because the term 'compara-tive theology' continues to be used in various ways. For example, David Tracy, in keeping with his view that theology in general be included in 'religious studies', thinks that comparative theology should be considered a sub-discipline within comparative religion.[11] Tracy's proposal begs the question of how com-parative religion itself is to be defined.[12] In the interest of a better understanding of comparative procedure carried out theologically, I will define comparative religion as a discipline located within the secular study of religions. Comparative religion holds up for itself the scholarly ideal of detached inquiry and seeks, as its primary public, the academic community of scholars. In contrast, comparative theology does not proceed from a religiously neutral starting point (however elusive this neutrality may be to begin with). Comparative theology understands itself as a procedure which is normative, constructive, and revisionist, and which is often done by believers for the benefit of believers, even as it includes the academy of scholars as a public to be addressed as well. Unlike comparative religion, comparative theology entails a 'faith seeking understanding' (*fides quaerens intellectum*). However, I do not think it wise to draw too sharp a distinc-tion between these two disciplines. The comparative theologian, perhaps more than any other theologian, should be interested in the methods of comparison and the findings of the non-theological study of religion.[13]

Comparative theology should also be distinguished from the theology of religions. By 'theology of religions', I mean the attempt to understand the

11 Tracy, 'Comparative Theology', 9126.
12 Tomoko Masuzawa, 'The Legacy of Comparative Theology', in *The Invention of World Reli-gions: Or, How European Universalism was Preserved in the Language of Pluralism* (Chicago: University of Chicago Press, 2005), 72–104.
13 Clooney, 'Comparative Theology', 664; and *Theology after Vedanta*, 4–6; Fredericks, *Buddhists and Christians*, 97–8.

theological meaning of the diversity of religions in keeping with the doctrinal requirements of a home tradition. This enterprise is not exclusively a Christian preoccupation and the comparison of these theologies itself is of interest.[14] Very often, the primary interest of theologies of religions is soteriological: can the one who does not follow my path be 'saved'? Generally, theologies of religions are not based on detailed studies of the specific teachings of the other religious traditions. They depend instead on meta-religious theories of religion or concern themselves with the doctrinal requirements of the home tradition.[15]

For the time being, at least, I maintain that Christian comparative theology should be seen as an alternative to the theology of religions. I recommend this because theologies of religions are not adequate to the purposes and practices of comparative theology as I envision it. This is the most controversial position I have taken in my proposals for doing theology comparatively.[16] Given the prescriptive (or should I say 'proscriptive'?) nature of my proposal, I want to restrict my argument about the theology of religions to Christian theology.

There are several reasons for concluding that comparative theology should be taken up as an alternative to the theology of religions. First, for most Christian theologies of religions, comparative procedures that require the careful and detailed study of other religious traditions have generally been secondary to the construction of comprehensive theological interpretations of other religions. Comparative theology seeks to resist this. A comprehensive Christian theological understanding of religious diversity, as David Tracy argues, should come only after detailed studies of other religions. This project has barely begun to have an impact on Christian theology.[17]

Second, none of the candidates for a Christian theology of religions is adequate to the hermeneutical requirements of doing theology comparatively. Interpreting the religious classics of other traditions in keeping with the doctrinal demands of Christian faith usually leads to systemic distortions in the reception of the Other. Moreover, these distortions succeed in what I have called the 'domestication of difference', in which the threat of the Other, as well as its transformative power, are muted.[18]

---

14 See Jeffery Long's essay in this volume and Kristin Beise Kiblinger, *Buddhist Inclusivism: Attitudes Towards Religious Others* (Aldershot, England and Burlington, VT: Ashgate, 2005).

15 For a dependable and insightful summary of the various positions, see Paul F. Knitter, *Introducing Theologies of Religions* (Maryknoll, NY: Orbis Books, 2002).

16 See Fredericks, *Faith among Faiths,* 163–8; and *Buddhists and Christians*, 198–202, 110–12. Frank Clooney takes a position that is similar to mine; see Clooney, SJ, *Oxford Handbook*, 666; *Theology after Vedanta*, 6–7, 193–6; and 'The Study of Non-Christian Religions in the Post-Vatican II Church', 489. In addition, see Klaus von Stosch, 'Komparative Theologie – ein Ausweg aus dem Grunddilemma jeder Theologie der Religionen?', in *Zeitschrift für Katholische Theologie* (124, 2002), 294–311; and Norbert Hintersteiner, *Traditionen überschreiten: Angloamerikanische Beiträgen zur interkulturellen Traditioneshermeneutik* (Wein, 2001), 318–20. For criticisms of my position, see footnote #10 of Kristen Beise Kiblinger's essay in this volume.

17 Tracy, 'Comparative Theology', 9127.

18 For a perspective on the hermeneutical importance of difference incorporating feminist discussions, see Michelle Voss Roberts, *Dualities: A Theology of Difference* (Westminster: John Knox Press, 2010).

Third, preoccupation with a theology of religions is not helpful in supporting Christians in their need to respond to the pluralism of religions not only with fidelity to their own tradition, but also with creativity in embracing the Other. I make this claim even as I admit that I am a Christian inclusivist. Among various candidates for a theology of religions, the inclusivist (or fulfillment) theology model is the most adequate to the demands of Christian faith. However, the apriorism of theologies of religion can function ideologically by protecting Christians from the necessity of changing their minds, at least about theologically significant matters, in response to the encounter with the Other. Moreover, the continued emphasis on a theology of religions hobbles interreligious dialogue by allowing Christians to continue to talk to themselves and place in abeyance the need to engage in and be engaged by the bewildering fact of religious diversity today.

Fourth, in the past, Christian theologies of religions have not been sufficiently attentive to the hegemony of their discourse. When theologies of religions function as a template for doing theology comparatively, the comparative theologian is placed in the unhappy position of knowing more about other believers than they know about themselves. Comparative theology, more so than theologies of religion, is able to be attentive to what Jean-Francois Lyotard famously called 'the postmodern condition' – the crises of grand narratives brought about by the growing proximity of all the grand narratives to one another. Religious or philosophical theories about the ultimate unity of all religions notwithstanding, this postmodern condition is where we all find ourselves in beginning to think theologically about ourselves and our world.[19]

Of course, all of the above is but the starting-point for a new generation of theologians who are doing theology comparatively, not their final destination. The theologians who have contributed essays to this volume have their own exciting ideas about what kind of map those who do theology comparatively should be using to find their way. The essays are noteworthy for the immense diversity of their concerns. As a group, the essays are confrontational and sagacious, discerning but also inventive. Tracy Tiemeier, toward the end of her essay in this volume, makes an astute observation: the discipline of comparative theology, at least as Frank and I have proposed it, is still quite young. If these essays are any indication, the discipline is growing up fast. The comparative theologians who have contributed to this volume are eager to take us to destinations as diverse as missiology and musicology.

Above, I claimed that comparative theology was defined by a tension established by fidelity to a home tradition and vulnerability to the Other. Bagus Laksana provides a new voice in comparative theology that helps us to see how

---

19 For my views on these four points, see Fredericks, *Faith among Faiths*, 103–18, 162–86; and *Buddhists and Christians*, 1–29, 96–115. See also, 'A Universal Religious Experience?', in *Horizons, Journal of the College Theology Society* (22:1, Spring 1995), 67–87; and James Heft (ed.), 'Off the Map: Roman Catholicism and the Dialogue with Buddhism' (forthcoming, 2010).

this tension asserts itself in both a global and a local context. Laksana does theology comparatively for his Christian community in Indonesia. His essay, 'Comparative Theology: Between Identity and Alterity', explores the tension of fidelity and vulnerability by recommending pilgrimage as a metaphor for how to maintain that tension. He takes as a model Ali ibn Abi Bakr al-Harawi, a thirteenth-century Syrian Muslim whose life was spent crossing the borders separating the three Abrahamic monotheisms. For al-Harawi, pilgrimage was never simply an act of piety, safely encircled by the boundaries of his own religious community. Pilgrimage was 'a privileged locus' for the 'creative negotiation of religious identity' by means of intimacy with the Other. Laksana offers al-Harawi's willingness to make pilgrimages as a model for comparative theologians as they try to find ways of resisting the temptation of reducing the Other to more of the same and externalizing the Other as insurmountable difference.

Kristin Beise Kiblinger's 'Relating Theology of Religions and Comparative Theology' offers a critique of the role that the theology of religions should play in doing theology comparatively. Kiblinger recognizes the weaknesses of inclusivism and pluralism, but draws our attention to alternative forms of these theologies that have been proposed by Paul Knitter, Schubert Ogden, Paul Griffiths, S. Mark Heim and herself. When comparative theology is construed as an alternative to the theology of religions, comparativists can be naïve about the presuppositions they have about other religions – presuppositions that shape their comparisons. Most challenging, for me at least, is her claim that even theologians who call for placing more emphasis on actual experiments in comparison have subconsciously adopted some version of these newer forms of inclusivism and pluralism.

Hugh Nicholson's essay, 'The New Comparative Theology and the Problem of Theological Hegemonism', takes Kiblinger's concerns to a very different destination. Nicholson agrees with my judgement that the debate about theologies of religions has reached an impasse and that we need to turn to comparative theology as an alternative. But where Kiblinger argues that the sharp separation of comparative theology and the theology of religions fails to take into account more recent developments in thinking about inclusivism and pluralism, Nicholson argues that separating the two promotes 'the comforting illusion' that the problem of hegemonism can be solved by renouncing our attachments to theologies of religions. In Nicholson's view, comparative theology, as it has been proposed by Frank Clooney and myself, is but the latest development in Liberal Theology's effort to transcend 'the political', which Nicholson understands as the inevitably antagonistic and exclusivist dimension of inter-faith relations.

David Clairmont's essay, 'On Hegemonies Within: Franciscan Missions and Buddhist Kings in Comparative Theological Contexts', takes Nicholson's concern about hegemonism in a decidedly unexpected direction. Clairmont documents the way in which hegemonies are at work not only between religious communities, but within them as well. As an example of these 'hegemonies within', he takes us to sixteenth-century Sri Lanka and the struggles of

Franciscan missionaries, whose encounter with Buddhism was complicated by the ambiguities of Christian theology and the politics of Portuguese colonialism. Playing off what Michelle Voss Roberts (citing Patricia Hill Collins)[20] calls 'outsiders within', Clairmont shows how the Franciscans became 'insiders without'. Reflecting on this example, he argues that comparative theologians need to reflect on specific historical encounters between faiths and to appreciate the conflicts – theological, political, and ethical – engendered by such encounters. The missionary efforts by the Franciscans in Sri Lanka show that an encounter with another religious community not only poses new theological challenges for understanding one's own faith, but also confronts us with the contradictions and ambiguities that are endemic to the home tradition. In this way, comparative theologians need not only to hear the voice of the Other, as Laksana argues in his essay, but also the voice of those marginalized by 'hegemonies within' their own tradition.

Hugh Nicholson calls us to recognize the inevitability of antagonism among religious communities and the ethical responsibilities of comparative theologians to do their work aware of these antagonisms. Daniel Joslyn-Siemiatkoski's essay, 'Comparative Theology and the Status of Judaism: Hegemony and Reversals', provides us with a concrete example of how comparative theologians have succeeded in skirting this very issue.[21] Joslyn-Siemiatkoski argues that, for comparative theology, Judaism has been a 'submerged tradition', cast either as merely another 'world religion' (heedless of its historical and theological relationship with Christianity) or studied only in terms of its scriptures (the 'Old Testament' and heedless of the post-scriptural Rabbinic heritage of Jews). In his essay, Joslyn-Siemiatkoski goes far beyond the widely acknowledged demand that Christians renounce their supersessionist theologies of Judaism. He wants us to rethink basic Christian doctrines in light of this renunciation and he holds up comparative theology as a way to accomplish this task. Moreover, his essay includes a concrete example of this revision of Christian understanding by providing a reflection on the Pauline critique of the Law (and Augustinian/Lutheran theologies of grace versus works) by means of a close reading of the Mishnah *Avot* and its discussion of Torah.

Michelle Voss Roberts' essay, 'Gendering Comparative Theology', demonstrates how comparative theology and feminist thought can be both a blessing and a challenge to one another. In doing so, she makes a significant contribution to our understanding of hegemonic discourse and its impact on comparative theology. Instead of theories of religion in general, comparative theologians study the specific truth claims of those who are 'insiders' to a tradition. But this has unintended and undesirable consequences because women and other marginalized people often remain 'outsiders within' the tradition. This problem is

---

20 See below, p. 110.
21 The same may be said for Daniel Joslyn-Siemiatkoski's *Christian Memories of the Maccabean Martyrs* (New York: Palgrave Macmillan, 2009).

compounded by the fact that the hagiographies of women are often written by men in a way that legitimizes an androcentric construction of the tradition. Comparativists need to recognize that women's voices do not represent 'the tradition' as their male hagiographers construct it. Women speak as 'outsiders within' their traditions in a way that requires and also empowers us to rethink traditions. To make her point, she compares the lives of two women, Mechthild of Magdeburg, a Christian contemplative, and Lalleswari, a Saivite poet-saint.

Up until now, comparative theology has been dominated, for the most part, by the concern of theologians who are North American or European, Christian and male. In the next generation, new voices will make the conversation considerably more complicated. Tracy Tiemeier's essay, 'Comparative Theology as a Theology of Liberation', aims to shape the way we do theology comparatively by getting comparative theologians to sit down and learn from Asian and Asian American theologians. In pursuing this goal, she singles out Aloysius Pieris, Peter Phan, and Sathianathan Clarke as conversation partners to show how, for Asian and Asian American theology, questions of culture and interreligious living are inseparable from questions of justice. Asian and Asian American theology will help to change the subject from western concerns with historical and systematic issues to the theme of liberation.[22] This shift provides a basis for her to critique the AAR comparative theology group's definition of the discipline. Tiemeier expects this dialogue to bring us to a revision not only of what it means to do theology, but what it means to work for liberation as well. To take a concrete step in this direction, she offers a reflection on Antal, a Hindu saint in the Srivaisnava tradition, as a way for Christians to raise questions about the embodiment of liberation.

Jeffery Long's essay, '(Tentatively) Putting the Pieces Together: Comparative Theology in the Tradition of Sri Ramakrishna', intersects with the stance Kristin Beise Kiblinger takes *vis-à-vis* the theology of religions in several ways. He is in agreement with her in holding that the theology of religions and comparative theology are not, in practice, separable. And significantly, he wants to alert his own tradition (the neo-Vedanta of Sri Ramakrishna) to the need for what he calls (citing Kiblinger) an 'open inclusivism'. This means that the pieces of the jigsaw puzzle of religions can only be put together 'tentatively', as he says in his title. In this respect, the essay can also be taken as a response to Kiblinger's call for constructing theologies of religion in dialogue with other traditions. Long carefully (and even courageously) chooses to revise the Sri Ramakrishna community's strongly held pluralist theology, a teaching central to the tradition, by constructing critical correlations with process thought and Jain theology.

---

22 See also, Tracy Sayuki Tiemeier, 'Retrieving "Asian Spirituality" in North American Contexts: An Interfaith Proposal', in *Spiritus: A Journal of Christian Spirituality* (6:2, Fall 2006), 228–33.

John Sheveland's essay, 'Solidarity through Polyphony', also brings us back to the question of a theology of religions in a new way. He proposes that 'polyphony', the musical form that arose in European music after plainchant, be used as a model for comparative theology. Polyphony provides for a unity-in-distinction of voices which produces 'a polyphonic whole more beautiful than the sum of its parts'. Moreover, the contrapuntal relation of the voices brings out a beauty in each voice that could not be heard in the voice apart from the polyphony. His goal is to move away from judgement of others (inherent in many theologies of religions) towards an 'aesthetic understanding' of religions which emerges in the polyphony the theologian creates in the work of comparison. The goal of this theological aesthetics is to promote a solidarity among religions based in the 'principle of non-competition' inherent in polyphonic form. A concern for the ethical import of doing theology comparatively is never far from Sheveland's reflections. In an approach quite different from my own, he argues that 'rival truth claims may be of interest in the distant future, but only after the laborious work of comparison, i.e., careful listening, takes place'. Therefore, 'the prospects for interreligious learning and conflict resolution are encouraging'.

Writing almost twenty years ago, Frank Clooney predicted that the divide between those who seek to construct general theories about 'religion' and those who proceed with limited experiments in comparison will dominate the theological debate over the next generation.[23] This prediction has proven correct, even though, in keeping with Buber's aphorism, the journey has taken us to destinations of which neither Frank nor I were aware when we began this trek. Buber was right: all journeys, or at least the really important journeys, are full of surprises and delights. Frank and I have been delighted with the journey so far. We believe these essays demonstrate that doing theology comparatively is a journey whose secret destinations have only begun to show up on the horizon.

---

23 Francis X. Clooney, SJ, 'The Study of Non-Christian Religions in the Post-Vatican II Church', in *Journal of Ecumenical Studies* (28:3, 1991), 483.

1

Comparative Theology: Between Identity and Alterity

A. BAGUS LAKSANA

Introduction

I roam the lands east and west; to many a wanderer and hermit was I a companion. I saw every strange and marvelous wonder, and experienced terror in comfort and misery. I have to come to be buried alone beneath the earth; I hope that my Lord will be my companion.[1]

These are the words written on the cenotaph of the tomb of Ali ibn Abi Bakr al-Harawi (d. 611 H/AD 1215), a curious and avid Muslim pilgrim who lived mostly in Syria, serving various Muslim rulers during the tumultuous years of the Crusades, including Saladin (r. 564 H/AD 1169–589 H/AD 1193) and his son, al-Malik al-Zahir Ghazi, the ruler of Aleppo. On the surface, these words might seem either too self-referential or too pious, but what might be much more interesting is what lies behind them. For al-Harawi, the 'strange and marvelous wonder' would not have been limited to Muslim cities and shrines, but also Jewish and Christian ones, for he visited many of them and treated them with deep respect. And the 'wanderer and hermit' to whom he was a companion might have included some Christian monks and pilgrims. As a Muslim servant of the Ayyubid rulers, he rejoiced at the chance of meeting with Byzantine Emperor Emmanuel Comnenos (r. 1143–80) and of imbibing the sacredness of Hagia Sophia. In the context of the tensions, not to mention a heightened sense of hostility between 'Muslims' and 'Christians' during the Crusades, it is indeed rather strange to find a personality like al-Harawi whose life was defined by a border crossing between the three Abrahamic religious worlds.[2] Obviously, he

---

1 Josef W. Meri's introduction to al-Harawi's *Kitab al-Isharat ila Ma'rifat al-Ziyarat* (*A Lonely Wayfarer's Guide to Pilgrimage*) (Princeton, NJ: Darwin Press, Inc., 2004), xxv.
2 Al-Harawi's personal life journey was also marked by border crossing: belonging to a family that originally came from Herat, he was born in Mosul, Iraq; after briefly serving the Abbasid caliph in

embodied a rare spirit of fostering an authentic religio-cultural identity that to a certain degree was marked by a constant act of including and communing with the other, rather than excluding the other, a strategy that was more common during his time. This was a pious Muslim who, even while serving Saladin, never hesitated to testify about the presence of saintly and righteous people among the 'Frankish' in Jerusalem, at a time when anything 'Frankish' would have represented the reality of demonic force for most of his fellow Muslims.[3]

So, if we may ask, what enabled al-Harawi to foster this attitude throughout his life? For his ability to negotiate his strong identity as a Muslim in a constant and rather intimate encounter with the other is rather unusual. I surmise that his passion for doing pilgrimage must have played an important part. For al-Harawi and his like-minded pilgrims, pilgrimage was never just an act of piety fully enclosed in the confines of a particular religious tradition. Instead, it was often a sustained encounter with the 'strange and marvelous wonders' of the other and Other, made possible by the audacity of the pilgrims themselves to cross the borders, be they religious, cultural or political.[4] As shown in the life and work of al-Harawi, pilgrimage has become a privileged locus in which a creative negotiation of religious identity in the proximity and intimacy with God, the Other, as well as with the religious other, occurs in all its complexity.[5]

Shifting our attention to our own world, the persistence of the challenge of encountering alterity that al-Harawi and his contemporaries had faced is stubbornly noticeable, if not made much more complex due to what had happened in the tumultuous centuries in between. The Crusades are certainly no longer the norm of the day, but our age has yet to overcome the many barriers that we have come to put in place precisely at the decisive junctures where we have to encounter the other. In our era, dealing with the specter of hegemony against the other becomes much trickier precisely because it is so real, complex and

---

Baghdad, he settled in Aleppo, Syria, working for various Ayyubid rulers, while doing an enormous amount of travels in the Near East, North Africa, Byzantium, and Mediterranean islands. He was buried in Aleppo. Besides being an avid pilgrim, al-Harawi was also an ascetic, preacher, counselor and emissary, as well as scholar and poet.

3 Amin Maalouf, *The Crusades through Arab Eyes* (New York: Schocken Books, 1984).

4 In the case of al-Harawi, both his passion for pilgrimage as well as his role as the emissary of Muslim rulers were marked by reaching out to the other. As a Muslim pilgrim, he visited Jewish and Christian sites, while as the emissary of various rulers, he worked for the rapprochement between the Caliph and the Ayyubids, between the Crusaders and the Ayyubids, and so forth. He was appointed a preacher of the congregational mosque in Baghdad by the Abbasid Caliph al-Nasir li-Din Allah (r. 575 H/1180 AD–622/1225), whose rule was marked by the rapprochement between the Sunnis and the Shiites. As a Sunni, he never hesitated in showing his deep respect for 'Ali, so much so that others might have seen him as a crypto-Shiite.

5 By stating this, I certainly do not view all forms of pilgrimage as belonging to this category. In some cases, pilgrimage can become narrow and exclusive, used as a sign of forging a distinct identity at the expense of the other. Even during al-Harawi's time, pilgrimage of this sort existed. The Crusaders were sometimes called 'soldiers-pilgrims'. In fact, part of their motivation was to regain the exclusive possession of the Holy Sites in Jerusalem, excluding even their eastern Christian brothers and sisters.

subtle at the same time. Furthermore, as postcolonial studies have made us aware, the complexities around the phenomena of migration of peoples, communities in diaspora, racial relations between the former colonial powers and their ex-subjects and so forth are signs that such encounters are by no means simple. At the same time, in the religious world, the old practice of pilgrimage in all its variety and forms has persisted, if not increased in its popularity. Oddly, I argue, this practice still retains its potentiality as a privileged space for forging an identity by encountering alterity in a fruitful and creative way, beyond the dichotomy between self (same) and other as well as beyond the easy conflation of the two.

As a discipline, the new comparative theology is born in precisely this context, where self meets with other in all its complexities and ambiguities.[6] It understands itself as a theological response to the opportunities as well as tensions in the encounters between peoples, religions, and cultures that are rife in the postmodern condition. It is also a practice that is based on the optimism that the delicate reality of encounters (the so-called 'pluralism', religious or otherwise) can be turned into a fruitful moment of self-growth and deeper mutual understanding, precisely by intensifying this encounter through committed cross-learning, as well as by making this scholarly process a constitutive part of the dynamic of identity formation of the comparativists themselves and, ideally, their respective religious communities. Thus, at the heart of comparative theology lies a dynamic of fostering an ever richer and deeper sense of religious identity through the arduous journey of productive encounters with alterity, respecting a certain degree of irreducibility inherent in the religious others – especially when this is put in the framework of God as the Wholly Other – while refusing to succumb to the idea of the absoluteness of this alterity. In this respect, comparative theology shares the profundity of the pilgrims' sentiment and passion of reaching out to the Other and other as well as of going home refreshed by this very act of reaching out.

This essay, taking pilgrimage and pilgrims as the guiding metaphors, intends to argue for the relevance and contribution of comparative theology as a theological art of forming identity (self) in the intimacy with the religious other and always in the bigger context of relationship with God, the Other.[7] This way,

---

6 Michael Barnes describes this context as 'an all-pervasive "context of otherness"'. See his *Theology and The Dialogue of Religions* (Cambridge: Cambridge University Press, 2002), 3. I use the term 'new comparative theology' to refer to the works of Francis X. Clooney (primarily), David Burrell, James Fredericks, and Roberts Neville, in contradistinction to the old comparative theology that was developed in the nineteenth century. See Norbert Hintersteiner, 'Intercultural and Interreligious (Un)Translatibility and the Comparative Theology Project', in Norbert Hintersteiner (ed.), *Naming and Thinking God in Europe Today* (Rodopi, 2007), 465–92.

7 Deviating a bit from the common usage in postmodern philosophy where the term 'the Other' might or might not include the mystery of God, I differentiate between 'the other' (other religious traditions) and 'the Other' (God). However, I would mostly use these two terms in a close proximity to each other, precisely because, at least in the context of Christian theology of religions and

comparative theology has arguably taken up in a theologically distinctive manner one of the most important challenges of our time. Based on the affinity between comparative theology and pilgrimage, I choose three categories that constitute major elements of both comparative theological practice and pilgrimage: *identity, imagination,* and *hospitality.*

Accordingly, this essay proceeds in three steps. In the first part, I attempt to take up the question of the place of the other in the identity formation of the self. Drawing insights from philosophy and postcolonial studies, I endeavor to show the futility of the ideology of 'purification' as well as the fecundity of border-crossing or 'in-between spaces' in the identity formation of the subjects. Like a pilgrimage to the other and Other, comparative theology is a practice that intentionally works in these in-between spaces. And, engaging Zygmunt Bauman, I argue that comparative theology, while sharing some of the postmodern values, also comes to present itself as a practice based on different values by retaining the older logic of pilgrimage that is marked by firmer commitment to God and to one's home religious tradition (rather than a postmodern free-floating state and radical fluidity), in the process of identity building.

The second part deals with the crucial role of imagination in comparative theology. As in real pilgrimage, where encounter with the Other and other is mediated through images, comparative theology's journey to the religious other also results in the confluences of various images. Comparative theology then presents itself as a milieu where the Other and other are imagined, alongside the familiar images of the self or one's own religious tradition. Learning from the world of the pilgrims, I argue that the meetings of images and attention to the traces of the other (and Other) are instrumental in the transformation of the self through the widening of our religious horizon.

The third part takes up the question of hospitality, one of the defining features of pilgrimage. Against the background of Derrida's idea of hospitality without reserve, I argue that comparative theology offers a hospitality that is so generous yet remains realistic; it is generous because it offers a hospitality to the religious other even when this other does not seem to need it, because hospitality belongs to the very essence of comparative practices. However, this hospitality is not without reserve due to its realism: it works on smaller scales, offering what can usefully be offered to the religious other.

---

comparative theology, the religious others ('the other') could only be understood fruitfully if placed in the larger framework of the mystery of God, the Other. Thus, the mystery of God is always implicated in the existence of these religious others. Rooted in a deeply Christian conviction of the unity of the love of neighbor and the love of God, there is no way to separate the religious others from the mystery of God himself. My designation of God as the Other also stems from the experience of the pilgrims, for whom the otherness of God's mystery could be intensified during the pilgrimage. However, this alterity of God is not absolute, because God is also experienced as the most intimate part of the pilgrims' identity. Thus God also belongs to the Same or Self. Nevertheless, I retain the designation of God as the Other to emphasize the unlimited horizon of God's mystery, something that I consider quite insightful in the encounter of comparativists with the religious others.

Comparative Theology, Postmodernity, and Identity

Contrary to the expectations of many commentators, the dawn of the so-called postmodern age and the development of globalization did not dispel the need for a distinct identity. For despite the high level intensity of encounters between different peoples, the need for more distinct identities for certain groups seems to be reinforced, resulting perhaps from the realization that one's identity is made even more fragile by these very encounters. Along this line, the rise of the religio-political forms of the ideology of purification is alarming due to its radical commitment to viewing the other as sworn-in enemy.[8] For within this ideological framework, a true identity of the self can be achieved only by wiping out any traces of alterity, or, if necessary, wiping out this alterity altogether.

In the context of postmodern philosophy, Richard Kearney talks about the externalization of alterity among some post-phenomenological thinkers, such as Levinas and Derrida, who externalize the category of alterity to the point that any contact with self smacks of betrayal or contamination.[9] This externalization is quite benign in its initial intention – namely, to respect the integrity of the other and to avoid violating the dignity of the other in a way that could stem from the hegemony of ontological or logocentric hermeneutic. However, as Kearney argues, this stand actually amounts to a denunciation of any form of dialogical interbeing between self and other. Within this framework, he says, 'the God beyond being becomes an abyss beneath being; the Other becomes Alien'.[10]

It is very telling to note that the other side of this philosophical move can be found in the religio-political ideology of purification that is basically founded on precisely the same ontological opposition between identity and alterity, self and other. Although the intention and starting point are different – the post-phenomenological thinkers externalize alterity out of the awareness of the absolute respect and inaccessibility of the other, while the proponents of the purification ideology are moved by a completely different agenda of preserving the purity of their identity – the end result is strikingly similar: total separation from one another. The other becomes so other, both in a positive and negative sense, so as to render any contact with it neither possible nor beneficial. Furthermore, as Kearney reminds us, this thinking is by no means foreign to the tradition of western philosophy that 'equated the Good with notions of self-identity and sameness' and linked the experience of evil with notions of exteriority.[11] In

---

8 An example of this kind of discourse in Indonesian context can be found in: Muhammad Iqbal Ahnaf, *The Image of the Other as Enemy: Radical Discourse in Indonesia* (Chiangmai: Silkworm Books, 2006); Noorhaidi Hasan, *Laskar Jihad: Islam, Militancy, and the Quest for Identity in Post-New Order Indonesia* (Ithaca, NY: Southeast Asia Program Publications, Cornell University, 2006).
9 Richard Kearney, *Strangers, Gods and Monsters: Interpreting Otherness* (London and New York: Routledge, 2003), 9.
10 Kearney, *Strangers, Gods and Monsters*, 65.
11 Kearney, *Strangers, Gods and Monsters*.

this respect, alterity is 'considered in terms of estrangement which contaminates the pure unity of the soul'. As Kearney points out further, the contemporary anathematization of what is unfamiliar as evil is the offspring of this philosophical tradition: 'it is this proclivity to demonize alterity as a menace to our collective identity which so easily issues in hysterical stories about invading enemies'.[12]

In the context of this discourse, comparative theology can be viewed as a modest effort to build a hermeneutic bridge that would allow the back-and-forth dynamic between identity and alterity.[13] However, what is much more essential for comparativists is to actually do the crossing, to dwell in the realm of the other, and finally to come home (and to do all these three repeatedly). In my view, the fruitfulness of this back-and-forth dynamic reveals the illusory nature of the purification of identity in the sense we just discussed. Moreover, I would argue that precisely for this purpose – namely, to debunk the ideology of purification and show the fertility of border-crossing in identity formation – comparative theology can draw some constructive insights from various disciplines like postcolonial studies. In this regard, it is striking to notice that the major proponents of this discipline, such as Frants Fanon, Edward Said, Homi Bhabha, and Gayatri Spivak, are themselves border-crossers, or, to borrow Bhabha's words, they are 'complex figures of difference and identity, past and present, inside and outside, inclusion and exclusion'.[14] To some, they might appear as typical postmodern intelligentsia whose life-world is shaped by the postmodern facility of moving across borders. Obviously, they are not theologians. However, I would argue that in many respects, especially in terms of their spirit of life and in their strategies for encountering the other and negotiating their complex identities, they are not completely foreign to al-Harawi, a pious pilgrim from many centuries before.

For our limited purposes, I take these postcolonial authors to help us see the hitherto undermined yet pervasive reality of the fecundity of the so-called 'in-between spaces'. On this crucial point, Homi Bhabha argues categorically:

What is theoretically innovative, and politically crucial, is the need to think beyond narratives of originary and initial subjectivities and to focus on those moments or processes that are produced in the articulation of cultural differ-

---

12 Kearney, *Strangers, Gods and Monsters*.
13 On this, Kearney argues: 'I will argue that what is needed, if we are to engage properly with the human obsession with strangers and enemies, is a critical hermeneutic capable of addressing the dialectic of others and aliens. Such a hermeneutic would have the task of soliciting ethical decisions without rushing to judgement, that is, without succumbing to overhasty acts of binary exclusion.' Richard Kearney, *Strangers, Gods and Monsters*, 67.
14 About himself, Bhabha writes: 'Growing up in Bombay as a middle-class Parsi – a member of a small Zoroastrian-Persian minority in a predominantly Hindu and Muslim context – I never imagined that I would live elsewhere. Years later, I ask myself what it would be like to live without the unresolved tensions between cultures and countries that have become the narrative of my life, and the defining characteristic of my work.' Homi Bhabha, *The Location of Culture* (Routledge Classics, 2004), x.

ence. *These 'in-between' spaces provide the terrain for elaborating strategies of selfhood, singular and communal, that initiate new signs of identity, and innovative sites of collaboration, and contestation, in the act of defining the idea of society itself.*[15] [italics mine]

For a discipline like comparative theology, Bhabha's point about the role of 'the in-between spaces' could not be more insightful, since it points to the spaces where communal and individual identities are forged and negotiated through both collaboration and contestation. For Bhabha, this dynamic forms the society itself as an entity where identity is always negotiated in the face of, and with, the other, in the very act of interaction, in between, not solely inside the self, nor in the idea of purity. He goes on to argue:

> Once again, it is the space of intervention emerging in the cultural interstices that introduces creative invention into existence. And one last time, there is a return to the performance of identity as iteration, the re-creation of the self in the world of travel, the resettlement of the borderline community of migration.[16]

In this respect, the challenge of comparative theology, itself an offspring of some cultural and religious interstices of our time, is then precisely to seek out further, or to create if necessary, these in-between spaces. Within the discipline of comparative theology, these spaces might be taken as pointing to different realms such as comparative methods and their textual results, the discourse spaces that are inhabited by the interaction among comparativists (as well as with the readers, religious communities and so forth), the interfaith communities that inspire and are inspired by comparative works, and perhaps the subjective realm of the comparativists themselves, including their identity formation as theologians. However, because comparative theology is a theological discipline, the in-between spaces here should also be understood, ultimately, as a milieu of divine revelation, a space of our struggle to understand God better.

As I see it, however, the main insight of postcolonial studies seems to gravitate more towards the dynamic interconnection between values or ideas and the very realities from which these values stem and in which they come to be embodied. Thus, for postcolonial theorists, it makes little sense to talk about the fecundity of in-between spaces or hybridity, without resorting to the realities and personalities of diasporic communities.

It is this kind of dynamic that, I argue, renders the metaphor of pilgrimage fruitful in our discourse about the place of comparative theology not only within the current academic interdisciplinary discourse but, perhaps more importantly, within the realm of lived experience of our contemporaries whose world is

---

15 Bhabha, *The Location of Culture*, 2.
16 Bhabha, *The Location of Culture*, 12.

shaped by the persisting phenomenon of migration as well as other forms of movements and encounters between peoples. In this context, pilgrimage can indeed be viewed as a precursor as well as a spiritual and theological companion to these phenomena. As al-Harawi and countless other pilgrims have shown, pilgrimage is a particular kind of 'performance of identity as iteration, the re-creation of the self in the world of travel', to again borrow Bhabha's words. The religious and theological nature of pilgrimage renders the whole dynamic of this performance of identity special. This is because what the pilgrims seek is not just a re-creation of the self, but a communion with the Divine. Thus, the travel goes deeply inward, to the deep recess of the self, as well as upward, in a journey of ascent to God. And the identity constructed is always relational both to God and to fellow human beings.

For our purpose of shedding some theoretical light on the dynamic of identity formation in the practice of pilgrimage in general, I turn to Zygmunt Bauman, the noted Polish-born sociologist-cum-philosopher. Although not based on specific case and not strictly theological, his theoretical insights on pilgrimage as a world-view and other postmodern alternatives to it, I believe, would help us understand the major dynamics of comparative theology, itself a kind of pilgrimage to the other, Other, and the self.

In his critical response to the argument that 'identity continues to be the problem it was throughout modernity', Bauman categorically argues that:

> At no time did identity 'become' a problem; it was a 'problem' from its birth – was *born as a problem* (that is, as something one needs do something about – as a task), could exist only as a problem; it was a problem, and thus ready to be born, precisely because of that experience of under-determination and free-floatingness which came to be articulated *ex post facto* as 'disembeddedment'.[17]

While Bauman clearly points out the perennial dimension of the task of identity making, he does not lose sight of the fact that postmodernity poses a specific challenge in this regard.

Bauman argues that, in the context of Judeo-Christian culture, pilgrimage was the guiding metaphor of humanity seeking to perform the task of identity making. To a certain degree, inspired by St Augustine, the Church came to understand herself as a 'pilgrim through time', seeking to dwell in the Eternal City of God in heaven. In this context, says Bauman, identity making is akin to doing pilgrimage, which is basically a journey to the final destiny of humankind, God, which involves some experiences of dislocation and homelessness in this world. So, 'going to the desert' came to be appropriated as an enactment of pilgrimage in the early and medieval period of Christianity. The desert was the

---

17 Zygmunt Bauman, 'From Pilgrims to Tourists – or A Short History of Identity', in S. Hall and P. du Gay (eds), *Questions of Cultural Identity* (London: Sage, 1996), 19–20.

place where 'pilgrims' recreated themselves in the intimacy with God. In a sense, to be like God was their task of identity building, self-construction.

In modernity, however, the Protestants gave a new twist to the pilgrimage world-view: they became inner-worldly pilgrims. They did not go to the deserts, but instead 'worked hard to make desert come to them, to remake the world in the likeness of the desert'. They worked hard to give meanings to the empty world of theirs, both social and cosmic. Thus, Bauman concludes:

> In such a land, commonly called modern society, pilgrimage is no longer a choice of the mode of life; less still is it a heroic or saintly choice. Living one's life as pilgrimage is no longer the kind of ethical wisdom revealed to, or initiated by, the chosen and the righteous. Pilgrimage is what one does of necessity, to avoid being lost in a desert; to invest the walking with a purpose while wandering the land with no destination.[18]

In this framework, identity building is precisely the act of bringing in meaning to the desert-like world. One crucial element in this process is the distance between the goal and the present moment. Pilgrimage becomes fascinating because of this distance, and pilgrims' ethos is marked by a commitment to never losing sight of the goals down the road, as Bauman writes:

> Pilgrims had a stake in the solidity of the world they walked; in a kind of world in which one can tell life as a continuous story, a 'sense-making' story, such a story as makes each event the effect of the event before and the cause of the event after, each age a station on the road pointing towards fulfillment.[19]

Then, Bauman continues, the so-called postmodern condition offers a rather different world-view. For everything now becomes fluid, and commitment to any overarching goal is not required.[20] If one considers daily life as just a succession of minor emergencies, instead of as meaningful moments within an architectonic journey of life, then no such goal is even thinkable. I find Bauman's analysis interesting despite its striking generality, especially his four postmodern typological models of life metaphors in place of pilgrimage. The first is the stroller, the kind of postmodern mall-goers who are obsessed with 'pure beauty', evading the grimmer facts of life. The second is the vagabond, the one who is forever a stranger, who never goes native, for whom the idea of a stable home is repulsive. Then comes the tourist (a third model), an avid seeker of novelty or new experience, out of sheer boredom with the familiar, for whom a home is just a part of

---

18 Bauman, 'From Pilgrims to Tourists', 21.

19 Bauman, 'From Pilgrims to Tourists', 23.

20 On this point, Bauman argues: 'I propose that while it is true that identity continues to be the problem, this is not the problem it was throughout modernity. *Indeed if the modern problem of identity was how to construct identity and keep it solid and stable, the postmodern problem of identity is primarily how to avoid fixation and keep the options open*' [italics mine]. Bauman, 'From Pilgrims to Tourists', 18.

the safety package, a place to return to when the world of new experience is not that exciting any more. And finally there is the player, for whom the thing that matters most is how well he plays his hands, whose world knows no necessity or determination, whose life is governed by the rule of each self-enclosed game to which he has no permanent commitment, for when he doesn't want to abide by the rules, he can just opt out.

Bauman's typologies, like all others, can sound too general at times, as well as too simple and neat as to be able to reflect the whole truth of human life that, for the most part, continues to be stubborn in its ambiguities and complexities, as postcolonial theorists are wont to indicate. However, prudently employed, they still retain a real force for shedding some light on our discourse about the particularities of comparative theology as a pilgrimage in which we endeavor to find our identity anew, to understand ourselves and the other and Other better, through serious and sustained encounter with other religious traditions. However, as we can readily detect, this self-understanding is of course counterintuitive in the context of late capitalistic or postmodern ethos Bauman has aptly described. In my view, in choosing to be a rather traditional pilgrim like al-Harawi, comparative theology refuses to be a mere stroller, vagabond, tourist, or game-player. Unlike the business of a stroller, comparative theology is not founded on the premise of enjoying some risk-free pleasure that can be derived from just passing or stopping by some 'spiritual stores' in a nice-looking 'religious shopping-mall', so to speak, where each religion is displayed in its pure beauty and charm. On the contrary, comparative theology is born out of a commitment to always seeking to dwell in the not always pretty and comfy intersections in which our religious tradition encounters the other. Even when comparativists rightly relish the joy of achieving some breakthrough in their works, they need to be reminded of the difficult and still unresolved questions that persist. Again, in this regard, the words of al-Harawi are instructive: 'I saw every strange and marvelous wonder, and experienced terror in comfort and misery.' Like al-Harawi, comparativists are ready to dwell in the world of contradiction and irony, hoping still to understand even deeper. However, in the case of believing comparativists, it is helpful to be reminded that, according to various mystical and theological traditions, the mystery of God should be understood at times in terms of irony, contradiction, and darkness.

In the same way, the passion of the vagabond is foreign to comparative theology, precisely because the journey of the comparativists into the world of the other is anchored in its firm rootedness in their own religious traditions and is placed in the framework of a commitment to returning home. The aloofness and perpetual foreignness that mark the identity of the vagabond *vis-à-vis* the visited lands stand in a stark contrast to the desire and longing of the comparativists to be always 'at home' even during the most alienating moment of the journey to the religious other. For comparativists, homeliness can mean both becoming relatively at home in the other tradition due to their ever-deeper immersion in it, as well as within their own tradition to which they ideally return time and again with fresh insights and better informed commitment. Some persistent elements of alterity in both home and visited traditions can be taken positively as signals that invite deeper engagement and probing. Thus, instead of rendering real understanding of self and other impossible, they make the journey to the other (and to the Other, too) a lifelong commitment. In my view, comparative theology rightly sees no finish line in terms of this dynamic movement into the other, the Other, and the self. For this reason, it intentionally creates room for respecting this aspect of alterity, the ever-present surplus of meanings contained in the other and Other, by refusing to arrive at a totalizing claim as well as by humbly acknowledging its own limited achievement *vis-à-vis* the unlimited possibilities of making sense of the religious other. Together with similarities, it is these differences that make other religious tradition perpetually appealing to comparativists, and that render every encounter with the other continually imbued with surprising promises and novel experiences.[21] Potentially, it is this feature of persistent alterity that keeps the comparative journey even more desirable and fruitful.

However, unlike the postmodern tourists, I would argue that comparativists do not seek this novelty for the sake of novelty or sheer enjoyment of it, but rather for a better understanding of the self, the other, and more importantly, the Other, even if this involves some pains and hardships. Unlike the tourists who might treat their own homes as a part of safety package, comparativists feel the need to have an ability to stay put where the pains and struggle seem to reign supreme. They endeavor not to see their home traditions as a mere safe place where they can easily return when things get rough or boring in the encounter, or when they have exhausted their own enthusiasm. Rather, much more than part of a safety package, their home traditions would constitute places where comparativists can draw out the first impulse for setting out in the comparative journey as well as the strength to sustain the whole journey. Like pilgrims, they keep the home traditions dearly with them at every moment of the journey.

However, not unlike the world of the game player, the world of the comparativists is filled with risks that can come with every act of comparison, the risks of misunderstanding the other tradition and thus potentially offending the religious sensibility of the insiders of this tradition, of unsettling the comfortable world of their own as well as that of the readers, of being misunderstood or even rejected by their home communities, of feeling occasional sense of being alienated from both their own tradition and the other traditions too, and so forth.

In this respect, Francis X. Clooney, SJ, talks about the risk of throwing one's self into an ambivalent or unsettling situation in the practice of cross-readings, namely, the situation where after a deep immersion into the text of the other,

---

21 In this regard, Francis Clooney argues: 'My goal has been to show how even the more difficult and stubborn points of religious and theological difference remain places where the mind can willingly visit, think, speak, and thus infuse new vitality and insight into believing lives.' Francis X. Clooney, SJ, *Hindu God, Christian God* (Oxford: Oxford University Press, 2001), vi.

one starts to feel to 'be neither here nor there, or perhaps both here and there'.[22]
In other words, to be a back-and-forth reader is to be vulnerable. However, this
lot is not the monopoly of the comparativists, for it has been shared by countless
others who live and work in the 'in-between spaces'. Indeed, as Bhabha has
shown, living and working within the 'in-between spaces' can be so enchanting
and fruitful, but its fruits come only after we pay the price of passing through
some periods of feeling either alienated or not completely at home both in the
visited land and the motherland. In this respect, it is insightful that al-Harawi,
despite his numerous encounters with other pilgrims or monks, still wanted to
emphasize the loneliness of his journey precisely because what he seeks was far
greater than human companionship. He seeks the companionship of God.
Likewise, I would argue, comparative theologians, in their loneliness, can find
comfort in feeling closer to God through meeting him in many unusual places,
through wonder and terror. As theologians, comparativists rightly take the
mystery of God as the ultimate reference.

Again, different from the world of the player, the risky practices that the
comparativists have embraced, as well as the vulnerabilities that come with them,
are not just a succession of moves aimed at winning the prize and beating the
opponent, thus scoring more numerous comparative winning points, moves that
are governed by a combination of luck and cunning. Rather, they are founded
on a deeper commitment whose fruitfulness can be achieved by the performance
of humility and patience as well as professional knowledge and skillful mastery of
the discipline's method and whose ultimate goal is never lost, even if some
particular comparisons seem to have met a dead end. In this regard, some comparativists might even dare to sign up for a commitment to personally struggle to
understand the other and, more importantly, the Other, unlike the tourists or
game-players who opt out once the adventures have gone sour or the games lost
their appeals. Again, I would argue that for comparativists, seeking to understand
the Mystery of God, the Other, is the ultimate horizon and goal.

Nevertheless, comparativists do need to find different ways of amending the
rules of the 'games' of comparison when the real dynamics of each comparison
signal to demand it. In this respect, comparative theology has the advantage of
having relative freedom compared to other, much more well-established disciplines. This methodological move might appear to be similar to the flexibility of
the postmodern player, but it is nevertheless different because of the nature of
the goal and commitment. If each individual game has its own final goal and
result (being either won or lost), the significance of each comparative project
also lies within the bigger commitment to the home tradition and the other as
well as the meeting between the two. Furthermore, each comparative endeavor
can be done and redone in a countless number of ways, yielding to different
insights. As such, it might strike us like a game due to the presence of 'trial and

22 Francis X. Clooney, SJ, *Beyond Compare: St Francis de Sales and Sri Vedanta Desika on Loving Surrender to God* (Georgetown University Press, 2008), 82.

error', but the theological commitment of the comparativists makes these trials and errors fundamentally different from those of the players.

Thus, we might say that comparative theology shares the postmodern conviction about the pervasive reality and fecundity of moving back and forth between different entities or worlds, but it should, in my view, remain rather skeptical about the extreme fluidity that postmodern thinkers come to understand the nature of phenomena such as traditions (and people's commitments to them), personal and communal identities and so forth. There is a tendency among these writers to minimize the power of a rather 'fixed' (or better, stable) tradition in the process of negotiation. They tend to over-emphasize the imaginary nature of this tradition as mere grand narratives. They seem to advocate a radical fluidity of the in-between movement, as if nothing is stable. In reality, this might not be as extreme as they seem to think. I am not sure that this reflects the experience of the vast majority of those border-crossers and in-between inhabitants themselves. Arguably, it is not the typical experience of the pilgrims who cross religious boundaries like al-Harawi. Over against this radical position, comparative theology, as I understand it, assumes that firmer rootedness in a religious tradition whose relative stability one can rely on, will prove to be much more fruitful and realistic in terms of enriching the tradition in question, so that comparative insights are still recognizable by the home tradition and hopefully by the visited tradition as well. As Catherine Cornille has remarked, this desire to help the tradition grow will in fact be made smoother by the visible commitment to the tradition on the part of those who engage in interreligious dialogue.[23] After all, comparativists are not on a constant lookout for a completely new identity, as if they were religious vagabonds. Their passion is closer to that of seekers who start the journey not from nowhere, but rather from a rather definite somewhere. They are pilgrims who, while enjoying every bit of the process of transformation on the road, are resolute to come back home, knowing full well that this on-the-road experience, which involves a certain degree of unhomeliness (*unheimlich*), will be made much more meaningful and fruitful in terms of self-transformation when it is placed in the context of the homeliness of their traditions.

Comparative Theology, Pilgrimage, and Imagination

In this second part of the essay, I want to address the role of imagination in comparative theology's journey to the other. One of the important features of comparative theology is its attempt to find the various ways in which religious traditions can be re-imagined afresh much more vividly, and thus enriched, by putting them in contact with the others. If pilgrimage is used here as a metaphor

---

23 Catherine Cornille, *The Im-Possibility of Interreligious Dialogue* (New York: The Crossroad Publishing Company, 2008), 72. On p. 60 she calls the function of the tradition 'a solid point of departure and a critical place of return'.

for better understanding the major dynamics at play in comparative practice, it is also because of its distinctive force in enabling the re-imagination of religious traditions in light of one another. For, under certain circumstances, pilgrimage could become a privileged moment where pilgrims are put in direct contact with otherness while searching to understand themselves and God. The vividness of this encounter with the other, resulting from the sensory experience with it, makes the whole experience quite memorable.

In turn, this sensory encounter with the other will lead to the re-imagination of the religious world where the other is hosted in one way or another. It was this movement that occurred, for example, in the context of Christian pilgrimage to the monks and monasteries in the desert as a natural extension of Holy Land pilgrimage; the pilgrims were eager to have a sight of the desert monks because this sight would bring them much more vividly and intimately to the biblical world and truth.[24] Thus, these pilgrims were re-imagining the biblical world by taking into account some new realities that can somehow be connected to it by association and extension. It is fascinating in this regard to see how the pilgrims deal with the question of alterity in the forms of the extreme features of these ascetics. For the major appeal of these ascetics is precisely their 'alterity', namely, the fact that they are no ordinary Christians. That is why the most extreme and peculiar ascetics got the most attention, as the case of St Simeon the Stylite has shown.[25] At the end of the day, though, this alterity does not pose a problem since the pilgrims could still find biblical models or *typos* for these. However, they were also insistent on maintaining this visible aspect of alterity of the ascetics within the familiar world of the Bible.

In this respect, it is insightful to note the role of seeing through the 'eye of the faith' (*oculis fidei*) that some Church Fathers like St Jerome use to refer to the modality in which Christians could enter more fully and personally into the biblical time and relish the transcendent moments there.[26] In my view, the power of this *oculis fidei* in bringing the pilgrims into a spiritual realm of imagination cannot be limited to the rather familiar world of the Bible. For the richness and fuller horizon of the biblical world could also be imagined anew by taking into account a plethora of different images, including the images of the other, of course through careful discernment and always with the help of this *oculis fidei*. In this respect, any pilgrimage that involves seeing the other seems to be always in need of this *oculis fidei* as a kind of hermeneutic of the heart in the face of this other. A recent example, narrated by Richard Kearney, might be insightful here.

---

24 Georgia Frank, *The Memory of the Eyes: Pilgrims to Living Saints in Christian Late Antiquity* (Berkeley, Los Angeles, London: University of California Press, 2000).

25 In late antique Syria, the cult around St Simeon the Stylite (c. 386–459) grew spectacularly, even during his lifetime, due to the fact that he was no ordinary ascetic. For it was he who founded the dramatic 'stylite asceticism'. See Susan Ashbrok-Harvey, *Asceticism and Society in Crisis: John of Ephesus and the Lives of Eastern Saints* (University of California Press, 1990), 15ff.

26 St Jerome, Letter XXII to Eustochium; also *The Pilgrimage of the Holy Paula* (Adamant Media Corporation, 2004).

Some participants of an interfaith conference in Bangalore concluded their conference by embarking on a pilgrimage from the holy town of Kalady – birthplace of the Hindu sage, Sankara – in Kerala to the caves of Ajanta and Ellora north-east of Mumbai. These ancient caves, which mark a site of interreligious sharing between Hindus, Buddhists, and Jains, caught their imagination. On this, Kearney writes:

> One image in particular struck us as we entered Cave 29 of Ellora: a Jain earring and a Buddhist hand salute. It was the last day of our travels and this icon of cross-religious hospitality seemed to epitomize for us, weary pilgrims, a fitting culmination of our odyssey into the 'cave of the heart' (*guha*).[27]

More directly relevant to comparative theology, Francis Clooney gives a personal account of his visit to a Hindu shrine of Laksmi:

> To visit this temple and stand before the goddess Laksmi opened for me *new possibilities of vision beyond what I had seen or thought before.* I was face to face with a reality – a kind of real presence – from within a living religious tradition other than my own. I did not have, nor do I have now, some easy words by which to explain this concrete and in some ways very foreign moment of encounter.[28] [italics mine]

This kind of sensory encounter with the other is one of the forms of encounters that enables each religious tradition to re-imagine themselves beyond normal boundaries. As Catherine Cornille puts it, 'whereas the religious imagination is usually shaped by a particular religious tradition, encounter with other religions may allow the imagination to stretch beyond its established religious boundaries and to conceive of symbolic universes hitherto unimagined'.[29]

Perhaps more importantly, these newly imagined symbolic universes then become the context in which the question of identity, at least part of it, is framed. For if identity is a perennial human task, as Bauman argues, and if this task can only be done properly in encounter with alterity as the postcolonial theorists insist, what more do we need than this kind of symbolic universes where both the self and the other are represented and evoked in a rich tapestry of images? On this question Bhabha muses:

---

27 Richard Kearney (ed.), *Religion and the Arts* (A Journal from Boston College) (12:1:3, 2008), 4.
28 Francis X. Clooney, SJ, 'Learning to See: Comparative Practice and the Widening of Theological Vision', in *CTSA Proceedings* (58, 2003), 1. See also his work *Divine Mother Blessed Mother* (Oxford: Oxford University Press, 2005), which can be seen as the comparative fruit of his struggle to understand this experience of seeing the other and Other. In my view, this work is a good example of how we can apply *oculis fidei* creatively in a robust comparative discourse.
29 Catherine Cornille, 'Empathy and Interreligious Imagination', in Richard Kearney (ed.), *Religion and the Arts* (12:1–3, 2008), 114.

In the postcolonial text the problem of identity returns as a persistent questioning of the frame, the space of representation, where the image – missing person, invisible eye, Oriental stereotype – is confronted with its difference, its Other.[30]

In this regard then, comparative theology could offer itself as that kind of frame, precisely because it is committed methodologically to embracing the other with all their images and to becoming a discipline where the other and the self can be re-imagined through hermeneutics working on the richness of the confluences of images.

As Francis Clooney argues in his recent work *Beyond Compare*, the practice of comparative reading will have to deal with the ways in which we decide to make sense of the inundation of new images, exemplars, words, and so forth. Complexity comes in precisely where these new images and the familiar ones seem to jostle and unsettle each other. What should we make of the confluences between, say, the Christian images that Francis de Sales mentions in his work – Mary, Paul, Francis of Assisi, and Francis Xavier – and the Srivaisnava exemplars that Vedanta Desika mentions – Sita, Laksmana, Vibhisana, etc.? Or, to refer back to the world of the pilgrims: if Christian pilgrims in the past could without much difficulty picture St Simeon the Stylite alongside his biblical model like John the Baptist, could Christian pilgrims of our time, having been exposed to the religiously other ascetics – Hindu and Buddhist monks, Sufi saints and so forth – include these strikingly similar yet also so different in their religious imagination alongside the familiar ones, possibly through a discerning application of the same *oculis fidei*?

This challenge can appear to be overwhelming. However, it is reassuring to find that it is also here, in this vast universe of images, that the fruits can be reaped, provided that we become skillful in our use of imagination.[31] For, isn't it true that challenges like this one have inspired such captivating works like the statue of Ellora mentioned earlier? While it is true that such works did not have to be born out of an explicitly comparative works, it certainly means that a discipline like comparative theology, due to its very nature, should make itself useful in this regard precisely because it understands itself to be not only the place where these confluences of images occur, but also the arena in which this imagination bears some more visible fruits, first in the forms of discourse, but then, ideally, in various forms like religious arts, architecture, liturgy, and so forth, that in turn could inspire further comparative discourse. In the context of comparative practice, the act of 'seeing' the other is not discarded but intensified through

---

30 Bhabha, *The Location of Culture*, 66.
31 In this work, which he says is different from his much more explicitly comparative works, imagination presents itself as a crucial step in comparative practice, perhaps much more important than, and definitely comes before, any rational systematization of insights. See Clooney, *Beyond Compare*, 141.

cross-reading and probing. In short, comparative theology can indeed present itself as a unique pilgrimage to the other where a complex interreligious imagination is sustained by serious comparative discourse.

Comparative Theology as Hospitality

This third part of the essay takes up the subject of hospitality to the other. The questions to be addressed here are the continuation from our previous discourse on imagination. For if comparative theology is ready to take into account the images of the other or to let the other leave its traces in the self in various forms, and if this gesture is in itself a hospitality to the other, questions as to how far this hospitality can go or whether this hospitality is at all adequate in response to the reality of the other and Other, can still be posed. In this respect, it is insightful to take up Jacques Derrida's challenge to the monotheist religions of Judaism, Christianity, and Islam to, in the words of Georges De Schrijver, 'return to their [Abrahamic] roots and to revive the "messianic" dream of the "impossible" ideas of justice and hospitality without reserve'.[32] This celebrated postmodern philosopher, who himself returned to his Jewish roots later in life, lamented the fact that the Abrahamic hospitality has been restricted in its Jewish, Christian, and Muslim application to their respective fellow-believers, to the exclusion of the strangers. To a discipline like comparative theology, this idea of hospitality without reserve seems to be particularly challenging. Again, as we have examined, comparative theology intends to be hospitable to the other by presenting itself as a milieu where the self is re-imagined in the presence of the other. Furthermore, if comparative theology, different from theology of religions, seeks to not only welcome the other but to dwell in the realm of this other, then the question about the nature or limits of hospitality seems to be crucial.

However, before responding modestly to this Derridean challenge, I would like to return to the guiding metaphor of this essay, the pilgrims, in order to learn a lesson about the dynamic of hospitality. Hospitality is, of course, a crucial element of pilgrimage. Although more so in the past than in the present, there is no pilgrimage without hospitality offered to pilgrims (strangers) by the hosts (who are also strangers in the eyes of the pilgrims). Al-Harawi, as a Muslim pilgrim, could not possibly have visited a Frankish-controlled Holy City of Jerusalem without the hospitality of the Christians. The degree of hospitality requested by the pilgrim varies greatly, but a pilgrimage that involves a religious other requires a lot more.

Interestingly, the Latin word *peregrinus* designates both stranger and pilgrim, and of course these two meanings stem from the same semantic domain: a

---

32 Georges De Schrijver, SJ, 'The Derridean Notion of Hospitality as a Resource for Interreligious Dialogue in a Globalized World', in *Louvain Studies* (31, 2006), 79.

pilgrim becomes a stranger upon leaving the familiar world of his own home.[33] However, the identity of a stranger or pilgrim could only make sense against the background of hospitality offered by the hosts (*hospis*). In the context of this dynamic, comparative theology as a form of pilgrimage finds itself in a unique situation. For, it wants to be a pilgrim (stranger, *peregrinus*) and a host (*hospis*) at the same time. And the way it goes about doing this double task is rather unusual. This is so partly because its offer of hospitality to the other is not based on the need of this other for a shelter (although in some cases, this might be so), but rather because this hospitality has become the condition of the possibility of the comparative project itself. It is part of the complex identity of the comparativists themselves. Comparative theology then attempts to be hospitable to the other, not by receiving the visit of the other but instead by reaching out to this other. In other words, comparative theology seeks to be hospitable by being a pilgrim.

In the context of this dynamic, it is indeed tempting to embrace the idea of hospitality without reserve, for this idea seems to show the highest degree of our commitment to the other. To a certain degree, comparative theology takes up the Derridean challenge by offering hospitality to the other even if this other does not seem to need it, or even if this hospitality is not instrumental in the life of the other. Furthermore, it might be the case that in principle, comparativists work as if there is nothing that prevents any comparative probing. For even surmountable theological differences that exist between religious traditions should not be taken as a hindrance, but rather as an invitation to further comparative probing, assuming that real differences, when read back and forth, can yield to unforeseeable fruits of understanding the self and the other. In this respect, comparativists might seem to work under a Derridean framework of hospitality without reserve. However, the fruitfulness of comparative works does not depend on this framework, but rather on their concreteness.

In fact, what I find rather problematic about the idea of hospitality without reserve is its formlessness, something that goes against the comparative theology's insistence on concreteness and its theological commitment, which is rooted in some particular tradition. For, despite its honorable intention of respecting the other, this idea can only exist as a principle meant to lure people into acting accordingly, but is not supposed to be realized in reality due to its impossibility. In reality, it is rendered almost meaningless by its own claim for absoluteness. Obviously it does not guide us in concrete terms, in the context of life's complexities where abuse and violence, or simply confusion, can also occur in the dynamics of encounters between different parties, of course alongside charity and benevolence. In other words, it is formless due to its overly general statement of generosity to the other. Again, in this framework, comparative theology

---

33 For a very insightful analysis of the use of this term in the context of Christian pilgrimage in antiquity, see Stephen Davis, *The Cult of St Thecla: A Tradition of Women's Piety in Late Antiquity* (Oxford: Oxford University Press, 2001).

rightly refuses to succumb to this very general idea, but tries instead to express this hospitality in small and concrete steps.

As a theological discipline seeking to fecundate the in-between spaces, the discernment of comparative theology is governed by the principle of fruitfulness, guided by humility and respect for the Mystery of God and his will on the one hand, and respect for the integrity and distinctiveness of each religious tradition on the other. Thus, it is a principle that after comparisons, Christianity will remain distinctively Christian, and Islam distinctively Islamic and so forth, but affirming this would have a different meaning after comparison since each has become part of the identity of the other in various ways, both visible and subtle, both through words and silence. In other words, no conflation of religions is desired, even if it were possible. In this sense, comparative practice agrees with the postmodern notion of respecting the relative integrity of the other.

For some, this reasoning might seem rather instrumentalist, one-sided, or even hegemonic, but it does not have to be so. The one-sidedness of comparative generosity should fade away as soon as the community of comparativists becomes larger, where theologians of different traditions take the other seriously for their own growth. Furthermore, the other tradition is not treated simply as an instrument but rather as something much more valuable than that. For, in the words of Francis Clooney, the comparativists make themselves 'vulnerable' to the attractiveness and cogency of these other traditions.[34] Thus, through a sustained practice of dwelling in the realm of the other, the comparativists make the other part of his complex identity, avoiding a crude hegemony of the other.

Concluding Remarks

Besides his work *Kitab al-Isharat,* al-Harawi also recorded his impressions on the wonders of the lands he visited in a no longer extant work entitled *Kitab al-'Aja'ib wa al-Athar wa al-Asnam (The Book of Wonders, Antiquities and Idols).* Al-Harawi was a pilgrim who became intensely enchanted by the kinds of images that he saw, no matter how profane they might have appeared. For him, 'the lands east and west' then became one vast and rich spiritual landscape where God is found in all his wondrous and diverse manifestations.

Indeed, visits to the other can result in the confluences of images that will never be erased from the memory of the pilgrims. These images are often too complex for neat and rigid categorization. Al-Harawi might have noticed the presence of Greek or Roman-styled religious arts in various Byzantine churches he visited, or the same cupolas that marked both Muslims and Christian shrines, or the fact that Jewish, Muslim, and Christian pilgrims uttered their prayers in Arabic. Like al-Harawi, pilgrims nowadays can also be struck by the presence of the Byzantine architectural forms in the Umayyad Mosque in Damascus, for

---

34 Clooney, *Beyond Compare*, 16.

example, a mosque that was built on the former Byzantine Cathedral of St John. After such visits, the other has then become part of oneself in a way that is far too complex and subtle, yet so real and powerful. The other has left its indelible traces, and hopefully the pilgrim has also left some traces on the visited land. In fact, one of al-Harawi's habits during pilgrimage was that he would write his name on the wall of every site he visited.[35] After such encounters, otherness also becomes much more nuanced, thus resisting easy and simple generalization. If the pilgrim is serious enough in taking these images and traces of the other, his identity is no longer the same. This essay has attempted to show that comparative theology works similarly. It is a pilgrimage, a generous visit to the other and Other, and as such it creates spaces where the traces and images of the other are taken seriously in the identity formation of the pilgrim-cum-comparativists and their communities. It goes intentionally deeper than ordinary pilgrims in terms of discourse about the other. Now the challenge, of course, is far greater, but the promise is hopefully more bountiful.

---

35 According to Ibn Khallikan (d. 681 H/1282 AD), al-Harawi's fame as a pilgrim was indebted to this practice. See Josef Meri, *op. cit.*, xxi.

2

Relating Theology of Religions and Comparative Theology[1]

KRISTIN BEISE KIBLINGER

Introduction

Theology of religions involves formulating an understanding of other religious systems that accords with one's own theology. Perry Schmidt-Leukel concisely defines key theology of religions terms: exclusivists assert that '(s)alvific knowledge of a transcendent reality is mediated by only one religion'; inclusivists assert that '(s)alvific knowledge of a transcendent reality is mediated by more than one religion . . . but only one of these mediates it in a uniquely superior way . . .'; and pluralists assert that '(s)alvific knowledge of a transcendent reality is mediated by more than one religion (not necessarily by all of them), and there is none among them whose mediation of that knowledge is superior to all the rest'.[2] Related to but distinct from theology of religions, comparative theology designates the work of doing one's own theology while drawing upon the resources of other faith systems.

This essay re-examines the relationship between theology of religions and comparative theology. Leading comparative theologians James Fredericks and Francis X. Clooney, SJ, desire to distance themselves from theology of religions and have been reluctant to endorse any particular theology of religions stance as a presupposition for their comparative projects. In my view, the problems that they see with theology of religions do not hold up under closer inspection. Comparative theologians' complaints about the theology of religions too often apply only to old forms of inclusivism and pluralism, lacking reference to

1 I am grateful to Francis Clooney, James Fredericks, Daniel Joslyn-Siemiatkoski, Bagus Laksana, Jeffery Long, Hugh Nicholson, Michelle Voss Roberts, John Sheveland, and Tracy Tiemeier for their helpful comments on earlier drafts of this essay.
2 Perry Schmidt-Leukel, 'Exclusivism, Inclusivism, Pluralism: The Tripolar Typology – Clarified and Reaffirmed', in Paul F. Knitter (ed.), *The Myth of Religious Superiority: A Multifaith Exploration* (Maryknoll, NY: Orbis Books, 2005), 19–20. As will become clear later, this typology is complicated by variations within these basic categories.

advances in the field. The same complaints were leveled as well within theology of religions circles, which has led to improved, newer forms of theology of religions positions. While perceiving themselves as shifting away from theology of religions to an alternative endeavor, another way to see certain comparative theologians is as exemplifying these new forms of theology of religions.

It seems to me impossible to deeply engage others on theological matters without having some preliminary theological presuppositions about those others. Recognizing and disclosing these theology of religions leanings upfront, stipulating them clearly, is preferable to leaving them implicit, I will argue, and so I recommend this as we eagerly look to the future of comparative theology in this volume. After describing prominent comparative theologians' reasoning regarding theology of religions, as I understand it, and rebutting their views, I then turn to Buddhist theology of religions materials and the work of Christian–Buddhist comparative theologian John P. Keenan in order to demonstrate in more detail why comparative theologians need to affirm newer forms of theology of religions.

Leading Comparative Theologians' Views on the Theology of Religions

In his *Faith among Faiths* as well as his *Buddhists and Christians*, Fredericks claims that theology of religions fails to help Christians engage others.[3] The theology of religions, from Fredericks's perspective, becomes a sophisticated way to avoid others, because it makes theologians feel good that they are considering others, while in reality they end up talking about dialogue more than practicing it. Talking only among themselves and constructing their theology entirely out of home system materials, theologians of religion meanwhile defer the actual engagement with non-Christians and their resources.

Of the three basic theology of religions options, Fredericks thinks that inclusivism is the most faithful to the Christian tradition and that promoting an inclusivist stance was an important step, but that theology of religions is now hindering Christians' ability to learn from others in part because it makes decisions about the others in advance of engagement, predetermining the outcome rather than approaching the other with genuine openness. Inclusivism, Fredericks also charges, embraces others by presupposing similarities between Christianity and non-Christian systems. Other systems are seen merely as lesser versions of the same truth as Christianity, which means that the incentive for dialogue is undercut as we lose the point of engagement in the first place – i.e., to learn from the encounter with difference. Not only is inclusivism dismissive of differences

---

3 James L. Fredericks, *Faith among Faiths: Christian Theology and Non-Christian Religions* (Mahwah, NJ: Paulist Press, 1999); and *Buddhists and Christians: Through Comparative Theology to Solidarity* (Maryknoll, NY: Orbis Books, 2004). See also his 'Interreligious Friendship: A New Theological Virtue', in *Journal of Ecumenical Studies* (35:2, 1998), 159–75.

between the home system and the other, but the theology of religions generally tends to be dismissive of the differences *within* other traditions, too, because it generalizes about entire traditions rather than attending closely to more limited particulars. In addition, when we inclusivistically insist on seeing others as anonymous Christians (or pluralistically force traditions into a universal, vague mold), we are imposing our concepts and seeing ourselves in others rather than seeing others on their own terms. Thus we distort rather than interpret adequately; we disregard the others' voices and self-descriptions, presumptuously claiming to know more about what they are doing and meaning than *they* do. Fredericks's solution is to turn away from theology of religions, instead favoring practice over theory. Comparative theology, seen as a process, is the way out of the impasse of theology of religions, seen as only armchair theorizing.

Relative to Fredericks, Clooney has had less to say about theology of religions. What he has said, however, indicates that he shares some of Fredericks's concerns. In addition, Clooney thinks that theology of religions is an unnecessary precursor to comparative theology, because there are more modest reasons for reading comparatively, such as that others' texts are great classics already assumed to be worth reading in and of themselves or that once we read we will stumble upon reasons for continued reading.[4] And we should wait a century or more, Clooney counsels, until the implications of the engagement are clearer, before drawing theology of religions's sorts of overarching conclusions about other traditions and relations among them; because learning through comparison makes answering such large questions difficult, we need to wait patiently and see what happens with our comparative explorations.[5]

Whereas theology of religions requires being clear about one's starting identity and loyalty, comparative theology raises complicated questions about these matters; namely, the comparative theologian's identity and loyalty can be hard to pin down. On the one hand, in Clooney's recent *Beyond Compare*, he identifies himself as a Roman Catholic who seeks to remain so, not 'letting new affinities shatter original commitments and loyalties'. On the other hand, he also describes losing the devotion possible for those who know only their own tradition and now being unable to submit entirely to either.[6] In 'Neither Here nor There' he describes immersing himself in Hindu culture in order to approximate seeing it as an insider would, being 'very much caught up into that Srivaisnava world', saying that he 'tried hard to think, imagine, even pray as would an insider' and contending that indeed one can, to some extent, learn to see the world through the eyes of the other. Clooney thereby complicated his identity and 'was neither

---

4 Francis X. Clooney, SJ. 'Reading the World in Christ', in Gavin D'Costa (ed.), *Christian Uniqueness Reconsidered* (Maryknoll, NY: Orbis Books, 1990), 68–9.

5 Francis X. Clooney, SJ. 'Comparative Theology', in J. B. Webster, Kathryn Tanner, and Iain R. Torrance (eds), *The Oxford Handbook of Systematic Theology* (New York: Oxford University Press, 2007), 666–8.

6 Francis X. Clooney, SJ, *Beyond Compare: St Francis de Sales and Sri Vedanta Desika on Loving Surrender to God* (Washington, DC: Georgetown University Press, 2008), 204–5, 209.

here nor there, though in a way both'.[7] For Clooney, then, the ideal comparative reader creates a 'new, intratextual space' where 'boundaries are ideally blurred' and where 'there are no longer settled groups of interlocutors, religiously identified, who come and constitute the expected sides of the dialogue'.[8] Aspiring to see Hindu texts in Hindu terms, therefore, his ultimate intention is *not* to read Hindu scriptures through Christian eyes[9] (which, I gather, he associates with the theology of religions approach).

Challenging the Current Views

The desire to shift away from theology of religions, or to proceed with comparative theology without first setting out theology of religions presuppositions about the religious other, has been treated with suspicion and challenged by numerous respondents: David Cheetham, Paul F. Knitter, Catherine Cornille, Perry Schmidt-Leukel, Stephen Duffy, Paul Ingram, and Gavin D'Costa.[10] Knitter, for example, writes that we always bring perspectives and histories governing our attitudes toward others that influence how we converse with the other.[11] Cornille argues, regarding comparative theology, that 'there remains a need for further reflection regarding what appear to be the presuppositions and methodology of this approach'. She maintains that comparative theology 'requires and even presupposes' theology of religions.[12] Agreeing, Schmidt-Leukel has argued forcefully that there is not a way out of theology of religions if one wants to resist falling back to mere phenomenological comparison and aims to keep comparative theology genuinely theological, for the typology of exclusivism, inclusivism, and pluralism is fully disjunctive and logically comprehensive and thus forces a choice.[13] Duffy calls theology of religions the 'condition

---

7 Francis X. Clooney, SJ, 'Neither Here nor There: Crossing Boundaries, Becoming Insiders, Remaining Catholic', in José Ignacio Cabezón and Sheila Greeve Davaney (eds), *Identity and the Politics of Scholarship in the Study of Religion* (New York: Routledge, 2004), 102–3, 109–10.
8 Clooney, *Beyond Compare*, 25, 30.
9 Clooney, *Beyond Compare*, 30.
10 David Cheetham, review of *Faith among Faiths* by James Fredericks, *Reviews in Religion & Theology* (7:3, 2000), 359; Paul F. Knitter, review of *Faith among Faiths*, *Theological Studies* (62:4, 2001), 874; Catherine Cornille, review of *Faith among Faiths*, *Buddhist–Christian Studies* (21, 2001), 132; Perry Schmidt-Leukel, 'The Limits and Prospects of Comparative Theology', in Norbert Hintersteiner (ed.), *Naming and Thinking God in Europe Today* (Amsterdam: Rodopi, 2007), 494–6; Stephen Duffy, 'A Theology of the Religions and/or a Comparative Theology?', in *Horizons* (26:1, 1999), 106–12; Paul O. Ingram, review of *Buddhists and Christians* by James Fredericks, *Buddhist–Christian Studies* (26, 2006), 225; Gavin D'Costa, preface to *Christian Uniqueness Reconsidered*, Gavin D'Costa (ed.) (Maryknoll, NY: Orbis Books, 1990), xiv–xv.
11 Paul F. Knitter, *Introducing Theologies of Religions* (Maryknoll, NY: Orbis Books, 2002), 235–6.
12 Cornille, review, 132.
13 Perry Schmidt-Leukel, 'The Limits and Prospects', 494–6. (A fourth option, atheism or naturalism, cannot be a *theological* option, he points out. I would add that any hybrid or multiple allegiance is to be treated as the home framework, from which one still responds theologically to others in one of these three ways.)

grounding the very possibility' of comparative work, for comparative study is not self-justifying.[14] The consensus of voices here should give comparative theologians pause.

Some of the critics mentioned above have, I admit, remained in the realm of theology of religions rather than doing much comparative theology, seemingly vindicating the worry that theology of religions tends to postpone or replace actual entry into others' worlds. Although a legitimate danger to bear in mind, this does not *have* to be the case. As Cornille observes, there are plentiful counter-examples of theologians of religions who have 'written very detailed works on other religions' and have enhanced their 'understandings of truth through dialogue with other religions'.[15]

However, I will not maintain that comparative theologians must necessarily divide their time in order to do extensive theology of religions as well as comparative theology. I support comparative theologians' determination to keep the bulk of their energy on the direct exploration of others' materials. Detailed debates on theology of religions may be left to others in a division of labor. But I *will* argue that comparative theologians should disclose the bare outline of the working theology of religions guiding their comparative engagement, stipulating some favorite(s) among the currently debated options.[16]

The concern that theology of religions predetermines the outcome should not be prohibitive. To say that one has some theological assumptions about the other, and that some such assumptions are preferable to others, is not tantamount to saying that one's theological presuppositions are set in stone; rather, certainly they are revisable, in light of the findings.[17] Indeed, certainly engagement with others and comparative theology, whether done by theologians of religions themselves or just studied by them (for, again, we all have limited time), should speak back to and inform the evolution of theology of religions paradigms.

Furthermore, the objection that theology of religions amounts to a conversation only among Christians with just Christian resources is no longer accurate in

---

14 Duffy, 'A Theology of the Religions', 106–12.

15 She cites, in particular, Wilfred Cantwell Smith on Islam and John Hick on conceptions of death and the afterlife (Cornille, 131). I would add as further examples Perry Schmidt-Leukel and Paul J. Griffiths, both Christian scholars of Buddhism who have done significant theology of religions work as well as in-depth studies showing skilled engagement with the finer points of other traditions.

16 Just because comparative theologians are tired of or uninterested in theology of religions conversations does not mean that they do not have theology of religions positions (Michelle Voss Roberts, e-mail message to author, 24 March 2009).

17 Hugh Nicholson has said that what makes prejudices productive rather than distorting is their capacity for change; thus he refers to a dynamic inclusivism in contrast to a static one (Hugh Nicholson, 'A Correlational Model of Comparative Theology', in *Journal of Religion* (85:2, 2005), 193, 198.) Knitter concurs: 'Theology guides dialogue; but dialogue will also guide, even transform, theology.' 'While we have to be aware that we bring our theological baggage to the journey of dialogue, that doesn't mean that during the journey we may not have to rearrange, or even dispose of, some of that baggage' (Knitter, 235–6).

light of recent developments in the theology of religions literature. Explicit theology of religions, with the terminology of exclusivism, inclusivism, and pluralism, is starting to take place in non-Christian traditions. I am most familiar with Buddhist cases, having myself done research in this area. For example, in June 2007, the European Network of Buddhist–Christian Studies sponsored an international conference in Salzburg on Buddhist theology of religions. It resulted in the 2008 book *Buddhist Attitudes to Other Religions*, of which Part One is titled 'Buddhist "Theologies of Religions"'.[18] Elsewhere too, Buddhists such as John Makransky, Sallie King, and Kenneth Tanaka have self-identified as Buddhist inclusivists or pluralists and have argued for their respective theology of religions positions in various articles.

Even more important are the advances from older to newer forms of inclusivism and pluralism.[19] The theology of religions has evolved to distinguish variations among these positions according to their particular methodologies and justifications. The new subtypes identified within theology of religions categories separate features of inclusivism (and also, but more rarely, pluralism) that have been heavily criticized, from alternative strategies that seem less prone to certain difficulties.[20] Paul Knitter has distinguished inclusivism types as fulfillment vs. acceptance, S. Mark Heim as single-end vs. multiple ends, and I as problematic vs. preferred models. The work of Joseph A. DiNoia is also relevant here, as are Paul Griffiths's distinction between open and closed inclusivism and Schubert M. Ogden's division between indicative claims and those that are modalized (that is, recast in terms of possibility). David Ray Griffin divides pluralists in ways parallel to some of the inclusivism divisions in his *Deep Religious Pluralism*.[21]

---

18 Perry Schmidt-Leukel (ed.), *Buddhist Attitudes to Other Religions* (St Ottilien: EOS, 2008). See also Kristin Beise Kiblinger, *Buddhist Inclusivism: Attitudes Towards Religious Others* (Aldershot, England and Burlington, VT: Ashgate, 2005). An example of theology of religions work in Hinduism is Jeffery D. Long, *A Vision for Hinduism* (London and NY: I. B. Tauris, 2007).

19 First, I am not the only one who feels that comparative theologians' rejection of theology of religions was premature and based on older models, that newer ones deserve a second look. See Ingram, 225 and Duffy. Second, the section beginning here is indebted to my 'Buddhist Stances Towards Others: Types, Examples, Considerations', in *Buddhist Attitudes to Other Religions*, 24–46.

20 To come down in favor of either inclusivism or pluralism would involve more argument than is possible here. For now, I am concerned only to show the significance of old vs. new patterns that cut across both. The old pattern complicates categorizations between inclusivism and pluralism anyway, with old forms of so-called pluralism seeming inclusivistic upon analysis. For more on this, see my 'Buddhist Stances Towards Others'.

21 Knitter, *Introducing Theologies of Religions*; S. Mark Heim, *The Depth of the Riches: A Trinitarian Theology of Religious Ends* (Grand Rapids: William B. Eerdmans, 2001); and *Salvations: Truth and Difference in Religion* (Maryknoll, NY: Orbis Books, 1997); Kiblinger, *Buddhist Inclusivism*; J. A. DiNoia, *The Diversity of Religions: A Christian Perspective* (Washington, DC: The Catholic University of America Press, 1992); Schubert M. Ogden, *Is There Only One True Religion or Are There Many?* (Dallas: Southern Methodist University Press, 1992); Paul J. Griffiths, *Problems of Religious Diversity* (Malden: Blackwell, 2001); David Ray Griffin, 'Religious Pluralism: Generic, Identist, and Deep', in David Ray Griffin (ed.), *Deep Religious Pluralism* (Louisville, Kentucky: Westminster John Knox Press, 2005).

The older sort of inclusivism (or pluralism), now generally discredited and unpopular, has been characterized as seeing how they do in their way what we do in ours. It often exemplifies the anonymous other move, named for Karl Rahner's 'anonymous Christianity'. Inclusivists of this stripe commonly espouse an experiential-expressivist understanding of doctrine, to use George Lindbeck's term.[22] This theory of doctrine de-emphasizes particular expressions by conceding 'priority . . . to a pre-verbal world of experience'.[23] Claims of distinctiveness are easily dismissed and particularities of language are not taken seriously, because various expressions can all be seen as inadequately approximating the same experience. Experiential-expressivism is often found alongside a common core theory of religions, according to which all religions are said to share a common essence (such as a religious object or salvific function) but to vary merely due to cultural and historical circumstances. Accompanying this too is sometimes the assumption that salvation or liberation is singular – that there is one process that is taking place within all time-honored religious traditions.

These methods (i.e. the anonymous other move, experiential-expressivism, common core theory, positing a singular ultimate end) are faulted for assuming a significant level of agreement. To see truth, they look only for similarity. According to detractors, these methods tend to misunderstand others because they interpret them in the home system's terms and impose home tradition-influenced categories as though they are universally valid.[24] In the end, these methods can lead to such massive reinterpretation that something foreign is remade so that it is no longer recognizable to the foreigners. Traditions are gutted of their distinctiveness. Therefore the comparative encounter is disingenuous; it pretends to embrace diversity but in practice snuffs it out.[25]

I agree with comparative theologians that these forms are not helpful for empowering Christian engagement with non-Christians. But these are objections that Fredericks seems to have about inclusivism and pluralism as a whole, rather than leveling these charges only towards the older theology of religions forms. When Fredericks complains about theology of religions forms and then commends a shift to comparative theology as an alternative, his argument rests on the incorrect assumption that all theology of religions is implicated in the transgressions that bother him.[26] On the contrary, there are improved forms of inclusivism and pluralism that do not fall prey to these problems.

---

22 George Lindbeck, *The Nature of Doctrine: Religion and Theology in a Postliberal Age* (Philadelphia: The Westminster Press, 1984).

23 Clooney, 'Reading the World in Christ', 67.

24 This is not to be confused with *evaluating* others by home system standards, which happens eventually, but the argument is that *what* we evaluate should be understood correctly, which means understanding it in its own context first.

25 Not to mention that experiential-expressivism, in particular, falls prey to problems with the category of direct or unmediated experience itself.

26 The work that seems to represent theology of religions in Fredericks's books is that of such figures as Karl Rahner, John Paul II, Jacques Dupuis, and Roger Haight.

The newer types of inclusivism and pluralism – variously known as accept-ance, multiple ends, open, deep, and preferred – typically eschew common core theory and leave differences standing. They are open to the possibility of an authentic variety of ultimate ends and think that traditions can be understood well only in the context of their own salvations or fulfillments. New inclusivists and pluralists will note rootedness of their evaluative and selective criteria in a home tradition rather than claiming for them neutrality or universality. They refrain from telling others what their concepts mean, insisting on valuing others' self-descriptions and making sure those interpretations are recognizable to the other. Not seeing others as anonymously practicing the home tradition or doing in their way what we do in ours, they will find ways to value differences without undoing them or directing attention away from them. Since others are not seen to be doing in their way what we already do in ours, there is more incentive for engagement, increased potential for learning that is truly new, and a turning to the concrete details. These theologians dislike experiential-expressivism and think of religions and religious language instead according to a cultural-linguistic model. Therefore the differences and particularities of religious language and their contexts are studied in depth to learn the grammar from a native speaker's point of view rather than writing off the distinctiveness of others' expressions as something that could be quickly translated to the home system's language. New forms of inclusivism support an *a priori* inclination to look for things to learn from others, but respect for such theologians of religion is less about acceptance than it is about open consideration. They feel that it is more respectful to hear others as they are and leave their distinctiveness intact, even if in the end aspects are rejected due to incompatibility with the home system, than it is to concoct similarity and compatibility in order to be able to affirm. The latter, in this view, is not respect but domination.

Unfortunately, I cannot summarize here numerous book-length arguments for the advantages and varieties of new theology of religions forms, but one example involves seeing the implications of closed vs. open inclusivism up against Fredericks's concerns. Closed inclusivists feel that their home tradition is wholly and exhaustively true, so that any insights found in another tradition would have to be assimilated onto already known home tradition insights in order to be embraced. Open inclusivists, in contrast, not asserting exhaustive truth for their own system, affirm that an alien religion(s) may teach truths not already explicitly taught by the home tradition – truths that may expand the home tradition – without anonymous Christian-style assimilation. So open inclusivists look for genuinely new and different insights, not just familiar wisdom in different guises.

As another example, consider the advantages of a rule theory of doctrine (beyond the advantage of avoiding experiential-expressivism's problems, already covered above). If doctrines were understood as propositions, an inclusivist would be interested in and could accept only those doctrines from other tradi-tions that overlap or do not conflict with the home system. If one understands doctrines as rules, however, there are more options for reconciliation in cases of apparent conflict. Lindbeck gives the example of the claims that we should drive on the left side of the road versus the right, which flatly clash when understood propositionally. When understood as rules, though, the two claims may both be seen to have their own logic in certain circumstances within their own systems, and attention is thereby directed to their holistic contexts. Rule theory directs us to describe more thickly the system of which the doctrines are a part, extending the period of openness and keeping alive longer the possibility of truth until our understanding is deeper and more nuanced. And yet rule theory does not dictate resolvability, for in the end elements of one game may not find acceptance from the standpoint of another game. If and when acceptance happens, though, it will not be as quick, superficial, or problematic as some of the older forms' methods because the items in question will have been understood on their own terms. Understanding religions as analogous to language games (as Wittgenstein-influenced rule theory does) means that we cannot presume to know equivalences in advance or assume that our categories are valid cross-culturally, instead forcing us to enter the others' worlds and see from their points of view, learning their culture and language. A third example, the move to modalize one's theology of religions (e.g., by claiming only that *it is possible that* there is truth in other religions and/or that others could be saved) likewise avoids definitively mapping the territory before one explores the territory. Yet it has the virtue of coming clean about the hypothesis and hopes guiding the travel.

But even if comparative theologians can applaud such newer options in theology of religions, they may remain impatient to get on with the actual practices of engagement rather than getting bogged down at the theology of religions theoretical set-up stage. Here I sympathize. I do agree with Clooney that 'no amount of reflection on the presuppositions, methods, or importance of one's own tradition can succeed in obviating the need actually to read and learn from other traditions'.[27] But we cannot skip over getting clarity on our theological presuppositions about the other and just jump into the practice of reading, because so much hangs on *how* we read, which is determined by our theology of religions in the first place.[28] This is why theology of religions is properly prior to comparative theology (even if comparative theology in turn leads to theology of religions adjustments). The theology of religions obviously implies reading strategies. Without the proper theology of religions foundation established ahead of time, we may read differently (e.g., seeing others as saying what we are saying, presuming a singular end or an experiential-expressive theory of doctrine, looking for flaws rather than new truths and insights, etc.). When comparative

---

27 Clooney, 'Comparative Theology', 662.
28 Work by Amos Yong supports me here. The third chapter of his book discusses how various theology of religions positions condition particular interreligious practices such as approaches to dialogue. See his *Hospitality & the Other: Pentecost, Christian Practices, and the Neighbor* (Maryknoll, NY: Orbis Books, 2008), 65.

theologians describe the kind of reading they have in mind – whether in their own books or in discipline-defining works such as the 'What is Comparative Theology?' website of Boston College, the founding statement of the American Academy of Religion's comparative theology group, and the *Oxford Handbook of Systematic Theology*'s entry on 'Comparative Theology' – they clearly point to unadmitted theology of religions inclinations, in spite of their professed distaste for theology of religions.[29] They end up sounding an awfully lot like those championing new forms of the theology of religions.

Fredericks does, after all, specify the theology of religions that he is *not* starting from (e.g., one that presumes that religions are talking in two ways of the same thing). With every critique is Fredericks not thereby actually revealing his preferred or alternative theological presuppositions about the other? Clooney, in his review of S. Mark Heim's work, admits that Heim's type of inclusivism is important for comparative theology and lets us move on to ask how we might learn from others.[30] Does this not mean that Heim's is precisely the sort of groundwork that infuses, implicitly, Clooney's own projects? Clooney, in 'God for Us: Multiple Religious Identities as a Human and Divine Prospect', contemplates a verse about how God comes to us in ways appropriate to the ways we love God, as a key to what occurs in his own comparative theology. When we cross religious boundaries, God meets us there, Clooney thinks.[31] Surely, this suggests something about Clooney's theology of religions and affects how he reads.

Discipline-defining documents and authors envision the comparative theologian openly confessing a base religious framework (even if that framework is non-traditional or hybridized) and representing faith seeking understanding, in action. If there is a need to confess explicitly that one comes from, say, the Roman Catholic tradition, why would the same logic not necessitate confession as well that one is an inclusivist or pluralist of a certain kind?

Moreover, Fredericks acknowledges that there has been much talk about the need to identify a foundation for interreligious dialogue, much attention to what Christians must do in order to prepare to encounter others honestly and authentically. Yet Fredericks rejects this on the grounds that we should not revise our religious view in order to *prepare* for dialogue but rather ought to revise *after and in light of* dialogue. He discusses the mistake of watering down points of difference to make ourselves more agreeable to the other in order to prepare for the

---

29 Francis X. Clooney, SJ, 'What is Comparative Theology?', Boston College, http://www.bc.edu/schools/cas/theology/comparative/resources/articles/ct.html (accessed 23 December 2008); Clooney, 'Statement for the Comparative Theology Group for the AAR', American Academy of Religion, http://www.aarweb.org/upfiles/PUCS2007/AARPU145/CTGroupAAR.doc (accessed 5 June 2009); and Clooney, 'Comparative Theology'.

30 Francis X. Clooney, SJ, review of *Depth of the Riches* by S. Mark Heim, *International Journal of Systematic Theology* (3:3, 2001), 329–31.

31 Francis X. Clooney, SJ, 'God for Us: Multiple Religious Identities as Human and Divine Prospect', in Catherine Cornille (ed.), *Many Mansions? Multiple Religious Belonging and Christian Identity* (Maryknoll, NY: Orbis Books, 2002), 44–60.

encounter and thus losing the value of the conversation (i.e., the juxtaposition of differences).[32] Yet, again, the new theology of religions does not require watering down differences, nor does it rule out theological revision as a result of dialogue, but at the same time new theology of religions can provide an otherwise lacking foundation for engagement that people seem to think is needed.

Still, self-reflective scholars worry about the vexing problem of how to negotiate the tension between commitment and faith, on the one hand, and true openness and the lure of the other tradition, on the other. There has been much discussion about the potentially worrisome power dynamics of comparative work. Red flags go up with comparative theologians' talk of using other religions as resources and seeing other traditions as opportunities for self-enrichment. This makes an object of the other and raises the buzzword problems of colonialism, imperialism, hegemony, consumerism, etc. Yet we cannot deny that self-enrichment and appropriation of others' resources are a large part of the motive for comparative theology. So it is better to own up to this fact, and temper the distrust by confessing one's theology of religions in conjunction with one's religious framework, so that the practice of engagement is presented as part of a larger process of one's quest for the true and the good that goes beyond self-centeredness, greed, and competition. New forms of theology of religions have been developed with better sensitivity to the political ramifications and can help here.

It is impossible to get around principles of selection, guiding structures, categories, etc. that will always be biased to our own interests and backgrounds. If we admit working from within a certain religious and theology of religions framework, it makes the imposition of these more honest. (Following the work of such figures as Alasdair MacIntyre, Alvin Plantinga, and Nicholas Rescher, I believe that privileging one's home framework in the first place is justified because it is an unavoidable consequence of our epistemic situation.[33]) If one admits one's theological biases about the other in advance – to the extent that it is possible to be conscious of them – and holds them tentatively, not dogmatically, then one is in a better position to catch and correct cases where one's lens could be skewing the interpretation. Declaring one's theology about the other in advance is also more respectful to those in the tradition studied. Being forthcoming about one's intentions and where one stands may help foster improved co-operation on the part of the other, which the comparativist likely needs.

Can the eschewing of theology of religions theory about the other really get you to an intratextual, neither-here-nor-there space? Clooney champions the

---

32 Fredericks, *Buddhists and Christians*, 106–8.

33 Kiblinger, *Buddhist Inclusivism*, 19–23; Alasdair MacIntyre, *Three Rival Versions of Moral Enquiry: Encyclopaedia, Genealogy, and Tradition* (Notre Dame: University of Notre Dame Press, 1990); Alvin Plantinga, 'Pluralism: A Defense of Religious Exclusivism', in Thomas D. Senor (ed.), *The Rationality of Belief and the Plurality of Faith* (Ithaca: Cornell University Press, 1995); and *Warrant and Proper Function* (New York: Oxford University Press, 1993); Nicholas Rescher, *The Strife of Systems* (Pittsburgh: Pittsburgh University Press, 1985).

ideal of trying to see as an insider, but it is just that: an ideal. He speaks not of being an insider but of doing things as an insider would. That is a key difference. His status *vis-à-vis* the other tradition is 'more or less' insider. He can 'to some extent, in some way, learn to see the world through the eyes' of the other.[34] I do not begrudge him this; I can understand what he describes and can empathize with his frustration with cut-and-dried categories that do not do justice to real-world complexities. I know that religious identity is not fixed but fluid in response to experiences and that one can gradually near an insider's understanding of another system.[35] But this asymptotic approach towards an insider perspective of the other may not necessarily complicate or suspend identity as much as Clooney suggests, because it is possible to see it instead as a certain kind of inclusivism. While we yearn for the ideal of complete openness and the insider's view, the hedge, the qualification is always there.

When, in *Beyond Compare*, Clooney speaks of surrendering himself lovingly to Desika's words, initially without plans and strategies, without knowing exactly where it will lead, he *does* know that he is looking for ways to better understand and practice loving surrender; he *does* surmise that Desika will teach him something about those things. Clooney may aspire to enter two worlds back and forth, being in an undefined situation, taking both seriously but also being distanced from both, and yet he also admits that the hermeneutic in *Beyond Compare* (i.e., loving surrender) was a value deep in his own tradition and is exemplified by Jesus on the cross ('Into your hands I commend my spirit').[36] We are better off admitting our locatedness and presuppositions, not only in terms of our religious and cultural baggage but in terms of our theology of religions as well.

Listening to Others' Voices, Being Clear About Our Own

Yet does this very essay, composed of methodological reflection and a review of some theology of religions issues, validate comparative theologians' worry that work such as mine here displaces or postpones the more primary – and, let's face it, more interesting – work of actually engaging others? 'Where are the Buddhist voices in this paper?' Clooney asked in response to an earlier, shorter version of this paper at the AAR.

Recognizing this point, I will now draw from my research examining Buddhist voices responding to non-Buddhists – in effect, from Buddhist theology of religions, demonstrating that even our theology of religions work can be done in conversation with other traditions and is not necessarily, as Fredericks has

---

34 Clooney, 'Neither Here nor There', 109–10.
35 Though admitting being subject to correction by Buddhists, I myself, though a Christian, have made similar claims about my ability to reason from a Buddhist perspective (even with my experience and knowledge of Buddhism terribly anemic compared to Clooney's with Hinduism).
36 Clooney, *Beyond Compare*, 3, 24.

claimed, only Christians talking among themselves driven solely by Christian problems.[37] This section provides illustrative cases to support 1) that theology of religions shapes comparative theology because it determines how we read others (which is why getting one's theology of religions ducks in a row first is key), and 2) that preferred new forms of inclusivism or pluralism result in the motivations for and methods of comparison that best align with and affirm the vision of comparative theology set out in the AAR Comparative Theology Group's statement.

Some Buddhists, like the Christians criticized in theology of religions literature, can be faulted for unacknowledged privileging of the home tradition, distorting when interpreting others, and inadequate attention to differences. They too need to develop improved forms of theology of religions, constructed in accord with their own theological resources, which will facilitate comparative theology and other sorts of dialogic learning.[38]

Exploring Buddhist sources for examples of Buddhists' reasoning about non-Buddhists, I came across many instances of pragmatic thinking, in one form or another. The famous parable of the raft is typically cited in the context of evaluating other religions. Religious traditions, the reasoning goes, are a means for reaching the far shore. Parallel to experiential-expressivism's treatment of linguistic expressions (i.e., deemphasizing them in favor of the common experience to which they point), the variations in and specifics of the means are deemphasized in favor of the ostensibly common end to which they lead, and thus others' religious beliefs and practices are to be judged pragmatically by their abilities to help us to the far shore. The *Kalama Sutta* is used similarly. As the Buddha advised the Kalamas, the thinking goes, we should see which teachings and activities help lessen our suffering and attachments. Various ideas and methods can be affirmed as long as one is moving with them to those goals, and clinging to any particular set of means over others can hinder one's progress. In this way, room opens for valuing aspects of non-Buddhist systems.[39]

The doctrine of skillful means (*upaya kausalya*), I found, has been another tool used by some Buddhists to justify appreciation of other traditions. According to this teaching, the Buddha skillfully adapts and calibrates his message to the particular needs of his diverse audiences. So, a plurality of teachings and practices, appearing to conflict, may be harmonized when recast as means being used skillfully – that is, as means aiding progress towards Buddhist goals but suitable for different cultures, for persons at different stages, for persons with different spiritual aptitudes, etc. The Dalai Lama, for example, has appealed to skillful means this way, explaining in his *Spiritual Advice for Buddhists and Christians* how

---

37 For our purposes here, I will stick to examples of inclusivistic and pluralistic reasoning, rather than exclusivistic, although one can find examples of the latter, too, among Buddhists.

38 I borrow again in this section from my 'Buddhist Stances Towards Others'.

39 Phra Khantipalo uses this sort of reasoning, for example. See his *Tolerance: A Study from Buddhist Sources* (London: Rider and Company, 1964), 39–40.

and why this doctrine helps him to respect and affirm aspects of non-Buddhist traditions.[40]

Three-body doctrine has also proved convenient for negotiating difference. Three-body doctrine specifies that Buddhahood has three aspects: dharma body (ultimate source reality), enjoyment body (heavenly or visionary appearances), and transformation body (earthly persons or projections). This has been used to interpret non-Buddhist figures as enjoyment or transformation bodies. For example, Tendai and Shingon schools responded inclusivistically towards Shinto by teaching that kami (Shinto deities) are manifestations of buddhas and bodhisattvas who are their true natures (*honji-suijaku*).[41]

Buddhists draw on the theory of the two truths – conventional and ultimate (*samvrti-* and *paramartha-satya*) – as well. Bhikkhu Buddhadasa of Thailand, for instance, relies heavily on this theory in his thinking regarding religious plurality. One can see the implied common core theory and experiential-expressivism as he relegates religious differences to a low level. At the high level, the level of Dhamma as he calls it, he sees only agreement. In addition to the literal and conventional language, there is something 'essential', a 'special kind of religious language embodying the "inner world"', a 'truth hidden in between the letters or behind the sound of speech', he writes. If people can understand this 'Dhammic language' then differences will evaporate and Buddhists 'can accept all the passages of Christianity as in agreement with the Buddha's teaching', interpreting 'the language of Dhamma in the Bible in their own terms'. 'God and the "Law of Karma" are one and the same thing', he insists. '(W)hich term is used depends (merely) upon how we were taught to label things or how we were brought up.'[42]

Exiled Vietnamese Buddhist Thich Nhat Hanh demonstrates common core theory and experiential-expressivism as well. In the context of discussing religious diversity in his *The Raft is Not the Shore*, he writes, for instance, that 'it is not the words and the concepts that are important but something within'.[43] In *Going Home: Jesus and Buddha as Brothers*, he asserts that the Apostles' and Nicene Creeds contain equivalent teachings to the Five Mindfulness Trainings, provided that we do not get 'caught in words'. 'Whether you call it nirvana or Father, it's not important', he says. 'What is important is that there is another dimension that should be touched.'[44] (Note that 'dimension' is singular.)

---

40 His Holiness the Dalai Lama, *Spiritual Advice for Buddhists and Christians* (New York: Continuum, 1998), 15–18.

41 American Buddhist John Makransky discusses how several Mahayana sutras talk of 'apprehending venerable teachers of non-Buddhist religions as if they were Bodhisattvas . . . who use non-Buddhist means to prepare their followers for the Buddha's path to liberation'. See his 'Buddhist Perspectives on Truth in Other Religions', *Theological Studies* (64, 2003), 334–61.

42 Bhikkhu Buddhadasa, *Christianity and Buddhism: Sinclaire Thompson Memorial Lecture* (Bangkok: Karn Pim Pranakorn Partnership, 1967), 3–7, 22, 32, 66, 71, 79.

43 Thich Nhat Hanh and Daniel Berrigan, *The Raft is Not the Shore: Conversations Toward a Buddhist/Christian Awareness* (Boston: Beacon Press, 1975), 112.

44 Thich Nhat Hanh, *Going Home: Jesus and Buddha as Brothers* (New York: Riverhead Books, 1999), 135, 99. Japanese Zen Buddhist Masao Abe would be another case in point here. See my *Buddhist Inclusivism*, 102–12.

These patterns are symptomatic, I contend, of the one-vehicle theory that underlies them. One-vehicle theory, such as that found in the *Lotus Sutra* (*Saddharmapundarika Sutra*) and the *Srimaladevisimhanada Sutra*, was originally developed by Mahayana Buddhism in relation to non-Mahayana Buddhist schools, although this theory has grown to affect Buddhist attitudes towards non-Buddhist others, too. It contends that all beings will eventually attain ultimate fulfillment through the Mahayana and that other paths are just preparatory for advancing to the Mahayana. Significant plurality, in other words, in the end is only apparent or provisional. This is a Buddhist version of what Heim would call the problematic single-end sort of inclusivism, with its attendant difficulties that obstruct comparative learning.

The theory of two truths, as used by some Buddhists, assumes a single end, because differences and particularities at the conventional level of real expressions are dismissed in favor of a posited, vague, deeper commonality (i.e., end) at a higher level. With three-body theory, when non-Buddhist figures are reinterpreted as Buddha bodies, others' claims to distinctiveness are discounted; their ends evaporate. Pragmatically judging other religions by their fruits requires criteria that come from considering the home tradition's end as normative, rather than trying to understand others on their own terms in the context of their own aims. With skillful means, others' teachings and practices are seen to be ways by which non-Buddhists can advance towards the Mahayana Buddhist end. When, as John Makransky says, skillful means are used to 'explore how others' symbol systems and modes of thought might serve to communicate, in their own ways, the very truths the Buddha had taught', then it is an anonymous Buddhism move.[45]

According to my research, Buddhist inclusivists' and pluralists' favorite tool, however, is often emptiness (*sunyata*), the notion that all phenomena lack independent and enduring essences and thus that all things are relative and conditioned. Buddhists want to treat emptiness as an antidote to all positions rather than itself one position alongside others. This concept, they want to say, is exceptional in this way and therefore can ground dialogue particularly well. Masao Abe, a Japanese Zen Buddhist, is a case in point.

With emptiness, Abe treats as normative a 'positionless position' that he thinks is 'inherently non-dogmatic and free from one-sidedness or bias'. It is, he says, 'a position which is completely free from any particular position that is surreptitiously taken as the absolute or universal standpoint'.[46] So, when dialoguing with others, Abe wants this to be a criterion that floats above all systems, and by which all other systems are measured. Against the accusation that this smacks of a commitment to Buddhism over other religions, Abe retorts that emptiness is

45 Makransky, 'Buddhist Perspectives', 335.
46 Masao Abe, in Steven Heine (ed.), *Buddhism and Interfaith Dialogue* (Honolulu: University of Hawai'i Press, 1995), viii, 13.

unsubstantial and negates itself.[47] In addition, he argues that the Christian notion of kenosis means the same thing as emptiness, if Christians could only understand it rightly (never mind that Abe's Christian interlocutors at the time unanimously denied this). He maintains that emptiness can serve as a common basis for our pluralistic situation if only the religions would 're-examine themselves radically and grasp the quintessence of their own faiths'.[48] Although Abe may deny it because of the ostensibly special nature of emptiness teaching, this amounts to positing a non-neutral hermeneutic as if it were neutral. The kenosis part and the bit about others needing to re-examine themselves to grasp their own faiths also makes the anonymous other move, telling members of other traditions what their traditions really mean. Buddhadasa acts similarly when he takes further his hermeneutic of the theory of the two truths. For him, at the lower level, religions seem different. At the level of Dhamma, they share an essence and at the level of emptiness they explode the my-religion-versus-your-religion duality. 'Everything', Buddhadasa says, 'is void of self and there is no Buddhism, no Christianity, or Islam . . .' Hence his title, 'No Religion!'[49] In this way, without admitting it, he builds a supposedly universal or neutral truth from the Buddhist concepts of non-duality, no-self, and emptiness.

These Buddhists are vulnerable to the same critiques that have plagued Christians employing outdated forms of theology of religions, and accordingly their faulty theology of religions will impede their involvement with and learning from others for the same reasons. Will the above Buddhists be ideal or productive comparative readers, given the problematic nature of their theology of religions, which causes them to refuse to hear self-descriptions, impose their own norms, see their own notions in others' notions, etc.?

Let's take Thich Nhat Hanh, for example. In his *Living Buddha, Living Christ*, he argues that while the historical Jesus and the historical Buddha may differ, the 'living Christ' and the 'living Buddha' amount to the same thing.[50] He says that the Jesus who teaches the Dharma is the 'true Jesus'.[51] He sees in the Christian notion of incarnation the Buddhist concept of non-duality and equates the 'seed of the Holy Spirit' with the 'seed of mindfulness' and Buddhahood.[52] Nhat Hanh thinks of himself as celebrating the Eucharist, which he sees as a practice that Jesus taught to awaken his disciples to mindfulness. So, when he eats his muesli

---

47 Like Abe, Makransky insists that the stress on emptiness is not just a sneaky way of identifying Buddhist representations of truth more closely with *the* truth than the representations of other traditions, because it is not the representations themselves that are upheld as Truth; they just point (Makransky, 'Buddhist Perspectives', 359).

48 John C. Cobb and Christopher Ives (eds), *The Emptying God: A Buddhist–Jewish–Christian Conversation* (Maryknoll: Orbis Books, 1990), 36, 40–51.

49 Bhikkhu Buddhadasa, 'No Religion!', in Donald K. Swearer (ed.), *Me and Mine: Selected Essays of Bhikkhu Buddhadasa* (Albany: SUNY Press, 1989), 146–55.

50 Thich Nhat Hanh, *Living Buddha, Living Christ* (New York: Riverhead Books, 1995). See especially p. 56.

51 Hanh, *Going Home*, 139.

52 Hanh, *Living Buddha*, 36 and *Going Home*, 46, 91.

in a slow and meditative way, that, to him, is taking Communion. He recommends that Christians take Communion not in a church but outside, the way that his community at Plum Village eats breakfast.[53] Nhat Hanh seems to reinterpret radically this central Christian ritual, leaving it unrecognizable to Christians. Presenting himself as profoundly respecting – indeed as practicing – Christianity along with his own Buddhism, in fact he maps Christian ideas onto Buddhist ones, privileges Buddhism without admitting doing so, ignores crucial differences, and interprets Christian teachings and practices very inadequately. In the process, he offends Christians, whose help he presumably needs if he wishes to learn more from Christianity. The commonalities he asserts have the vagueness problem for which old-style pluralists are notorious, and his writing is rife with anonymous Buddhism (i.e., telling others how they should understand their own teachings). (My favorite example of the latter is that he tells Christians to portray Jesus sitting in the lotus position rather than on the cross, because the cross is to Nhat Hanh a disturbing image that 'does not do justice to Jesus'.[54] As I have argued elsewhere, there is something very peculiar and deeply questionable about doing such violence to the other while supposedly embracing the other.)

I should clarify that not all Buddhists whom I researched were found to share these theology of religions deficiencies. Although I do not have time to describe his work in detail here, American John Makransky, a Tibetan Buddhist lama, for instance, moves toward the newer and improved form of inclusivism, explicitly endorsing Heim's multiple ends inclusivistic approach in his 'Buddha and Christ as Mediators of the Transcendent'.[55] Nor are Buddhists necessarily bound to one-vehicle theory. I have argued elsewhere that if Buddhists have an interest in developing their inclusivism more along these newer lines by recognizing the possibility of finally different soteriological ends, three-vehicle theory as found in the *Mahayanasutralamkara* is a very important possible resource and alternative to the one-vehicle theory of the *Lotus* and *Srimaladevisimhanada Sutras*. I discuss this and other Buddhist resources for constructing improved inclusivist forms in my *Buddhist Inclusivism*.[56]

Admittedly, Thich Nhat Hanh is an extreme case, but his writing shows, I hope, how well-intentioned but problematic inclusivism and pluralism shape our approach to others, and how under the friendly surface of comparative thinking, dominance and disrespect can be found lurking. Thus, one's theology of religions makes a significant difference in one's comparative theology, and

---

53 Thich Nhat Hanh, *Peace is Every Step: The Path of Mindfulness in Everyday Life* (New York: Bantam, 1992), 22–3; *Living Buddha*, 30–3; *Going Home*, 106–8.
54 Hanh, *Going Home*, 46.
55 John Makransky, 'Buddha and Christ as Mediators of the Transcendent: A Buddhist Perspective', in Perry Schmidt-Leukel (ed.), *Buddhism and Christianity in Dialogue: The Gerald Weisfeld Lectures 2004* (London: SCM Press, 2005), 189. See also his 'Buddhist Perspectives' and his 'Buddhist Inclusivism: Reflections Towards a Contemporary Buddhist Theology of Religions', in Perry Schmidt-Leukel (ed.), *Buddhist Attitudes to Other Religions* (St Ottilien: EOS Verlag, 2008).
56 Kiblinger, *Buddhist Inclusivism*, 44–8, 78–89.

getting the former right is essential to doing the latter well and to framing what one is doing properly.

Now I turn to the work of Christian–Buddhist comparative theologian John P. Keenan. Keenan's writings, too, instantiate a problematic form of inclusivism, and recognizing this fact relates the otherwise disconnected criticisms of his comparative theology and suggests that reframing his project could help redeem it.

Keenan is professor emeritus of religion at Middlebury College and an Episcopal priest with extensive academic training in Buddhist Studies and relevant languages. His major works in comparative theology are his *The Meaning of Christ: A Mahayana Theology*, *The Gospel of Mark: A Mahayana Reading*, and *The Wisdom of James: Parallels with Mahayana Buddhism*.[57] The motivation for his Mahayana Christian theology arises from his view that Christian faith need not depend exclusively upon any one philosophical system and that it can be enriched by enunciating it from alternative perspectives. Christian theology's reliance on Greek philosophy, Keenan contends, arose from historical accident and so need not be set for all time.[58]

Keenan explains that when Greek thinking was adopted, an unfortunate division developed between theoretical meaning and practical or mystic understanding. A subject–object mode of understanding accompanied by a view of language as able to capture absolute truth came to dominate Christian thinking and to color Christian doctrines of salvation. With that, the tradition strayed from the experience and awareness of the first Christians.[59] Keenan argues that a Mahayana hermeneutic can help to retrieve this mysticism. Mahayana thought insists on the inadequacy and conditioned nature of all views and warns against any clinging to literal meaning. Emptiness is not a new view but rather the deconstruction of all views, which tend to generate delusions of essences. The focus is on wisdom, or direct awareness of no–self, which comes before explanation and theorizing. The distinction of conventional from ultimate truth allows re-engagement in worldly convention, but with a crucial understanding of it as just convention. In this way, Mahayana Buddhism strives for the awareness that is unmediated by words.

The Yogacara movement applied concepts such as emptiness, dependent co-arising, etc. to consciousness, unpacking the implications for reading scripture. With their notions of the container consciousness and the active consciousness, they explained how we mistake appearances for permanent realities and take

---

57 John P. Keenan, *The Meaning of Christ: A Mahayana Theology* (Maryknoll, NY: Orbis Books, 1989); *The Gospel of Mark: A Mahayana Reading* (Maryknoll, NY: Orbis Books, 1995); *The Wisdom of James: Parallels with Mahayana Buddhism* (Mahwah, NJ: The Newman Press, 2005).

58 John P. Keenan, 'The Emptiness of Christ: A Mahayana Christology', in *Anglican Theological Review* (75:1, 1993), 48–63.

59 Keenan, *The Meaning of Christ*, 62.

ourselves to be perceivers distinct from what is perceived. With the resultant subject–object pattern of knowing, we forget that these patterns derive from karmic seeds in our container consciousness, and these patterns in turn engender more seeds. Awakening can occur only when the seeds are slowly destroyed, which is called the transformation of the basis (*asraya-parivrtti*) and which re-orients the consciousness to mystic understanding. Wisdom is such contact with what is ineffable, and valid discrimination about the scriptures flows from this wisdom. Discriminative thinking is now valid only because the ideas and images generated are not understood to imply essences or absolute truths.

Keenan favors doing Christology through the lens of Mahayana Buddhism because Nagarjuna's dialectic is vigilant about resisting clinging to doctrine rigidly, constantly admitting doctrine's contextuality and thus avoiding idola-trous images of Christ. Another virtue is that it keeps mystical experience central: 'Mahayana Christology remains true to the faith of the Christian com-munity', and its 'deconstructive themes will deepen insight into the gospel'.[60] Keenan argues that the 'Markan rhetoric of indirection and irony is the narrative analogue to Madhyamika dialectical' in Nagarjuna's work.[61]

Responding to Keenan's comparative theology, it is helpful to understand his reviewers' reactions in terms of criticisms leveled at outdated forms of inclu-sivism.[62] Multiple reviewers emphasize that they do not object to Keenan's ambition to theologize as a Christian while drawing on Buddhist resources, but rather applaud the effort by Christians to make use of insights from other faith traditions.[63] Instead the reviewers' objections parallel my objections to the moves of Buddhists mentioned above. Keenan's use of emptiness parallels that of Abe and Buddhadasa and thereby tries to make a meta-claim using a Buddhist claim. Keenan wants to rule out the idea that any language about ultimate reality can be ultimately valid rather than merely conventionally valid. Reviewers such as Robin Matthews dislike this because it seems to them inconsistent. It seems to make not just a conventional but also an absolute claim (about all claims being conventional).[64] On the one hand Keenan does say that using these Buddhist concepts is only one of many possible frameworks, and so in this sense his use of emptiness is conventional. Yet in the claim that Christology is amenable to many philosophical approaches and that no one should be taken as more than

---

60 Keenan, *The Meaning of Christ*, 262, 223.

61 Keenan, *The Gospel of Mark*, 4.

62 In addition to the reviews discussed here, see my own review of *The Wisdom of James* by John P. Keenan, *Journal of Religion* (86:1, 2006).

63 Joseph O'Leary, 'The Significance of John Keenan's Mahayana Theology', in *The Eastern Bud-dhist* (30:1, 1997), 132; John B. Cobb, Jr, 'Response to Mahayana Theology', in *Buddhist–Christian Studies* (13, 1993), 46; Paul J. Griffiths, 'Response to Mahayana Theology', in *Buddhist–Christian Studies* (13, 1993), 51.

64 Robin Matthews, 'Response to Mahayana Theology', in *Buddhist–Christian Studies* (13, 1993), 53–4.

convention, in that claim itself, emptiness is sneaking through as an absolute. There is a Buddhist imposition here.[65]

This ties in to typical objections to Keenan's work relating to his reliance on mystic experience and ineffable silence.[66] As Griffiths explains, Keenan's use of emptiness leads to experiential-expressivism. In fact, Keenan's is, says Griffiths, a 'textbook example' of this theory of doctrine.[67] In addition, Keenan's whole book on Mark, to put it crudely, could be seen as arguing that what we Christians should understand Mark to be conveying about Jesus is what Mahayana Buddhists mean when they speak of emptiness, the two truths, dependent origination, and so on. Thus, as Joseph O'Leary suspects, Keenan supposes that 'Mark is an anonymous Buddhist'.[68]

Many accuse Keenan as well of implying a common core. As with many of these accusations, Keenan denies this.[69] If there is no significant difference between the Buddhist and Christian traditions in the end, he admits that that would undermine his effort, for it is only because of differences that a Mahayana reading yields new insights. Yet it seems that he does not want to admit a true diversity either. He insists that ultimate awareness is ineffable due to consistent descriptions of it as such by those who have had mystic experiences. And although those experiences within various faith traditions are described differently, to admit ultimate diversity in such experiences would be to maintain that language in these cases refers to ontological realities. He feels that his Mahayana outlook avoids both options.[70] Nevertheless, the insistence on ineffable experience makes diversity impossible to establish and functionally irrelevant.

When we stop to ask what, according to Keenan, are the final differences between the Christian gospel and Mahayana Buddhist teachings, his common core and single end assumptions are quite clear. When he considers likely contenders, the differences, he sometimes says, are derived from accidental historical and cultural factors and thus are unnecessary accretions.[71] Other times Keenan

---

65 Buddhists and Keenan are aware of this problem and claim that when emptiness becomes a view, it is misunderstood. This is parallel to a much older controversy between Nagarjuna and his opponents: the question of whether emptiness itself can really be empty and not itself another view. Nagarjuna is careful to guard against this problem in his *Vigrahavyavartani,* in which he compares his statement (that all is empty) to a phantom, indicating that in one sense it is not real but that in another sense it is not totally non-existent, for it is capable of performing a function – in this case communicating meaning. Keenan here stresses the unreal aspect of the phantom without acknowledging that there is a meaning conveyed by that phantom that must be treated as one meaning on a par with others, rather than imposed categorically.

66 See Francis X. Clooney, SJ, Review of *The Meaning of Christ* by John P. Keenan, in *Spirituality Today* (43:4, 1991), 389–90; and O'Leary, 'The Significance'.

67 Griffiths, 'Response to Mahayana Theology', 48–9.

68 O'Leary, 'The Significance', 128.

69 See Keenan's 'Mahayana Theology: A Dialogue with Critics', in *Buddhist–Christian Studies* (13, 1993), 15–44; 'Hybrid Theology (A Response)', in *Eastern Buddhist* (31:1, 1998), 139–49.

70 Keenan, *The Gospel of Mark,* 190–2.

71 Again, this parallels the formal structure of Buddhist inclusivist moves. For example, the *Aganna Sutta* reinterprets the Vedic vanna system in order to make it accord with Buddhism, and

says that the oppositions are not in fact mutually exclusive (due to the experien-tial-expressivist's means of reconciling conflicts) and/or that there are analogues for the Buddhist teachings in non-mainstream strands of Christianity, which should be retrieved and highlighted.[72] In short, Keenan refuses to pay much attention to differences.

This is why people have asked, in response to Keenan's work, whether in fact a Mahayana Christian theology can be a Christian theology. Not only does his emptiness move make Buddhism his starting point, but interestingly, even though Keenan certainly claims to be doing work in the service of Christianity, his moves and concluding interpretation with respect to Jesus parallel closely many Buddhist inclusivists' ones. And this is why O'Leary comments that Keenan comes close to reducing the 'meaning of Christ' to Madhyamika doc-trine and why Cobb deems Keenan's Christology 'essentially a Buddhology'.[73] The most telling reaction to Keenan's work may be this sense among readers and reviewers that, despite Keenan's rhetoric, he is a closet Buddhist, that while he presents his writing as using a Buddhist framework for doing Christian work, it strikes many instead as inscribing Christian scripture into the margins of the Buddhist text.

Despite these lengthy complaints, however, I do find Keenan's work creative, knowledgeable, stimulating, detailed, and skilled. If he would just frame what he is doing differently, I would feel better about it. I would suggest that the Keenan corpus is really most accurately presented upfront as inclusivistic. Because he uses a Mahayana lens that must be seen as one lens among others rather than one that can rise above, Keenan's project works as Buddhist inclusivism. Presenting it that way would make the imposition of the guiding principles more honest and acceptable. Now Keenan just needs to upgrade to newer forms of inclusivism in order for his comparative theology to proceed unencumbered by the older forms' liabilities.

Conclusion

Clooney asks, in a review of a Paul Knitter book, which is the most fruitful theology of religions position? Which helps us to get on with the comparative reading and learning?[74] There is an answer. If we can agree that the comparative theologian best proceeds by inculturating herself to try to understand the other system as insiders do, then one arrives at the sort of dual perspective that

---

then justifies the reinterpretation with the claim that this is what the Vedic system itself taught orig-inally, before it became corrupted over time.

72 Keenan, *The Meaning of Christ*, 197–212.

73 O'Leary, 'The Significance'; Cobb, 'Response', 47.

74 Francis X. Clooney, SJ, review of *Introducing Theologies of Religions* by Paul F. Knitter, in *New Theology Review* (17:3, 2004), 83–4.

Clooney struggles to categorize, affirming its tensions and challenges as positive. One arrives simultaneously in the realm of the new theology of religions forms. Comparative theologians need to be self-conscious and forthcoming about the effects of their theology of religions on their comparative theology. They gave up on theology of religions prematurely, missing an opportunity for help easing the hegemony concern by framing work in terms of more politically sensitive theology of religions. New forms of inclusivism and pluralism should be explicitly endorsed, disclosed upfront, and used by comparative theologians.

3

The New Comparative Theology and the Problem of Theological Hegemonism

HUGH NICHOLSON

The New Comparative Theology as a Fresh Alternative to the Theology of Religions

In the 1920s, when the great phenomenologist Edmund Husserl was asked to explain what the then relatively unfamiliar phenomenological movement in philosophy was about, he is supposed to have declared, 'Phenomenology: that is I and Heidegger, and no one else.'[1] One could well imagine Francis X. Clooney, James Fredericks, Robert Neville, and a handful of others responding to the question, 'What is comparative theology?' with a similar reference to proper names. Comparative theology is only just beginning to win recognition from the wider theological community as an autonomous discipline transcending the varied practices of its individual founders. Even so, it remains in a more or less inchoate state. A clear consensus as to what exactly comparative theology is has yet to emerge. It will be the task of the next generation of comparative theologians to develop a relatively precise conception of the discipline as they take up the practice of theologically informed comparison from their teachers.[2] At the

---

1 Hans-Georg Gadamer, in David E. Linge (trans. and ed.), *Philosophical Hermeneutics*, (Berkeley: University of California Press, 1976), 143.
2 In this essay I have focused on the work of Fredericks and Clooney as representative of the new comparative theology. I am keenly aware of the fact that in my effort to engage directly the work of the two editors of this volume, I have given insufficient attention to the work of other contemporary comparative theologians that differs in certain respects from that of Fredericks and Clooney (e.g., the work of Robert Neville, John Berthrong, Lee Yearley, etc.). In particular, I have rather arbitrarily privileged more 'confessional' forms of comparative theology over more 'academic' ones, that is, those defined by a dual allegiance to church and academy as opposed to those whose primary allegiance is to the academy. An adequate treatment of the latter type would require a more in-depth treatment of the relationship between comparative theology and the academic study of religion ('comparative religion') than I have given here.

same time, they will seek to broaden the conception of the discipline to include more voices and perspectives, as the essays by Michelle Voss Roberts and Tracy Tiemeier in this volume attempt to do. As I understand it, the aim of the present volume is precisely to advance this dual task of clarification and inclusion.

We might best approach the question of what comparative theology *is* by first specifying what it is *not*. Comparative theology is not, as Fredericks and Clooney both insist, simply another theology of other religions like exclusivism, inclusivism, or pluralism. That is to say, the new discipline is not another theoretical, *a priori* theological position on the 'problem' of religious diversity considered in the abstract. Fredericks, in fact, makes this contrast with the theology of religions the basis of an understanding of comparative theology that I consider to be paradigmatic. In his book *Faith among Faiths*, he presents comparative theology as a fresh alternative to a form of theological discourse that he believes has become increasingly unfruitful. Fredericks argues that the debate between pluralists and inclusivists – a debate which has pretty much dominated recent theology of religions literature – has reached an impasse.[3] On the one hand, pluralist theologians like John Hick, Wilfred Cantwell Smith, and Paul Knitter have exposed the inadequacies of the more traditional theologies of Christian fulfillment currently labeled 'inclusivist'. The notion that Christianity fulfills the fragmentary and adulterated truths of other religions implies an arrogant presumption to know non-Christians better than they know themselves, an assumption epitomized by Karl Rahner's well-intentioned, if somewhat patronizing proposal that Christians regard non-Christians as 'anonymous Christians'.[4] Christian inclusivism, with its claim that Christianity fulfills, and thereby renders obsolete, other faiths, harbors a half-concealed intention to convert and dominate the latter. In the final analysis, pluralists see little real difference between inclusivism and the religious imperialisms of the past.[5] Put differently, the pluralists have exposed classic fulfillment-model inclusivism as a form of unacknowledged exclusion or, to introduce a concept that I will develop throughout this essay, theological hegemonism.

On the other hand, critics of pluralist theology like Mark Heim and Kenneth Surin have argued that these pluralist theologies of religions, ironically enough, are vulnerable to precisely the same criticism.[6] The universalist claim that the various religions represent only so many responses to a transcendent Real (Hick), express a unitary concept of personal faith (W. C. Smith), or evince a common concern for justice (Knitter) effectively renders the differences

---

3 James Fredericks, *Faith among Faiths* (New York: Paulist Press, 1999), 8 and *passim*.

4 This charge is mitigated by the fact that Rahner intended the concept of anonymous Christianity only for a Christian audience. Cf. Paul F. Knitter, *Introducing Theologies of Religions* (Maryknoll, NY: Orbis Books, 2005), 73–4.

5 John Hick, 'The Non-Absoluteness of Christianity', in John Hick and Paul F. Knitter (eds), *The Myth of Christian Uniqueness* (Maryknoll, NY: Orbis Books, 1994), 22.

6 Kenneth Surin, 'A "Politics" of Speech: Religious Pluralism in the Age of the McDonald's Hamburger', in Gavin D'Costa (ed.), *Christian Uniqueness Reconsidered* (Maryknoll, NY: Orbis Books, 1990); S. Mark Heim, *Salvations* (Maryknoll, NY: Orbis Books, 1995).

between them theologically insignificant.[7] The pluralist presupposition that all religions are fundamentally saying the same thing betrays an incapacity truly to respect religious difference, to respect the religious other *qua* other.[8] In the final analysis, pluralist theologies like those of Hick and Smith are little more than inclusivisms in disguise.[9] On the basis of this line of critique, Fredericks judges pluralist theologies, no less than inclusivist ones, to be 'strategies that effectively allow Christian believers to escape the necessity of taking other religious believers seriously'.[10]

However devastating this critique of pluralist theology may be, it is important to recognize that in itself it does nothing to vindicate inclusivism, let alone exclusivism, from the earlier pluralist critique. The net result, then, is an unproductive stalemate. The theology of religions, at least in its present configuration, finds itself at an impasse. In light of this mutual critique, Fredericks judges neither inclusivism nor pluralism, to say nothing of exclusivism, as being adequate to the task of responding 'creatively and responsibly' to religious diversity in today's world.

Fredericks proposes comparative theology as a way out of this impasse. The new discipline does this by abandoning the pretension to work out a stance towards other religions independently of a study of the specific teachings of those religions. In eschewing the apriorism of the theology of religions, comparative theology abandons a global, totalizing perspective on other religions.[11] Comparative theology thus renounces any presumption to know non-Christians better than they know themselves, whether as vain products of human presumption, as in Barth's exclusivism; as various expressions of 'anonymous Christianity', as in Rahner's inclusivism; or as various forms of 'Reality-centeredness', as in Hick's pluralism. The fundamental presupposition of Fredericks's critique of the theology of religions is that any unfalsifiable, *a priori* interpretive framework – whether exclusivist, inclusivist, or pluralist – functions as a protective screen against the challenge posed by the claims of meaning and truth of other religions.[12] By

---

7 Fredericks, *Faith among Faiths*, 113ff.
8 Kathryn Tanner, 'Respect for Other Religions: A Christian Antidote to Colonialist Discourse', in *Modern Theology* (9:1, 1993), 11–12 and *passim*.
9 Fredericks, *Faith among Faiths*, 110, 115 and *passim*; Heim, *Salvations*, 30 and *passim*.
10 Fredericks, *Faith among Faiths*, 115.
11 Fredericks, 'A Universal Religious Experience? Comparative Theology as an Alternative to a Theology of Religions', in *Horizons* (22:1, 1995), 83–4; Francis X. Clooney, SJ, 'The Study of Non-Christian Religions in the Post-Vatican II Roman Catholic Church', in *Journal of Ecumenical Studies* (28:3, 1991), 483, 488.
12 Fredericks, *Faith among Faiths*, 167; cf. 108–10. Cf. also Clooney, *Hindu God, Christian God* (New York: Oxford University Press, 2001), 12: 'I leave my judgements – that there is a God, that one can know something of who God is, that God can become embodied, and that God does speak to us and instruct us – open to further comparative and dialogical testing and do so contentedly, since there is no urgency to finalize such judgements before one has actually conversed and even argued in an interreligious context. Theologians not engaged in comparative work are quite often willing to be tentative in their conclusions, which remain open to revision and correction, and there is no reason to demand speedier progress of comparative theologians.' Epitomizing an under-

removing this screen, the comparative theologian is able to experience the full force of the interreligious challenge and, with it, the possibility of deepening, indeed transforming, his or her own theological understanding. Comparative theology distinguishes itself from the theology of religions, then, by its willingness to revise Christian self-understanding in light of the teachings of other traditions.[13]

We can be grateful to Fredericks for a conception of comparative theology that lends to the discipline a clear sense of identity and purpose. For this reason his understanding of comparative theology as a solution to the theology of religions impasse will serve as the basis for my reflections below on the nature and task of comparative theology in relation to the problem of theological hegemonism. At the same time, however, one could argue that a conception of comparative theology based on an invidious contrast between the essential openness and flexibility of comparative theology and the rigid apriorism of the theology of religions lends clarity to the former only at the cost of caricaturing the latter. As Kristin Beise Kiblinger argues in this volume, the characterization of the theology of religions as a rigid dogmatism, while usefully exposing the pretensions of the classic forms of inclusivism and pluralism, ignores recent developments in the theology of religions. Schubert Ogden's proposed 'modalization' of the theology of religions, to cite but one example – the proposal, that is, that the theologian be committed to the proposition 'not that there actually *are* many true religions, but only that there *can* be'[14] – in principle reduces dogmatism to the vanishing point.[15] In this, Ogden's so-called 'fourth option' (the other three being, of course, exclusivism, inclusivism, and pluralism), *a priori* theological reflection serves to establish a hermeneutical stance of openness and receptivity – nothing more. And at the same time that the disjunctive contrast between the theology of religions and comparative theology implies a caricature of the former as a closed, dogmatic enterprise, it suppresses an acknowledgement of the constraints that antecedent theological commitment places on the practice of comparative theology, constraints which Fredericks freely acknowledges in the less polemical sections of his work.[16] In short, the theology of religions might be a little less

---

standing of comparison as an open-ended, self-corrective process is the comparative method set forth by Robert C. Neville and Wesley Wildman in the context of their Cross-cultural Religious Ideas Project. See, e.g., Robert Cummings Neville and Wesley J. Wildman, 'On Comparing Religious Ideas', in Robert Cummings Neville (ed.), *The Human Condition: A Volume in the Comparative Religious Ideas Project* (Albany: State University of New York Press, 2001).

13 Fredericks, 'A Universal Religious Experience?', 84 and *passim*.

14 Schubert M. Ogden, *Is There Only One True Religion or Are There Many?* (Dallas: Southern Methodist University Press, 1992), 83.

15 See Ogden, *Is There Only One True Religion*, 103: 'All that the fourth option claims a priori, in advance of actually encountering specific religions and validating their claims to truth, is that, if the Christian religion itself is true, then any and all other religions can also be true in the very same sense [. . .]'.

16 On the constraints operative in comparative theology (and interreligious dialogue) see Stephen J. Duffy, 'A Theology of the Religions and/or a Comparative Theology?', in *Horizons* (26, 1999), 107

rigid and dogmatic, and comparative theology a little less flexible and open, than Fredericks's rhetoric might suggest.

The Problem of Theological Hegemonism

Below I reflect critically on the disjunctive contrast that Fredericks and, to a lesser extent, Clooney draw between comparative theology and the theology of religions. In this respect my essay will complement Kristin Biese Kiblinger's from this same volume. At the same time, however, I affirm a presupposition of Fredericks's conception of comparative theology that she questions, namely, the thesis that the theology of religions currently stands at an impasse. And it is here that my critique of the putative separation between comparative theology and theology of religions moves in quite a different direction than hers. While Kiblinger argues that the stark contrast that Clooney and Fredericks draw between the two disciplines exaggerates – to the point, perhaps, of manufacturing – the crisis of the theology of religions by failing to take account of its more recent developments, I shall argue that this contrast tends to suppress the full dimensions of a crisis that I believe is real. It does so by fostering the comforting illusion that the problem of unacknowledged exclusion or theological hegemonism can be neatly solved by eliminating the two prominent features of the theology of religions, namely, its apriorism and its penchant for abstract theorizing.

In order to bring the full dimensions of this problem of theological hegemonism into view it is necessary to put the relation between the theology of religions and comparative theology into a broader historical perspective. A major problem I see in most presentations of the theology of religions is that they tend to present its basic positions in more or less systematic, as opposed to historical terms.[17] Exclusivism, inclusivism, and pluralism are presented as alternative contemporary theological responses to religious diversity. Each is typically represented by an important twentieth-century theologian whose thought is still taken seriously: for example, Barth for exclusivism, Rahner for inclusivism, and Hick for pluralism.[18] I contend that such a systematic treatment, while perhaps

---

and *passim.* Cf. the critical question Paul Knitter poses to Fredericks in his review of *Faith among Faiths*: 'Is F. aware of how much his own theological suppositions might be implicitly influencing what he sees in other religions?' (*Theological Studies* 62:4, December 2001, 874).

17 Or else they are arranged in a tendentious evolutionary sequence, starting with exclusivism, through inclusivism, and ending with pluralism, as in Alan Race's classic *Christians and Religious Pluralism* (London: SCM Press, 1983). So prevalent is this tendency to arrange theology of religions positions in such an evolutionary pattern that Paul Knitter, for example, finds it necessary to disabuse his readers of such expectations when putting forth a neutral, systematic treatment of the subject in his *Introducing Theologies of Religions*. See p. 216 of that book.

18 The limits of the systematic conception of the theology of religions become apparent when one considers the choice of a representative for the exclusivist position. In standard works in the theology of religions, exclusivism is typically represented by the rather idiosyncratic exclusivism of Karl Barth and Heinrich Kraemer. The exclusivism of Barth and Kraemer is idiosyncratic because, unlike classic Christian exclusivism of the *extra ecclesiam nulla salus* variety, it holds that all 'religion',

serving as a useful heuristic aid for theological reflection on interreligious issues, nevertheless obscures what I regard as the fundamental problem facing the contemporary comparative theologian. In the pages that follow, I shall develop the thesis that inclusivism and pluralism represent successive moments in a dialectic through which the tradition of liberal theology has vainly sought to overcome exclusionary, 'us' versus 'them' relations in the realm of religion. Throughout this essay, I shall sometimes find it convenient to refer to this antagonistic dimension of interreligious relations, borrowing terminology from the controversial political theorist Carl Schmitt, as 'the political'.[19] Since the Enlightenment, successive generations of liberal theologians have sought to eliminate this exclusionary, 'political' dimension of traditional theological discourse by projecting a universalist theological vision. In the nineteenth century, this universalist vision most frequently took the form of a Christian fulfillment theology (classic inclusivism); in the twentieth, the notion of a harmonious plurality of faiths established on a putative unity of religious experience (classic pluralism). But as the above-mentioned critiques of inclusivism and pluralism have shown, such attempts to 'de-politicize' theological discourse have only yielded more subtle and easily misrecognized forms of religious exclusion.[20] Contemporary critics like Kenneth Surin and Tomoko Masuzawa have argued that both forms of liberal universalism are expressions of what Arif Dirlik terms 'Western cultural hegemonism'.[21] Far from being eliminated, the principle of the political has been merely sublimated – forced, as it were, into the arguably more insidious form of unacknowledged exclusion or hegemonism. It is this problem of 'the inescapability of the political', I contend, that lies at the root of the impasse to which Fredericks refers.[22] It is a problem far more profound and intractable than I think he recognized.

---

including the Christian, is 'unbelief'. When the theology of religions discourse is understood in diachronic terms, exclusivism is revealed to be the discourse's other. Thus exclusivism proper does not represent a viable theology of religions position. It is hardly surprising, then, that systematic presentations that suppress the historical dimension of this discourse are forced to represent exclusivism with theological voices that poorly exemplify it.

19 Carl Schmitt, *The Concept of the Political* (trans. George Schwab) (Chicago: The University of Chicago Press, 1996), 25–37 and *passim*. I should perhaps mention that my use of Schmitt's concept of the political as a helpful analytical tool does not imply support for Schmitt's constructive political proposals. In this respect I follow a theorist like Chantal Mouffe ('Carl Schmitt and the Paradox of Liberal Democracy', in Chantal Mouffe (ed.), *The Challenge of Carl Schmitt* (New York: Verso, 1990); *idem.*, *The Return of the Political* (New York: Verso, 1993)), who takes Schmitt's critique of liberalism seriously while drawing conclusions radically different from his.

20 As Heim (141–2) argues with respect to pluralist theology, the illusion of impartiality is maintained by a specious distinction between, on the one hand, the primary faith positions (i.e., Buddhism, Islam, Judaism, etc.) that it includes, and, on the other, the meta-theories of religion (exclusivism and inclusivism) that it excludes.

21 Surin, 'A "Politics" of Speech', 203–4; Tomoko Masuzawa, *The Invention of World Religions* (Chicago: University of Chicago Press, 2005), Ch. 9, esp. 315–17; 324–8.

22 This reading of the history of modern interreligious theology is influenced by Schmitt's provocative essay, 'Das Zeitalter der Neutralisierungen und Entpolitisierungen', in *Positionen und Begriffe im Kampf mit Weimar – Genf – Versailles 1923–39* (Berlin: Duncker & Humblot, 1988).

Enlarging our historical perspective thus reveals a depth dimension to the current crisis in the theology of religions. In doing so, it brings to light certain pitfalls and ambiguities awaiting the new comparative theology as it attempts to work around this impasse. In particular, an enlarged historical perspective disabuses us of any expectation that the problem of theological hegemonism can be solved simply by abandoning *a priori* theological reflection and integrating theological commitment with the comparative method. That an appeal to the notion of unprejudiced comparison represents a somewhat facile solution to this problem of theological hegemonism becomes clear when we trace the genealogy of the new comparative theology back to a theological discourse of the late nineteenth century which was also called, curiously enough, 'comparative theology'.

The Comparative Theology of the Late Nineteenth Century

'Comparative theology' was among the terms used to designate the nascent non-confessional, 'scientific' study of religion in the latter part of the nineteenth century.[23] Scholars of religion today, eager to disavow the theological pedigree of the science of religion, tend to assume a sharp distinction between 'comparative theology' and 'comparative religion'.[24] At the time, however, the two appellations did not mark, as they do today, an antithesis between theologically committed and scientific approaches to the study of religion. Scholars at the time who opted for 'comparative religion' over 'comparative theology' typically justified their preference for the former term not on the basis of its connotation of theological neutrality but rather on its comprehensiveness: whereas comparative *theology* restricted itself to the intellectual, doctrinal aspect of religion, comparative *religion* included its devotional, ritual, and mythological aspects as well.[25] On the other side, a scholar like Max Müller could argue that 'comparative theology' was a more fitting designation for the new science of religion because the term 'theology', inasmuch as it refers to the reflexive dimension of religious practice, aptly conveys a sense of the distance obtaining between a science and its object of study.[26]

Nineteenth-century comparative theology encompassed a range of works, from explicitly apologetical ones like F. D. Maurice's *The Religions of the World and Their Relations to Christianity* (1847), James Freeman Clarke's *Ten Great Religions: An Essay in Comparative Theology* (1871), or J. A. MacCulloch's *Comparative Theology* (1902) to works in which the authors' theological commitments are sublimated, qualified, or otherwise subdued, the best known of which is Müller's

---

23 See Henry Louis Jordan, *Comparative Religion: Its Genesis and Growth* (New York: Charles Scribner's Sons, 1905), 24–8.

24 Masuzawa, *The Invention of World Religions*, 22.

25 Jordan, *Comparative Religion*, 27; C. P. Tiele, 'On the Study of Comparative Theology', in Eric J. Ziolkowski (ed.), *A Museum of Faiths* (Atlanta: Scholars Press, 1993), 76.

26 F. Max Müller, *Natural Religion* (New York: Longmans, Green and Co., 1889), 45.

Introduction to the Science of Religion (1882). What the various works of comparative theology generally share, however, is a rejection of the traditional apologetical categories of revealed religion and natural religion to describe the relation between Christianity and other faiths.[27] By rejecting these categories, comparative theologians of the late nineteenth century sought to bring the study of religion in line with the liberal religious sensibilities of an age marked by rapidly expanding horizons of knowledge and experience. The rejection of these categories allowed them to recognize a place for non-Christian religions in an economy of salvation. In this way, comparative theology announced a decisive break with a tradition of exclusivist Christian apologetics that liberal Christians increasingly found distastefully intolerant, parochial, and reactionary.

The favorite categories of the late nineteenth-century science of religion were those of 'world religion' and 'national religion' (or, alternatively, 'universal' religion and 'ethnic' religion).[28] These categories were ostensibly based on an empirical distinction between those religions that have transcended a particular cultural milieu and those that have not. Unlike the dogmatic categories of revealed religion and natural religion, the empirically based categories of world religion and national religion allowed for a genuinely comparative – which meant, given the recent success of the comparative method in fields like anatomy and linguistics, *scientific* – approach to the study of religion.[29] At the same time, the privileged category of world religion embodied the normative liberal ideal of a form of religion transcending the principle of political division and strife. Accordingly, the categories could be used to frame what for a comparative theologian like James Freeman Clarke was the fundamental question of Christian apologetics:

> Is Christianity, as taught by Jesus, intended by God to be the religion of the human race? Is it only one of the natural religions? Is it to be superseded in its turn by others, or is it the one religion which is to unite all mankind?[30]

This question anticipates the typical course of argument. Works of this genre typically begin by recognizing a putative subset of religions as world religions, those, that is, which have managed to extend their influence beyond the con-

---

27 James Freeman Clarke, *Ten Great Religions: An Essay in Comparative Theology* (Boston: Houghton Mifflin Company, 1899), 4ff.; *idem.*, *Ten Great Religions, Part II: A Comparison of All Religions* (Boston: Houghton Mifflin Company, 1883), 24–5; F. Max Müller, *Introduction to the Science of Religion* (London: Longmans, Green and Co., 1882), 69; George Matheson, *The Distinctive Messages of the Old Religions* (New York: Anson D. F. Randolph and Co., 1894), 38ff.
28 See Masuzawa, *The Invention of World Religions*, 77–8.
29 Cf. Louis Henry Jordan's remark that the title, 'The Comparative Science of Religion', 'is clearly tautological' (Jordan, *Comparative Religion*, 26). On the use of the comparative method in anatomy and its parallel with comparative religion, see Jordan, *Comparative Religion*, 31–2. On the promise of the comparative method in religion based in its dramatic success in the field of linguistics, see Müller, *Introduction*, 8–12 and *passim*.
30 Clarke, *Ten Great Religions*, Part I, 14.

fines of a particular people or nation.[31] Typically, though with some exceptions, this list included Buddhism, Islam, and – of course – Christianity. These works then proceed to challenge the universalistic claims of the former two, concluding rather predictably that Christianity alone merits the title of 'world religion', that it is, in other words, the one religion which, by virtue of its inherent qualities, meets the religious needs of all humanity.[32]

In this way, comparative theological works present what is clearly a foregone conclusion – that Christianity is *the* world religion – as the outcome of an impartial empirical study. In the final analysis, comparative theology was no less dogmatic than the exclusivist apologetics it replaced. Its pretension of forging a decisive break with the tradition of Christian apologetics was largely illusory. Indeed, comparative theology, with its central concept of a world religion, gives paradigmatic expression to the nexus between liberalism and imperialism that characterized nineteenth-century European colonialism.[33] In its universalization of a particular conception of religion, comparative theology provides a textbook example of a hegemonic discourse in the realm of religion.

The Emergence of Pluralist Theology

What the universalist fulfillment theology of theologians like Clarke and Maurice was to the nineteenth century, the pluralist theology of religions of John Hick and Wilfred Cantwell Smith was for the twentieth. Each was the standard-bearer of Christian liberalism in their respective generations. The transition from the former to the latter can be understood in terms of two twentieth-century developments.

The first of these was a shift from Christian universalism to religious pluralism as the dominant paradigm in the non-confessional study of religion. During the first decades of the twentieth century there was a curious reversal of the nineteenth-century tendency to restrict the number of world religions by revoking – as we have just seen – the universal status of Buddhism and Islam. Now the

---

31 Exemplifying this pattern of argument are Clarke, *Ten Great Religions* (Part I); Abraham Kuenen, *National Religions and Universal Religions* (trans. P. H. Wicksteed) (London: Macmillan, 1882); and C. P. Tiele, 'Religions', in *Encyclopedia Britannica*, 9th edn (Edinburgh, 1885), 358–71, esp. 368–9.

32 A typical argument used against Islam's claim to world religion status appealed to the old apologetic stereotype of Islam as a 'religion of the sword': whatever conversions Islam managed to win outside of Arabia were through coercive, not persuasive means and were therefore invalid (for this argument, see, e.g., Kuenen, *National Religions and Universal Religions*, 102; Clarke, *Ten Great Religions*, Part I, 503 and *passim*.; F. D. Maurice, *The Religions of the World and Their Relations with Christianity* (London: Macmillan, 1886), 57 and *passim*). A typical argument used against Buddhism was that it was merely a 'philosophy', not a proper religion (Kuenen, *National Religions and Universal Religions*, 304). Whatever universal qualities it has are therefore irrelevant.

33 On the connections and tensions between nineteenth-century liberalism and European colonialism with specific reference to Britain's colonial project in India, see Thomas R. Metcalf, *Ideologies of the Raj* (Cambridge: Cambridge University Press, 1995), 28–65.

tendency was to *expand* the number of world religions to include religions
formerly classified as national religions, such as Judaism, Hinduism, and
Taoism.[34] The historical causes and conditions leading to the familiar notion of
seven to ten 'world religions' are complex, elusive, and, in any case, lie outside
the scope of this essay.[35] Here I might simply observe that at some point the
notion of national religion lost its currency, as it was evidently no longer seen as
compatible with the liberal sentiments of respect and tolerance. The corresponding concept of world religion, now deprived of its original contrasting term,
henceforth becomes a quasi-emotive – and obligatory – expression of recognition and respect. The term 'world religion' comes to refer blandly to one of the
recognized 'religions of the world'. These are in turn understood as so many historically conditioned manifestations of a conception of 'religion' that no longer
coincides – at least not explicitly – with Christianity.

The second twentieth-century development that led to pluralist theology as
we know it today was the divorce between Christian theology and the compar-
ative-phenomenological method in the so-called 'theological renaissance' of the
1930s. With its bold reassertion of the dogmatic categories of revealed religion
and natural religion, Barthian neo-orthodoxy rendered the comparative study of
religion theologically irrelevant, if not theologically suspect as well. The theological reception of the work of Rudolf Otto, a precursor of today's comparative
theology,[36] provides perhaps the most dramatic evidence of this shift in theological attitude towards the comparison of religions. Otto had the misfortune of
having his career trajectory coincide with the ascendancy of his critics, Barth,
Brunner, and Bultmann, in Protestant theology.[37] The apriorism of the present-
day theology of religions can perhaps be seen as the dubious legacy of Barthian-
ism. Pluralist theology thus developed – rather ironically in light of its profound
aversion to the Barthian dictum that 'religion is unbelief' – in an *a priori* mode.[38]

As mentioned above, pluralist theology is founded on a critique of the universalist fulfillment theology that had been standard-bearer of Christian liberalism.
Specifically, pluralist theology rejects as specious the latter's claim to have broken
decisively with exclusivist apologetics. According to John Hick, the inclusivist
notion of anonymous Christianity amounts to little more than 'a hangover from

---

34 See Jonathan Z. Smith, 'Religion, Religions, Religious', in *Relating Religion* (Chicago: University of Chicago Press, 2004), 191.
35 Tomoko Masuzawa acknowledges that the history of the usage of the term 'world religions' and
its variants is 'vexingly obscure' (*The Invention of World Religions*, 10). And, I might add, an adequate
explanation far exceeds my historical expertise.
36 In my opinion (and despite its well-known shortcomings), Otto's later comparative work represents a model for the kind of philologically rigorous and theologically sensitive comparison
espoused by contemporary comparative theologians.
37 See Gregory Alles's introduction to Gregory D. Alles (trans. and ed.), *Rudolf Otto: Autobiographical and Social Essays* (Berlin, New York: Mouton de Gruyter, 1996), 3–12.
38 Given this history of estrangement between a dominant strand of Protestant theology and comparison, it is not surprising that the recent revival of comparative theology would be centered in
Catholic circles.

the old religious imperialisms of the past'.[39] At the same time that it thus redescribes fulfillment theology as yet another form of Christian absolutism, pluralist theology introduces a hitherto unknown distinction between inclusivism and pluralism.[40] As captured by Hick's metaphor of the Copernican revolution in theology, the pluralist shift from a Christocentric to a theocentric model of religious salvation was supposed to mark a shift in paradigm from the tradition of Christian absolutism.

As we have seen, critics have since challenged this claim, arguing that Hick-style pluralism is little more than inclusivism in disguise. Pluralist theology, with its universalistic claim that all religions manifest the same fundamental experience or reality, is no less hegemonic than the inclusivist theology it was supposed to replace.

A Sequence of Binary Oppositions

The history sketched out in the preceding two sections should make us wary of any declaration of a radical break with the interreligious theology of the past. In particular, it raises the disconcerting possibility that the categorical distinction that a theologian like Fredericks makes between comparative theology and the theology of religions[41] will turn out to be just as specious as the putative caesura between fulfillment theology and traditional apologetics in the nineteenth century or, again, that between pluralism and inclusivism in the twentieth.

Here I would like to put forward the hypothesis that the disjunction between comparative theology and the theology of religions is merely the latest in a sequence of binary oppositions by which the tradition of liberal theology has vainly sought to transcend religious exclusion and antagonism, what I have been calling the political. I suggest this possibility with the constructive aim of flagging

---

39 Hick, 'The Non-Absoluteness of Christianity', 22.

40 To characterize nineteenth-century comparative theology as a form of Christian inclusivism is, strictly speaking, an anachronism. One can, in fact, discern pluralistic overtones in the expressions of Christian fulfillment found in these works, particularly when they emphasize that Christianity does not destroy, but rather preserves, the religions it fulfills. See, e.g., Matheson, 328. 'But the religion of Christ is not anxious to put things locally together, nor even to make them similar in appearance. It seeks to reconcile them in their differences, – to make them, in the very midst of their diversity, work out one common end. It is not eager for uniformity, not solicitous for the recognition of one mode of government, not desirous that all should think on the same plane; it desires that the air may run through the variations, that the diversity of gifts may enfold a unity of the spirit.' Later (p. 338) Matheson speaks of a Christian dominion, 'which extends from sea to sea without destroying the sea – without obliterating the boundaries that now divide, or annihilating the diversities that now distinguish'. Such statements would easily find themselves at home in contemporary pluralist theology.

41 Fredericks understands the distinction between the theology of religions and comparative theology in terms of a categorical distinction between theory and practice, with the latter being the privileged term. See *Faith among Faiths*, 9.

a potential pitfall in the conception of comparative theology that we should try to avoid, or at least be aware of.

The sequence begins with the recognition of the tradition of exclusivist Christian apologetics as the paradigmatic form of the political in religion. Nineteenth-century Christian liberalism then presents universalist fulfillment theology as a stark alternative to that tradition. When, in a second moment of the dialectic, classic fulfillment theology comes to be seen as itself an expression of religious imperialism, and thus as merely another modality of the political in religion, the liberal tradition responds with a new opposition between pluralism, on the one hand, and Christian absolutism in its twin forms of exclusivism and inclusivism, on the other. The subsequent critique of pluralist theology as disguised inclusivism sets the stage for the third moment in this dialectic. By setting itself over and against the theology of religions, the new comparative theology establishes yet another binary opposition between a fresh and promising new mode of interreligious theology and its recently discredited predecessors. The theology of religions, with its threefold typology of exclusivism, inclusivism, and pluralism, serves as a convenient shorthand for all those past forms of interreligious theology now recognized as only so many modalities of the political in theology. (See Figure 3.1 below.)

	Liberal Theology	*'Political' Theology*
Nineteenth century	Old Comparative Theology (Fulfillment Theology)	Traditional Apologetics (Exclusivism)
Twentieth century	Pluralist Theology	Christian Absolutism (Exclusivism; Inclusivism)
Twenty-first century	New Comparative Theology	Theology of Religions (Exclusivism; Inclusivism; Pluralism)

Figure 3.1: *Three Moments of Depoliticization in Modern Interreligious Theology*

This pattern comes even more clearly into view when we compare the new comparative theology directly to its nineteenth-century namesake. The distinction between the *a posteriori* and *a priori* methods forming the basis of comparative theology's presumptive split from the theology of religions carries an unmistakable echo of the methodological distinction between empirical comparison and dogmatic presumption that established nineteenth-century comparative theology over against traditional Christian apologetics. This parallel disabuses us of any expectation that the problem of theological hegemonism can be solved simply by adopting an *a posteriori* method, of integrating theological reflection with a knowledge of the actual teachings of other traditions. It warns us, moreover, that a given form of interreligious theology blinds itself to its own inherent ambiguities when it projects a political-dogmatic other.

I readily anticipate three objections to this thesis that the new comparative theology represents the latest moment in a dialectic of depoliticizing theology. The first is that today's comparative theologians are not apolitical in the ordinary sense of that term. James Fredericks, for one, sees the task of forging new forms of solidarity with other religious believers as an integral part of the practice of comparative theology.[42] The correlative practices of interreligious dialogue and comparative theology mobilize members of different religious traditions against two troubling symptoms of our present situation of late-stage, global capitalism: on the one side, a proliferating consumer culture that has eroded the bonds of community and tradition; on the other, virulent forms of religious militancy that threaten the peaceful coexistence of different religious and cultural populations in today's pluralistic societies.[43] It should be noted, however, that even in thus emphasizing the political dimension of the practice of comparative theology, Fredericks does not concede the specific aspect of the political that I am singling out as the 'other' of modern, 'liberal' theology: namely, social antagonism sustained by discourses of oppositional identity. Indeed, it is precisely this antagonistic dimension of social relations that is represented by those reactionary forms of religious revival that the practice of comparative theology resists. In developing his notions of interreligious solidarity and interreligious friendship,[44] Fredericks tacitly appeals to a distinction between what might be termed, following Sandria B. Freitag,[45] relational community and ideological community, that is, between localized forms of community developing out of a matrix of personalized, 'I–Thou' relationships, on the one hand, and large-scale forms of community mobilized by oppositional discourses, on the other.[46] To the extent, then, that comparative theologians refuse to countenance the oppositional discourses sustaining the latter form of religious community, we can say that comparative theology continues the liberal theological project of 'depoliticizing' religion and theology.

---

42 *Buddhists and Christians*, 100–2; 112–15, and *passim*.

43 *Buddhists and Christians*, 101–2.

44 James L. Fredericks, 'Interreligious Friendship: A New Theological Virtue', in *Journal of Ecumenical Studies* (35:2, Spring 1998), 159–74.

45 Sandria B. Freitag, *Collective Action and Community* (Berkeley: University of California Press, 1989), 88 and *passim*.

46 See, e.g., his emphasis on 'mutuality over polemics' (*Buddhists and Christians*, 114; note the reference to Martin Buber's conception of dialogue). This implicit distinction between relational and ideological communities dovetails with the practice versus theory distinction that Fredericks uses to distinguish comparative theology from the theology of religions. More than anything else, it is the ideological character of the latter discipline – its imposition of an unfalsifiable theoretical framework between a theological tradition and the potentially transformative experience of interreligious theological encounter – that distinguishes it from comparative theology.

The second objection has to do with my characterization of comparative theology as a form of 'liberal' theology, or, to be more precise, as a moment in the modern liberal project of depoliticizing theology. For many, perhaps most, comparative theologians today do not identify with the tradition of 'liberal' theology. There is, in fact, as Paul Knitter observes, a certain affinity between comparative theology and the 'postliberal' perspective of George Lindbeck.[47] But here, once again, the anticipated objection is largely a matter of semantics. As exemplified by Lindbeck's usage of the term in *The Nature of Doctrine*, 'liberal' theology refers rather narrowly to those forms of theology presupposing a foundational and universal religious experience, which he derisively – and, I might add, tendentiously[48] – terms 'experiential expressivism'.[49] In contrast to this usage, I understand liberalism in theology to refer more broadly to the modern project of liberating religious faith from social antagonism. In other words, I understand 'liberalism' as the contrasting term of 'the political' in the sense above. Lindbeck's so-called postliberal theology, to continue with his example, remains in the liberal tradition in this broader sense inasmuch as he is reluctant to concede an oppositional, 'political' dimension to the supposedly self-contained religious communities he champions.[50] The same can be said of the new comparative theology to the extent that it

47 Knitter, *Introducing Theologies of Religions*, 177 and *passim*. Clooney acknowledges the positive influence of Lindbeck on his conception of comparative theology. See, e.g., 'Reading the World in Christ: From Comparison to Inclusivism', in Gavin D'Costa (ed.), *Christian Uniqueness Reconsidered* (Maryknoll, NY: Orbis Books, 1992), 67–8; *idem.*, *Theology after Vedanta* (Albany, NY: SUNY Press, 1993), 115–18. Fredericks also accepts Lindbeck's cultural-linguistic understanding of a religion as 'a highly rationalized system of symbols that constitutes a resourceful and encompassing interpretive framework' (*Buddhists and Christians*, 98) as well as the latter's critique of 'experiential expressivism', but is critical of other aspects of Lindbeck's postliberal project, particularly its thesis regarding the alleged incommensurability of religious traditions. On Fredericks' assessment of postliberalism, see, e.g., 'A Universal Religious Experience?', 78–82.
48 David Tracy (among others) argues that Lindbeck's characterization of liberal theology as 'experiential expressivism' is a caricature. See David Tracy, 'Lindbeck's New Program for Theology: A Reflection', *The Thomist* (4:9, July 1985), 462–5.
49 Fredericks follows Lindbeck in understanding 'liberalism' 'as an aspect of German Romanticism' ('A Universal Religious Experience?', 68–9) and in crediting Friedrich Schleiermacher with being the 'founding father of Liberal Theology' (*ibid.*, 71). Against this reading of intellectual history, I would trace the origin of the tradition of liberal theology back to the Enlightenment, specifically, to the problematic of isolating an essence of religion from sectarian strife. For all its polemic against Enlightenment rationalism, Schleiermacher's *Speeches* preserves this characteristically Enlightenment problematic, as evident particularly in the crucial, but curiously neglected fourth speech, 'On the Social Element in Religion'.
50 This reluctance can be inferred from the rather dubious distinction between 'sociological' and 'theological' sectarianism that he uses to distinguish his postliberal Christian enclaves from militant, 'theologically sectarian' fundamentalist sects (see Lindbeck, 'Ecumenism and the Future of Belief', *Una Sancta* (25:3, 3–17); *idem.*, 'The Sectarian Future of the Church', in Joseph P. Whelan, SJ, (ed.), *The God Experience* (New York: Newman Press, 1971). Cf. also Kathryn Tanner's incisive critique postliberalism in her *Theories of Culture* (Fortress, 1997). As Tanner shows, the postliberal conception of Christian community rests on a problematic understanding of cultures as 'self-generating and self-contained' formations, that is, on the classic anthropological concept of culture that Lindbeck appropriates from Clifford Geertz. The recognition of this antagonistic dimension of religious com-

implicitly understands the differences between religious traditions to be substantive rather than contrastive in nature. In other words, to the extent that it presumes that interreligious differences are simply 'there', rather than being the contingent products of the complex processes of selection, emphasis, and recognition through which religious communities situate themselves 'politically' in relation to proximate rivals.[51]

The third objection has to do with my claim that comparative theology is defined by its rejection of exclusivism, inclusivism, and pluralism. One could argue that while such a characterization may indeed apply to Fredericks's and to a lesser extent Clooney's conception of the discipline, it overlooks the fact that many contemporary comparative theologians ally themselves with an inclusivist or (perhaps less commonly) pluralist theology of religions position. In her contribution to this volume, Kristin Beise Kiblinger argues in favor of such 'allied' forms of comparative theology. In order to uphold my thesis that the new comparative theology tends to define itself in opposition to exclusivism, inclusivism, and pluralism, I would appeal to the distinction that Kiblinger herself makes between older, 'problematic' and more recent, 'preferred' theology of religions models. When a comparative theologian like Kiblinger affirms an inclusivist theology of religions position, for example, it is invariably what Paul Knitter terms 'acceptance-model' inclusivism, which was itself developed as a clear alternative to the older, universalist forms of pluralism and inclusivism now recognized to be hegemonic.[52] To the extent, then, that comparative theologians clearly distinguish the forms of inclusivism and pluralism with which they identify from the older counterparts of these positions, their proposals can be understood, with only minor adjustments, in terms of the aforementioned dialectic.

The Improvements of the New Comparative Theology Over the Old

I have isolated a tendency in the conceptualization of the new comparative theology that establishes a relation of continuity with its discredited – and largely forgotten – nineteenth-century namesake. This tendency is offset, however, by

---

munity focuses attention on an aspect of doctrine that Lindbeck downplays, namely, their role in mobilizing Christian identity in opposition to rival communities. On Lindbeck's suppression of the political dimension of doctrine, see Hugh Nicholson, 'The Political Nature of Doctrine: A Critique of Lindbeck in Light of Recent Scholarship', in *The Heythrop Journal* (48:6, November 2007), 858–77.

51 Cf. the qualitative distinction Schleiermacher makes between intrareligious and interreligious differences, or as he puts it, between 'the plurality of the churches' and 'the plurality of the religions', in the 'Fifth Speech' (Richard Crouter, trans., *On Religion* (Cambridge, 1996), 96–7). The former are based on formal, political acts of exclusion and are therefore contingent and revocable. The latter, by contrast, are substantive and ineradicable.

52 Cf. Knitter's classification of comparative theology as an expression of the acceptance model, *Introducing Theologies of Religion*, 177 and *passim*.

other important elements in the conceptualization of comparative theology. As I see it, the new discipline differs sharply from its older namesake in at least three significant respects.

The first of these is its resistance to generalization and its consequent avoidance of the kind of religious and cultural stereotypes that fill the works of nineteenth-century comparativism. Clooney's work in particular exemplifies this focus on particular examples and a refusal to use these as mere stepping stones to advance more expansive theoretical claims. By keeping theological reflection closely tied to the careful reading of particular texts, Clooney's comparative theology maintains a healthy critical distance from reified conceptions like 'Buddhism' and 'Hinduism', which, as Jeffery Long notes in his essay with reference to 'Hinduism', often reflect and embody a history of asymmetrical power relations between the west and other religions and cultures. Lifting up a text or tradition of interest to the comparativist as representative of a larger cultural or religious formation lies at the root of the formation of invidious representations of the cultural other that reflect the interests and values of the west. In contrast to their nineteenth-century predecessors, today's comparative theologians are acutely aware of the internal diversity of the traditions they compare. They clearly perceive the problematic political implications of holding a single text or practice as representative of a tradition as a whole. Even when the decision is not wholly arbitrary, taking a particular text or sub-tradition as representative of the whole reinforces indigenous hegemonies, as, for example, when Orientalist scholars privileged brahmanical traditions in their construction of a 'Vedantized' concept of Hinduism.[53] As Michelle Voss Roberts argues in her contribution to this volume, comparative theology's sensitivity to the internal diversity of the compared traditions dovetails with the concern of feminist and liberation theologians to recognize marginalized voices in a given theological tradition.

The issue of representation leads us to the second feature of the new comparative theology that distinguishes it from the comparative theology of the nineteenth century: namely, a recognition of the importance of correlating interreligious theological reflection with the practice of interreligious dialogue.[54] In stark contrast to the armchair comparativists of the nineteenth century, who often evinced an astounding indifference to the self-understandings of the contemporary practitioners of the religions they studied, contemporary comparative theologians generally subscribe, even if only implicitly, to the principle, famously championed by W. C. Smith, that 'no statement about a religion is valid unless it

---

53 On the western 'discovery' of Vedanta as the essence of Hinduism, see, e.g., Richard King, *Orientalism and Religion* (Routledge, 1999), 118–24 and *passim*.
54 This dialogical dimension of comparative theology receives particular emphasis in Fredericks's work. While similarly stressing the importance of 'dialogical accountability' to religious others, Clooney broadens the concept of dialogue to include forms of interior dialogue prompted by a thoughtful engagement with the classic texts of another tradition (*Hindu God, Christian God*, 10).

can be acknowledged by that religion's believers'.[55] Or, as Fredericks argues, the teachings of other traditions should not be reformulated in an alien theoretical idiom in which they may no longer be recognizable to the members of the religion in question; in contrast to both the non-theological study of religion and the theology of religions, the comparative theologian strives to understand the religious teachings of others 'on their own terms'.[56]

The third characteristic feature of the new comparative theology is an honest acknowledgement of its own normative commitments and interests as the principal means – paradoxically – of avoiding the kind of distortion and bias of its nineteenth-century predecessor. A fundamental presupposition of the new comparative theology is that it is not bias as such that is responsible for cultural misunderstanding and distortion so much as it is the *masking* of bias under a false claim in objectivity. The answer to the problem of bias and distortion in the study of religion does not lie in the vain pursuit of the chimerical ideal of scholarly objectivity and neutrality but rather in a forthright acknowledgement of one's normative commitments coupled with a willingness to submit those judgements to critique and possible revision.[57] As Jeffery Long eloquently puts it, an openness about our interests and agendas is 'the postmodern equivalent to the modern stance of objectivity, inasmuch as it does the same work that objectivity was intended to do, only better'.[58]

Of course, both the non-theological study of religion and the theology of religions have also made this 'postmodern' turn to acknowledgement as requisite for the avoidance of ideological distortion in the treatment of other religions. Summarizing this turn in the theology of religions, Paul Knitter, a well-known advocate of the pluralist or 'mutuality' model, declares that 'we are all inclusivists now', in the sense that 'we are always – incorrigibly and incurably – going to view, hear, and understand the other religious person from our own religious perspective'.[59] One could perhaps argue, however, that the new comparative theology, particularly its more confessional forms, represents the paradigm of this recent turn to acknowledgement in the study of religion. Once again, we can refer to Clooney's work in order to illustrate this feature of comparative theology. Reflecting on his comparative theological reading of the South Indian Srivaisnava devotional text, the *Tiruvaymoli*, in his book *Seeing Through Texts*, Clooney writes:

---

55 Wilfred Cantwell Smith, 'Comparative Religion: Whither – and Why?', in Mircea Eliade and Joseph M. Kitagawa (eds), *The History of Religions: Essays in Methodology* (Chicago: University of Chicago Press, 1959), 42. This criterion must be qualified by a recognition that, given the internal diversity of religious traditions, such acknowledgement is not likely to be unanimous among the putative members of the tradition in question.

56 *Faith among Faiths*, 168, 169; 'A Universal Religious Experience?', 84.

57 Hugh Urban, 'Making a Place to Stand: Jonathan Z. Smith and the Politics and Poetics of Comparison', in *Method and Theory in the Study of Religion* (12, 2000), 373 and *passim*.

58 Jeffery D. Long, *A Vision for Hinduism: Beyond Hindu Nationalism* (London: I. B. Tauris, 2007), 4.

59 Paul F. Knitter, *Introducing Theology of Religions* (Maryknoll, NY: Orbis Books, 2002), 217.

In neither my reading nor writing was the goal to be entirely open; it was rather to make sure that our sympathetic reading would go forward with an acute awareness of our strictures of prior commitments, beliefs, attachments – according to linguistic community, profession, religion, etc. We have therefore studied *Tiruvaymoli* and its reception among the Srivaisnavas with a growing awareness of our own commitments, imaginations, desires.[60]

Contrast this description of the perspective of comparative theology with the scientistic outlook of the following passage from the opening pages of James Freeman Clarke's *Ten Great Religions*:

> The work of Comparative Theology is to do equal justice to all the religious tendencies of mankind. Its position is that of a judge, not that of an advocate . . . Its first problem is to learn what each system contains; it may then go on, and endeavor to generalize from the facts . . .
> [Comparative Theology] does dogmatize: it observes. It deals only with phenomena, – single phenomena, or facts; grouped phenomena, or laws.[61]

A comparison of the types of the theological claims corresponding, respectively, to these two methodological statements – the first modest and charitable, the second incautious and prejudicial – provides a striking illustration of the thesis that the way to truth and fairness runs through an honest acknowledgement of one's interpretive limitations rather than through an unexamined commitment, however sincerely held, to an ideal of scholarship as impartial and objective.

Living with Ambiguity

It is important to realize that a forthright acknowledgement and justification of the inevitably perspectival nature of one's approach to other religions is not a magic bullet for the problem of the political in religion. While it may indeed represent an advance in dealing with the problem of unacknowledged exclusion or hegemonism, it does so only at the risk of leaving the door open to a return to the kind of interreligious apologetics that the Enlightenment had hoped to banish for ever. Like Rahu, the Hindu deity of eclipses who swallows the moon only to have its other end reappear at the bottom of his neck, comparative theology, in its preoccupation with the problem of theological hegemonism in its twin forms of pluralism and inclusivism, finds itself conceding a polemical, 'exclusivist' dimension of interreligious theology. Thus, both Fredericks and Clooney affirm an apologetic dimension to the enterprise of comparative theology as a concomitant of its confessional nature.[62] Each is quick to emphasize, however, that the only

---

60 Clooney, *Seeing Through Texts* (Albany: State University of New York Press, 1996), 247.
61 *Ten Great Religions*, Part I, 3.
62 Clooney, *Hindu God, Christian God*, 11–12; Fredericks, *Buddhists and Christians* (Maryknoll, NY: Orbis Books), 109; 113–14.

kind of apologetics compatible with their vision of comparative theology is one that is well informed and respectful of its theological adversaries, and which is, in any case, somewhat peripheral to the comparative theological enterprise.[63] The chief justification for such an apologetics is its ability to highlight and clarify the substantive theological differences that exist between different theological traditions.[64] The kind of apologetics Clooney, Fredericks, and even Paul Griffiths have in mind is analogous to what the Indian logicians would have called *vada*, a debate motivated by a quest for truth, as opposed to *jalpa*, one motivated by a desire for victory.[65] Such a consideration, however, might be considerably easier to maintain in theory than in practice. In classical India, debates intended as quests for truth most likely degenerated into impassioned polemics employing questionable dialectical techniques to vanquish the other party.[66] Here too, attempts at rational persuasion might give way, when they fail – as they invariably do when passionately held convictions are at stake – to forms of subtle and not-so-subtle intimidation and manipulation.[67] One detects in the qualifications with which comparative theologians hedge the notion of a 'postliberal' apologetics a well-founded anxiety about the possible insidious influx of unsavory elements into interreligious theological discussion.

The foregoing remarks suggest that the delicate task of avoiding the twin pitfalls of hegemonism and polemic in comparative theology is ultimately a matter of theological judgement. When all is said and done, comparative theological method comes down to a balancing act between openness and commitment or, as Clooney eloquently puts it, 'between a necessary vulnerability to truth as one might find it [. . .] and loyalty to truth as one has already found it'.[68] Commitment and openness form the two poles of a dialectic, by which I mean the binding together of two logically irreconcilable claims in a necessary relation. Theoretically, such a dual affirmation of logically inassimilable claims is less than satisfactory, as it still leaves open the crucial question of where one draws the line between a sincere openness towards another religious perspective and a compromise of one's core convictions or, alternatively, between a robust commitment to one's own tradition and a narrow parochialism. *Practically*, however, it is sufficient for the operation of a faculty of theological judgement that is arguably

---

63 Fredericks remarks that such apologetics is 'occasional and preliminary' (*Buddhists and Christians*, 109).

64 Fredericks, *Buddhists and Christians*, 109.

65 Vindhyesvari Prasad Dvivedin (ed.), *Nyaya-Varttikam* (Delhi: Eastern Book Linkers, 1986), 148 and *passim* (commentary on Nyaya-sutra I.2.1).

66 Esther A. Solomon, *Indian Dialectics*, Vol. 1 (Ahmedabad: B. J. Institute of Learning and Research, 1976), 120, 129.

67 Cf. Talal Asad's somewhat pessimistic assessment of the viability of José Casanova's proposal that religious groups participate in a modern public sphere on the condition that they restrict themselves to persuasive means of influence (*Formations of the Secular* (Stanford, 2003), 185–7).

68 *Theology after Vedanta*, 4; cf. Fredericks, 'A Universal Religious Experience?', 87; *idem.*, *Faith among Faiths*, 169–71.

more supple and responsive – more *intelligent* – than an adherence to an explicit set of guidelines or procedures, however carefully and intelligently formulated, can be. In their implicit recognition of this distinction between judgement and method lies the kernel of wisdom in Clooney's and Fredericks' call for a moratorium on the theology of religions.

Towards the end of *Faith among Faiths*, Fredericks gives what I take to be a refinement of his earlier claim that comparative theology's superiority over the theology of religions consists in its greater openness to the transformative potential of other traditions. Here he suggests that what distinguishes comparative theology is its greater capacity to abide in the field of tension between openness and commitment, its refusal to defuse this tension by retreating to a meta-religious standpoint.[69] I might conclude by adding that a patient willingness to live with the inevitable tensions, ambiguities, and uncertainties of religious life, to learn to 'love the questions', as the German poet Rilke might put it, could well be a mark of intellectual and spiritual maturity.

---

69 *Faith among Faiths*, 170–1.

4

On Hegemonies Within: Franciscan Missions and Buddhist Kings in Comparative Theological Contexts

DAVID A. CLAIRMONT

Introduction

What lessons can comparative theologians learn if we place an ethical evaluation of mission encounters at the center of our future studies?[1] One important lesson considered here is that, when we study the history of how people share and explain their beliefs to others, we must acknowledge that their own failures to live by those beliefs are a significant part of what they communicate about them. Moreover, when theologians examine the contexts and reasons for these failures, they are led to another source for comparative reflection. Interreligious understanding, one of the principal aims of comparative theology, is often complicated not only by the linguistic and conceptual differences between traditions, but also by the histories of conflict and violence between traditions that give rise to related questions about the meaning and morality of certain theological notions. For Christian theologians, the notion of mission, as well as the related theological ideas that help to contextualize it, is one such example.[2]

---

1 Prior to conversations with Rabbi Michael A. Signer, who until his death on 10 January 2009 served as the Abrams Professor of Jewish Thought and Culture at the University of Notre Dame, I had not thought to explore the possible relationship of mission and ethics to both comparative theology and interreligious dialogue. This paper is a belated answer to a question he raised (in roughly the following form) during those conversations: How does one relate the study of interreligious dialogue to the study of comparative theology, given the changing nature of interreligious encounters through history? The question with which I begin this paper is my own reformulation of that question.

2 Throughout this essay, my focus will be the horizon of Christian comparative theologians, although I realize that the discipline is by no means limited to Christian theology. I limit my remarks to Christian theologians in part because of the centrality of mission to Christian theology. The applicability of a theological equivalent to the term 'mission' in other traditions is a topic that I

In what follows, I argue that comparative theologians should abide in, and then pass through, ethical moments – times when they reflect on the moral implications of how historical events marked by interreligious encounter and conflict are related to historically contextualized theological concepts. Moreover, by framing comparison in theology as a fundamentally ethical endeavor, I also want to argue that comparative theologians must think about how their work addresses two related communities as the primary 'publics' of their scholarship: the academy and communities of religious practice.[3] Their work exhibits a mode of engagement that may be understood in terms of two interrelated struggles which unfold within and before these publics: the intellectual struggles to understand the meaning and implications of their own beliefs, and associated moral struggles to live by those beliefs.[4]

In this essay, I explore how our interreligious encounters are affected by our sometimes failed attempts to live in accordance with what we say we believe, even if the complex nature of what we believe itself frustrates our best attempts to present such beliefs to others. Comparative theology, conscious of such struggles, will require careful attention to the relations among mission theology, history, and ethics. If we look carefully at particular mission contexts, we will see that mission cannot easily be subsumed under the more capacious language of hegemony – a frequent charge, explicit or implied, in much contemporary comparative scholarship in religion and one which, I suspect, makes many

---

cannot treat here. Similarly, although I focus here on mission history, I realize that even in the context of mission work there are other kinds of events and activities worthy of comparative theological study that are not related to proselytization (for example, a comparative account of apologetics). This essay is a reminder only that we not forget mission history in comparative theology, that it might indeed be central, and that studying mission actually calls us to think more closely about the moral dimension of comparative thought.

3 David Tracy has suggested that Christian theology in its varied modes always directs its discourse to three publics: the academy, the Church, and the wider society. While Tracy admitted that each theologian will tend, as a matter of course, to emphasize one public over the other two in her or his scholarship as research agendas unfold, the wider discipline of theology must address all three. What I would like to suggest, if only in a preliminary way, is that for Christian theologians it may be helpful to understand comparative theology, given the demands of preparation to engage it in and the close relationship between the meaning of theological concepts and the history of interreligious conflict, to envision its work as moving back and forth between the public of the Church and the public of the academy. Indeed I think that in comparative theology we see the most nuanced expression of why the Church and the academy must always be held in close if tense proximity. The extent to which comparative theology affects the wider society strongly depends, in my mind, on its ability first to relate the academy to local religious communities, although the empirical support for such a suggestion would be difficult to gather in the short term. For a further discussion of the publics of theology, see David Tracy, *The Analogical Imagination: Christian Theology and the Culture of Pluralism* (New York: Crossroad, 1981), 1–46.

4 Here I take my emphasis on the relationship of intellectual and moral struggle to express a similar comparative sensibility to Francis Clooney's suggestion that one aspect of comparative theological study is 'a necessary vulnerability to truth as one might find it and be affected by it in the materials studied'. See Francis X. Clooney, SJ, *Theology after Vedanta: An Experiment in Comparative Theology* (Albany: SUNY Press, 1993), 5.

comparative theologians uneasy when it comes to engaging missiological discourse as central to their work.

When we step into the details of interreligious encounters, we face a spiritually uncomfortable situation as we delve into the histories of our own traditions, marked as they are by religiously inspired violence, triumphalist claims, and oversimplifications of unfamiliar religious discourses. Yet those who engage in interreligious dialogue, in mission contexts as well as in more insulated and consoling environments, quickly become aware of how profound a place the violent histories of their own religious communities play in such discussions.[5] These are matters that comparative theologians cannot step around but must pass through, even if the conversations that such matters elicit leave scars on their way to honest confession, purification, and scholarship.

This kind of work cannot really be undertaken in a short essay, but I want nonetheless to chart some questions that even an initial examination of missionary encounters can offer as lessons for comparative theology. The particular historical example I shall consider here comes from the early sixteenth-century mission work by Franciscans in the Buddhist kingdom of Kotte on the southwestern coast of Sri Lanka during the period of Portuguese colonialism which lasted from 1506 to 1658 CE, after which time followed the Dutch (1658–1796) and British (1796–1948) colonial periods.[6] Sri Lanka was and continues to be a predominantly Buddhist land, by some estimates upwards of 70 per cent at the present time.[7] Yet throughout its history it has been the location of both peaceful and violent interreligious and multi-ethnic encounters, most recently displayed in the conflict between the governing Sinhalese and the minority Tamil community in the north. The case involves Bhuvanekabahu VII, King of Kotte, who ruled from 1521 to 1551 CE, and the peculiar kind of Christians who came to his land. The questions for comparative theology that arise by examining this

---

5 For Christian theologians, this is perhaps nowhere more acute than in how Christian violence (physical and ideological) against Jews has hindered Jewish–Christian dialogue. Although I will not explore the issue in depth here, it is important to acknowledge how difficult a theological idea mission is in this context, even as it must remain central to Christian comparative theology, as I shall argue.

6 Lakshmanan Sabaratnam, *Ethnic Attachment in Sri Lanka: Social Change and Cultural Continuity* (New York: Palgrave, 2001), 3. For a more precise division and detailed treatment, see also K. M. de Silva, *A History of Sri Lanka* (London: Hurst/Berkeley: University of California Press, 1981).

7 Citing the Sri Lankan government's 1981 census, Richard Gombrich summarizes the following characterizations of the country's population: '[Sri Lanka's] population was under 19 million. Of these, about 74 per cent are defined, primarily by their mother tongue, Sinhalese, 18.1 per cent as Tamil, and 7 per cent as Muslim. Most of the Muslims have a form of Tamil as their first language, though the majority of them live in predominantly Sinhala-speaking areas. Dividing the population by religion: 69.3 per cent are Buddhist, 15.5 per cent Hindu, 7.6 per cent Christian (mostly Roman Catholic), and 7 per cent Muslim. Almost all of the Buddhists are Sinhalese and all the Hindus are Tamils. The Christians, both Roman Catholics and Protestants, are fairly equally divided between Sinhalas and Tamils' (22). See Richard Gombrich, 'Is the Sri Lankan War a Buddhist Fundamentalism?', in Mahinda Deegalle (ed.) *Buddhism, Conflict and Violence in Modern Sri Lanka* (London and New York: Routledge, 2006), 22–37.

encounter are helpful to us now and, I suspect, might have been useful to the parties involved, as they were serious, engaged people struggling to make sense of their own beliefs, the religious differences that confronted them, and the impact that their own self-perceived moral failures had on the nature of those encounters.

The following remarks will be divided into three sections. First, in order to illustrate why such a case might be relevant to our discussions, and to position it relative to the discussion about hegemony and comparative theology which gave rise to many of the essays in this volume, I want to make some brief comments on what I understand to be some of the primary focal points of contemporary comparative theology. Among other considerations, I want to highlight the dominance of the comparative theology/theology of religions distinction and the almost complete neglect of the relationship between comparative theology and missiology.

Second, I want to explore in more detail the historical case just mentioned, namely the early Franciscan missionaries in conversation with the Buddhist kings of Sri Lanka. In this section, I want to make two points. First, the Franciscan missionaries that came to Sri Lanka during that period were wrestling with two important and unresolved issues: the theological debate in their own community about the extent to which the Franciscans ought to emulate in a most extreme form the voluntary poverty of their founder (the legacy of the so-called Spiritual Franciscans) and the influence on some of their members of the apocalyptic-prophetic character of that spiritual legacy (especially but not exclusively the expectation that their mission work was somehow related to the immanent end of days). Second, these same missionaries and their confrères in other mission lands were either uncertain about or strongly disturbed by the consort of economic colonialism and military force that accompanied their mission work. Indeed, these reservations, which to be clear did not prevent them from undertaking their work, nonetheless were brought into sharper relief by the particular nature of the land in which they were preaching, a land in which the relationship between the Buddhist king and the Buddhist monasteries he supported meant something very different from the kind of royal sponsorship that the missionaries enjoyed.

In the third and final part of the paper, I want to offer a series of images that I think communicate something of the mood or we might say spirituality of comparative theology as I have come to understand it. Here I will focus on the role of the comparative theologian as one who uncovers (and dwells with) the tragic and violent aspect of interreligious history, even as she or he tries to lay a new path out of those bloody remnants. While the work of comparative theology must exhibit this ethical component, I suggest that the spirituality of the comparative theologian might best be thought of as a confluence of two streams: the patience that comes with age and the sorrow and penitence that comes with an honest recounting of and meditation on, the history of one's own religious community. This is then related back to the mission context as the comparative theologian asks, 'Why are internal theological debates, honest confrontations with violent complicities, and even real doubts about one's own struggles to know the divine not foregrounded in actual interreligious encounters?' In this way, the comparative theologian provides an invaluable service to the religious communities of which she or he is a part.

There would appear to be a deep analogy between the interreligious understanding that results from the careful examination of theological ideas in a comparative style, and the truthful understanding about the moral tendencies of one's own tradition that comes through close attention to its historical encounters. We must pay attention to how the moral behaviors of those living within traditions affect the degree to which interreligious understanding is possible. My suspicion is that what comparative theologians are reacting against in their heightened sensitivities and the guarded or tentative mode of presenting their comparisons is not only the legacy of hegemonic theological language that reduces one form of religious thought to another more familiar form; rather, they are concerned also with how theological discourse becomes entwined with and subservient to military and economic power.[8] This is a use of theological language from which, it must be clear, Christians and others have for many years been trying to free themselves, well aware of their tendency to succumb to the allure of empire. This is what I hope the case of the Franciscan missionaries, in Sri Lanka and elsewhere, will illustrate.

---

8 · In contemporary discussions in religious ethics, which is the primary conversation community of the present author, the work of Stanley Hauerwas stands as an especially striking example. In his recent collection of essays on how the modern university has become an unreflective agent of the state especially through its dominant modes of discussing religion, entitled *The State of the University: Academic Knowledges and the Knowledge of God* (Malden, MA: Blackwell, 2007), he states: '[T]he challenge of the "new religious pluralism" has everything to do with Christian nonviolence. Just as [John Howard] Yoder had to challenge the claim that Christian pacifists were "irresponsible" so I must challenge the very terms used to describe the challenge before us. From my perspective, "pluralism" is the ideology used by Protestant liberals to give themselves the illusion that they are still in control of, or at least have responsibility for, the future of America. "Religion" is the designation created to privatize strong convictions in order to render them harmless so that alleged democracies can continue to have the illusion they flourish on difference. Indeed if there is anything "new" about the current situation it is that we are coming to the end of Protestant hegemony in America' (60). I think this criticism is helpful for comparative theology (and reminiscent of Hugh Nicholson's argument in his contribution to this volume) because it illustrates the depth of conviction among Christians such as Hauerwas that the argument about which kind of 'Christian' speaks for Christians in a context of alleged pluralism has not been settled. Indeed, Hauerwas thinks that the only basis on which Christians should enter into interreligious dialogue is from a position of what we might call 'nonviolent exclusivism'. Given how unlikely the pairing of these terms has been in actual Christian history, and how those working in theology of religions might react to it, Hauerwas' comment suggests the kind of honest self-critical exposition of religious history in which, I will argue, comparative theology must engage.

Comparative Theology, Theology of Religions, and the Omission of Mission

As I use the phrase in this essay, comparative theology denotes a certain style of theology which imbues each of the theological sub-disciplines as customarily understood (here I will pay particular attention to moral theology and missiology) with distinctive questions, pathways of study, and tones of conclusion. This style has two salient features. First, comparative theology proceeds with a purposeful movement outside of one's own tradition, that explores how the ideas and practices of one's own tradition are related, in theory and in history, to the ideas and practices in another tradition. Although comparative theology is relatable to interreligious dialogue, comparative theology can be (and is) carried on primarily though not exclusively through textual sources which offer a different mode of responding than one would see in two persons talking together about their religious lives. Second, the rationale for a comparative orientation in theology may be understood as intrinsic to the practice of theology itself.[9] Insofar as theology aims at increasing understanding of the truths about God, the human, and the Divine–human relationship, it must not be content with inaccurate, incomplete, or historically uninformed views of other traditions. For these traditions also claim to be saying something true about the subjects that theologians understand themselves to be studying, and the complexity of such claims must be acknowledged and respected.

Among the many questions that face the present generation of comparative theologians, one rather longstanding one continues to loom: why bother? With all that a theologian from any tradition has to learn about the tradition optimistically labeled 'home', why take a bold, tradition-challenging, and time-consuming comparative step? Why draw together in explicit juxtaposition ideas or persons or trajectories of thought that, certain accidental historical encounters notwithstanding, do not naturally converge? Many a comparative study has come to life without this question ever being posed, much less answered.

This looming question is less likely to be answered at all, much less answered well, if those who identify their scholarship as comparative theology do not take

---

9 In making this point, I am drawing, of course, on the ideas of Alasdair MacIntyre in his discussions of the relationship between practices and notions of virtue. MacIntyre says that a practice denotes 'any coherent and complex form of socially established co-operative human activity through which goods internal to that form of activity are realized in the course of trying to achieve those standards of excellence which are appropriate to, and partially definitive of, that form of activity, with the result that human powers to achieve excellence, and human conceptions of the ends and goods involved, are systematically extended.' See Alasdair MacIntyre, *After Virtue: A Study in Moral Theory*, 2nd edn (Notre Dame: University of Notre Dame Press, [1981] 1984), 187. I have explored the connection between MacIntyre's notion of practices and interreligious dialogue in more detail: see 'Moral Disagreement and Interreligious Conversation: The Penitential Pace of Understanding', in Lawrence S. Cunningham (ed.), *Intractable Disputes about the Natural Law: Alasdair MacIntyre and Critics* (Notre Dame, IN: University of Notre Dame Press, 2009), 97–129.

care to relate two often unexamined but related notions: ideological *hegemony* and the phenomenon of *mission*. My hypothesis, as I suggested earlier, is that too often these words have been assumed by those outside of comparative theology (and sometimes within it) to mean the same thing.[10] Yet there is an interesting incongruity present in their pairing: the first Greek derivative denotes power and dominance, a purposeful and will-crushing activity, while the second Latin derivative denotes an answer to a call, a received and consented-to passivity, a leading where one does not want to go. Mission can take on a hegemonic character, but the form of theological reflection that gives rise to it does not necessitate that it does.

Consider how little this difference seems to matter when one reviews the discussion about the relationship between comparative theology and the various theologies of religion and religious pluralism discussed in several of the essays of this volume. When comparative theology examines the important question of its Christian theological roots, and thereby its close historical connection to the mission discourse of the Christian churches, it helps a great deal to separate the hegemonies encoded in forms of thought from the hegemonies of physical power and violence that occurred and continue to occur in the wake and continued presence of colonialism. For if the former kind of hegemony is sometimes supported unintentionally through the very linguistic forms of our communication, such that comparative theological investigations by Christian theologians are dismissed because they originate as Christian discourse, the latter kind of hegemony continues to exert influence in part because of particular moral failures and political compromises. And moral failure – that is not living according to our own moral ideals – will always be with us.

---

10 I make this point primarily in reference to studies in comparative religious ethics (a discipline whose expositors are oddly not in frequent conversation with those working in comparative theology), where it has proved difficult to speak about the theological rationales for a comparative examination of moral matters without viewing the rationales as proselytizing impulses, or as hegemonic tendencies. It is for this reason that we find scholars such as Lee Yearley and Aaron Stalnaker engaging in finely detailed and linguistically sensitive comparative studies of basic moral ideas without ever asking, much less answering, this question: How do the rationales explicit or implied in their comparative studies relate to possible rationales for comparative engagement rooted in the thinkers or the traditions they compare? Yearley denies that such rationales can be easily discerned in his sources when he eschews the possibly of rooting comparisons in what he calls (finessing Robin Horton) secondary theories (those that put basic theological normative views about the world at their center). See his *Mencius and Aquinas: Theories of Virtue and Conceptions of Courage* (Albany: SUNY Press, 1990), 175–80. Stalnaker does somewhat better in this regard when he acknowledges that a turn to comparative notions of virtue or even the practices cultivated in liberal democratic society are not likely to be 'sufficient in themselves to cultivate virtuous citizens, in the absence of religious or quasi-religious traditions of personal transformations' (3). Even so, he continues to view comparison as primarily a tool to for 'theoretical critique' outside of traditions rather than a practice that emerges from within traditions themselves, even if intra-traditional comparative motives might actually advance Stalnaker's constructive 'regulative ideal' of 'global neighborliness' within the attitudinal context of a 'chastened intellectualism'. See his *Overcoming Our Evil: Human Nature and Spiritual Exercises in Xunzi and Augustine* (Washington, DC: Georgetown University Press, 2006), especially 279–80, 299–300.

Many of the contributions to the present volume exhibit concerns for the viability of a theology of religions in light of the development of comparative theology. For example, in responding to Kristin Beise Kiblinger's call for more attention to recent nuanced and multi-religious exercises in the theology of religions, Hugh Nicholson characterizes well the contours of the debate as he offers his own critique:

> While Kiblinger argues that the stark contrast that Clooney and Fredericks draw between the two disciplines exaggerates – to the point, perhaps, of manufacturing – the crisis of the theology of religions by failing to take account of its more recent developments, I shall argue that this contrast tends to suppress the full dimensions of a crisis that I believe is real. It does so by fostering the comforting illusion that the problem of unacknowledged exclusion or theological hegemonism can be neatly solved by eliminating the two prominent features of the theology of religions, namely, its apriorism and its penchant for abstract theorizing.[11]

The crisis in theology of religions, Nicholson suggests, is actually a situation far more challenging because it tends to ignore the 'antagonistic dimension of interreligious relations', or what he terms the 'political' dimension of comparative theology. Indeed for Nicholson, comparative theologians do not often give adequate attention to the historical contexts in which both the theology of religions and comparative theology designations arose and developed.[12]

I find Nicholson's critique very helpful because it highlights two points that contextualize my own suggestion that we ought to focus more on mission history. First, comparative theology and the theology of religions have their own histories, and only in knowing these histories can we appreciate their social, political and theological impact. Moreover, given these different histories, it would seem prudent to think about occasions when it is helpful to discuss comparative theology and the theology of religions together (namely, when historical contexts have given rise to the intersection) and when it is not. Second and more important for the present discussion, the focus on the 'antagonistic dimension of interreligious relations' is centrally important for understanding where comparative theology has been and might go in the future. The example I develop further on takes this 'political' dimension of theology in a different direction from what Nicholson considers by focusing on how particular moral failures, as well as the deep theological disagreements within communities frequently designated as 'traditions', have interfered with religious understanding. Such failures and disagreements complicate the situation in both theological directions: not only do they prevent understanding between those within one theological

---

11 Nicholson, this volume, p. 47.
12 Nicholson, this volume, p. 47

community and those from another community; these same failures prevent those in the theological 'home tradition' from understanding themselves in ways sensitive to how others understand and remember them.

Let me say more about this problem in light of recent discussions about how comparative theology relates to other approaches and specializations in theology. In an early review of the field, Francis X. Clooney, SJ, differentiated three senses in which the term 'comparative theology' might be used: 'the comparison of theology, the posing of theological questions in a comparative setting, [and] the doing of constructive theology from and after comparison'.[13] In another place, Clooney suggested that what differentiates comparative theology from other comparative endeavors in the study of religion is that 'Comparativists who are theologians are likely to believe that transcendence, revelation, truth, and salvation are real concerns, not simply components of the texts which talk about them; that they are concerns likely to affect not only explicit participants in the religious traditions which revere those texts, but also scholars who might read those texts seriously.'[14] Suggesting also that the term 'comparison' sometimes denotes a level of detachment from religious traditions that theologians should not emulate, he notes that perhaps the term 'collectio' theology better describes the foundational exercise of reading together that theologians working back and forth between traditions wish to practice.[15] Such descriptions as Clooney gives would not preclude a theology of religions but would delay it, as even the questions that structure theological reflection on religious pluralism might be significantly different after such together-reading has occurred.

In light of Nicholson's comments about the political dimension of theology, as well as his judgement that a theology of religions will be significantly hampered in its development if it neglects the histories of actual interreligious interactions, we need to ask whether the senses of comparative theology that Clooney distinguishes have been adequately accounted. Let me signal two elements of that accounting which I explore in more detail below: the form of belief and the connection between beliefs and behaviors (or in the more traditional Christian language, faith and morals). On the first score, while I think Clooney is entirely right that what distinguishes the comparative theologian as a comparativist is her or his commitment to the real powers of the traditions studied to disclose truth, especially some true aspect that is either missing or underdeveloped in the tradition from which resources the comparativist works, there is a further problem. The kind of belief that a comparative theologian learns to hold, while there may

---

13 Francis X. Clooney, SJ, 'Comparative Theology: A Review of Recent Books (1989–1995)', in *Theological Studies* (56, 1995), 522. The third of this threefold differentiation Clooney offers as a response to David Tracy's characterization of the field as attending to the first two senses. See David Tracy, 'Comparative Theology', in *Encyclopedia of Religion*, 16 vols (New York: MacMillan, 1987), 14.446.

14 Francis X. Clooney, SJ, *Theology after Vedanta: An Experiment in Comparative Theology* (Albany: SUNY Press, 1993), 5.

15 Clooney, *Theology after Vedanta*, 7.

be many nuanced versions, would be of a fundamentally open, critical, and gradually expressed kind. This form of belief is characterized, we might say, in its prematurely mature way of encountering and carefully considering what is revealed in light of together-reading. It is a form of belief that counsels against tendencies to assume that we know the fullness of meanings encoded in our own traditions precisely because comparative awareness develops sensitivity to questions unasked and together-readings unexplored. It is the kind of belief, were we to need an aural analogy, that sounds like the voice of old people explaining things slowly to young people. While oriented outward in its own way, it exhibits none of the uncritical urgency of the new convert or the freshly ordained. Comparative theology moves at a different pace than, say, moral theology; a paradoxical observation perhaps given how comparative theology is viewed as something new and current.

The second element, and the one which I will spend the rest of this paper developing, is the connection between beliefs and behaviors. If we take seriously Clooney's suggestion that working in comparative theology also entails a different shape for other specializations in theology, indeed asks different questions after together-reading has happened, we are led to another related observation. As much as the exercise of this together-reading affects the theological questions we ask, so too does the social and historical context in which this reading happens. I want to affirm the notion that James Fredericks has suggested in outlining the 'virtue of interreligious friendship', as we attend to the particularities of past religious encounters beyond meetings with religious friends: 'For all their ambiguity, texts are but static and limited snapshots of realities even more ambiguous – the religions themselves as they are realized in the lives of real believers. Interreligious friendships promote understating between believers in helping them to locate the text not merely within its historical context but also within its living, existential context.'[16] Put differently, one of the ways in which comparative theology changes the nature of theology itself is through its close attention to the particular theological questions that arise as a result of historically contingent interreligious encounters.[17] Such encounters are themselves often influenced by disputed interpretations of certain theological ideas, challenged as they were by the quite different theological ideas of the people encountered. They are also marked by the legacy of questions unasked and doubts unexpressed

---

16 James L. Fredericks, 'Interreligious Friendship: A New Theological Virtue', in *Journal of Ecumenical Studies* (35:2, 1998), p. 168.

17 This connection moves closer, I think, to the concern Nicholson expresses in the following lines: '[C]omparative theology, with its central concept of a world religion, gives paradigmatic expression to the nexus between liberalism and imperialism that characterized nineteenth-century European colonialism. In its universalization of a particular conception of religion, comparative theology provides a textbook example of a hegemonic discourse in the realm of religion' (p. 51). It also crosses the concerns that Laksana expresses around the topics of identity formation and what he takes to be the problematic trope of purification, for which he lifts up instead the ongoing usefulness of images of pilgrimage.

in the service of advancing a message. At least this is what I will try to show was the case for the sixteenth-century Franciscan missions, in Sri Lanka and elsewhere.

Christian Mission in a Buddhist Land – Moral Struggles and Disputed Ideals

The Franciscans appeared friendly, familiar, and even exemplary to Bhuvanekabahu VII, king of the western Lankan territory of Kotte, who ruled from 1521 to 1551 CE.[18] Sri Lanka had been a predominantly Buddhist area since the early third–second century BCE.[19] Bhuvanekabahu's reign roughly coincided with the rise of the Portuguese colonial presence in Sri Lanka and with the advent of Christian missionaries to that area. Discussing Portuguese explorations prior to the Franciscan missions, de Silva notes that

> One striking feature of Portuguese activities in Asia and Africa was that they did not aim at territorial conquest so much as the control of commerce by subduing and dominating, by means of naval power, the strategic points through which it passed. At no stage did they establish dominance over the politics of South Asia. What they did was to use their sea power and superior technology at points of weakness or where there were sharp divisions, and thus they attained an influence out of all proportion to their real strength.[20]

And there were plenty of divisions for the Portuguese to exploit.

---

18 Much of the summary information on Bhuvanekabahu VII is drawn from Alan Strathern, *Kingship and Conversion in Sixteenth-Century Sri Lanka: Portuguese Imperialism in a Buddhist Land* (Cambridge: Cambridge University Press, 2007).

19 Of the many histories of Sri Lanka, for an overview of the periods in question, see K. M. de Silva, *A History of Sri Lanka* (London: Hurst/Berkeley: University of California Press, 1981); and C. R. de Silva, *Sri Lanka: A History*, 2nd rev. edn (New Delhi: Vikas, 1997).

20 K. M. de Silva, *A History of Sri Lanka*, 100. Much of the subsequent history is summarized from de Silva's account. De Silva's observation is not unproblematic, as the Portuguese did subsequently develop significant imperial presence in many parts of the world, but his point centers on the pattern by which political influence and local control was a means to the stability of commercial interests, although both political and economic matters were bound up in religious conflict from the vey earliest Portuguese imperial actions. For example, A. R. Disney suggests that, with the beginning of Portuguese imperial activity in a military expedition from the Iberian peninsula across the Straits of Gibraltar into North Africa (the Moroccan town of Ceuta), one can discern three possible motives: military control of the Straits over against the kingdom of Castille; the economic benefit of controlling a central trading city; and as movement in what was known as the Reconquest of Muslim-controlled territory on the Southern part of the peninsula and in Northern Africa. Yet at the time of their contact with the people of Sri Lanka, the Portuguese had a network of trading cities in what was known in sixteenth-century Portuguese discourse as the Estado da Índia (or 'State of India') which extended in an arc from the East African coast to the West Indian coast. (145) (The West African Atlantic coast had seen the beginning of the Portuguese slave trade in the mid-fifteenth century with associated commercial settlements.) Of this network of cities, Disney notes the following. 'One of the most immediately striking characteristics of the formal *Estado da*

The Portuguese had first come to Sri Lanka very early in the 1500s and ten years later built their first trading settlements on the island in order to take advantage of Sri Lanka's cinnamon trade.[21] This event coincided with an important political division on the island resulting from 'succession disputes' among the sons of Vijayabahu VI, whose decision to appoint his youngest son by his second wife as his successor resulted in his assassination, engineered by his older sons including Bhuvanekabahu and supported by rulers of surrounding kingdoms.[22] While Bhuvanekabahu had gained the majority of his father's kingdom, he also inherited the same unease his father's subjects had over what they perceived to be Vijaya's subservient relationship to the Portuguese. Moreover, since Bhuvanekabahu had no male heir, his younger brothers who had been given only small portions of their father's kingdom assumed they would now inherit the rest of it. When the younger brother Mayadunne, who had been given the smaller eastern area of Sitavaka, proceeded to take more of his father's former territory, the Portuguese helped Bhuvanekabahu to resist the attack. Bhuvanekabahu hoped that his tentative support from the Portuguese would also help secure his throne for his grandson, Dharmapala. Trusting that his relationship with the

---

India was that it was largely urban. At the end of the sixteenth century only five of its twenty-four significant components – Goa, Damão, Bassein, Chaul and Colombo – possessed associated territories and rural populations of any significance. The *Estado da Índia*'s urban character was largely a product of function, for its raison d'être was to provide protected havens from which Indian Ocean maritime trade and communications could be dominated and as far as possible controlled. Such a focus provided little room or incentive to accumulate territory for its own sake, or to seek dominion over large subject populations.' See A. R. Disney, *A History of Portugal and the Portuguese Empire, Volume II: The Portuguese Empire* (Cambridge and New York: Cambridge University Press, 2009), 146. Disney makes the further point that, to the extent the Portuguese did undertake more substantial developments outside urban areas, such activity was driven by the need to supply material necessities to those urban centers. An interesting question in light of the present investigation, but outside its scope, is what impact this particular economic-political strategy might have had on the distinctive mode of evangelization (especially the morality of its methods) and urgency of conversion (with its concomitant hurried theological discernment) in cities such as Colombo and Goa.

21 Perniola's documentary history gives the date as November 1505, the first document recounting a sea voyage undertaken by Dom Lourenco de Almeyda from Cochin on India's south-west coast to the Maldives off the south-western tip of India, which was diverted to Colombo by a storm. In his company was a Franciscan friar named Vicente, the first Franciscan to visit and celebrate Mass in Sri Lanka. See V. Perniola, SJ, *The Catholic Church in Sri Lanka, The Portuguese Period, Vol. 1 – 1505–1565* (Dehiwala, Sri Lanka: Tisara Prakasakayo, 1989), 1–2.

22 As de Silva explains, 'Vijayabahu VI married twice, and had three sons by his first queen, and one by the second. When the king sought to secure the succession for his youngest son, the three elder princes obtained the assistance of the Udarata ruler, killed their father and shared the kingdom among themselves . . . While the ruler of Kotte, Bhuvanekabahu, lost a considerable amount of territory when that kingdom was partitioned in 1521, the region left to him was by far the richest and largest of the three with resources adequate to maintain his position as the most important if not the most powerful monarch on the island. But Bhuvanekabahu was no match for his more daring and ambitious younger brother Mayadunne, the ruler of Sitavaka, who aimed at control over the whole of the pre-partition Kotte kingdom. The Kotte ruler hoped that Portuguese protection would preserve his kingdom against Mayadunne, and willingly accepted the status of a Portuguese satellite.' (De Silva, 98–100).

Portuguese would dissuade a challenge from his rivals, he sent a delegation to King John III of Portugal for some indication of official support for his grandson to succeed him.

Thus far, the story of Bhuvanekabahu should not seem especially rich in theological themes, until one considers an event that happened in 1542, which has been well told by de Silva:

> [A group of Franciscan missionaries] came at his invitation as part of the price exacted for Portuguese recognition of the right of succession of Dharmapala to the Kotte throne. The Sinhalese envoys had exceeded their brief in giving the impression that Bhuvanekabahu himself would be willing to convert to Roman Catholicism. But while the king readily welcomed the missionaries and gave them permission to build churches and preach in Kotte, he categorically repudiated his envoy's promise of his own conversion. The Franciscans were not put off: they aimed at converting the king himself in the certain knowledge that if they succeeded they would pave the way for the conversion of large numbers of his subjects. Bhuvanekabahu, for his part, realized that there was no more certain way of alienating the affection of his people than by changing his religion. But despite his obvious opposition to the attempt to convert him, Franciscan pressure continued. In time Bhuvanekabahu became less favorable to Christian missionary activity, and there was a marked deterioration in relations between the Portuguese and the king of Kotte as a result.[23]

The outlines of the story signal the theological questions that arise in this interaction. Why was the king's conversion a condition of Portuguese support of his succession claims? What did it mean for him to convert? Who were these Franciscans that came to the island, and why did the king give them his initial support? How did the Franciscans understand the theological rationale for their mission, tied as it was to these political concerns?

It is unclear which Franciscan missionaries came to Lanka in 1540, with some accounts suggesting the party was led by Joao de Villa de Conde, presumed to be the voice recorded as addressing the king in the preserved documents.[24] Whatever the constitution of the group, they seem to have been members of a Franciscan community called the *piedosos* (the pious ones), 'established as the Province of San Gabriel de Estremadura'.[25] Members of this same group were the first to establish a mission in Mexico after its conquest by the Spanish, and

---

23 K. M. de Silva, *A History of Sri Lanka*, 104.

24 Lazaro Iriarte, OFM Cap., *Franciscan History: The Three Orders of St Francis of Assisi*, trans. Patricia Ross (Chicago: Franciscan Herald Press, 1982 [1979]), 321. Perniola's source, an account from a Franciscan friar Gaspar de Lisboa, records the other parties as Antonio Padram, Francisco de Montepradone, Simao de Coimbra, and Francisco de Braga (37, n.1).

25 Alan Strathern, *Kingship and Conversion in Sixteenth-Century Sri Lanka: Portuguese Imperialism in a Buddhist Land*, 86.

Alan Strathern speculates that 'it may have been this glamorous role in the conquest of New Spain that aroused the interest of the Lisbon court in the sister branch in Portugal'.[26] The so-called 'Province of Piety', in Spain and Portugal as well as in Mexico, was an informal continuation of an early Franciscan reform movement known as the Spirituals which had been officially disbanded two centuries earlier by Pope John XXII around 1317 CE.

The model that had motivated these friars, who sought a more strict interpretation of the Franciscan rule and a return to the early model of evangelical poverty, had never really left the order but took new expressions.[27] The name 'spirituals' was accorded them because this side of the order had been significantly influenced by the Gospel commentaries of Joachim of Fiore, a Cistercian abbot of the early twelfth century. The implications of his prophetic interpretations of Christian scriptural materials have been well summarized by Georges Baudot: 'Fiore presented an essentially historical reading of the Apocalypse and saw, based on the Old Testament, a prediction of the New Testament and the sign of a coming third time, the time of the Holy Spirit or of spiritual understanding.'[28] Although the Spirituals in name had been abolished much earlier, much of their spirituality and their link to Joachimite interpretation remained in the branch of the order that came to be known in the fifteenth century as the Observants (in distinction from the Conventuals) and the Capuchin division in the sixteenth century.

---

26 Strathern, *Kingship and Conversion in Sixteenth-Century Sri Lanka.*

27 I have been challenged by contributor Daniel Joslyn-Siemiatkoski to consider how the efforts by Franciscans in the high and late Middle Ages to convert Jews and Muslims might actually have impacted the strategies that the Franciscans in Sri Lanka adopted. By directing my attention to the Franciscan attempts to use 'native informants' to assist their conversion efforts, an important layer of complexity is added to the case I am arguing here. Unfortunately, I can find no direct evidence that the same strategy was used in the Sri Lankan context, and this may be in part attributable to how the Province of Piety approached their mission and its distinctive compromises. Yet Joslyn-Siemiatkoski has also suggested a helpful avenue for future research when he directed my attention to strategies of medieval Franciscan biblical exegesis that prioritized the study of Hebrew not only to assist the conversion of Jews (as other religious orders did) but also to understand the Hebrew Scriptures as best as possible on their own terms. See Deeana Copeland Klepper, 'Nicholas of Lyra and Franciscan Interest in Hebrew Scholarship', in Philip D. W. Krey and Lesley Smith (eds), *Nicholas of Lyra: The Senses of Scripture* (Leiden and Boston: Brill, 2000), 289–311. The relation of textual exegesis to mission as a topic for comparative theology is not explored here, but I take it to be essential to future work in the field, especially in regard to the Franciscans.

28 Georges Baudot, *Utopia and History in Mexico: The First Chroniclers of Mexican Civilization (1520–1569)*, trans. Bernard R. Ortiz de Montellano and Thelma Ortiz de Montellano (Niwat, CO: University Press of Colorado, 1995), 77. Baudot goes on to explain: 'The first age corresponded to the epoch of the secular Church; the next one lasted from Christ to 1260 and was the era of God the son and the Church of priests; the last era would be that of the Holy Spirit, a time that was coming, possibly beginning in 1260, and it would be the era of the Church of the monastic orders, which would abolish the earthly Church. This third age would be inaugurated by a new Christ, the founder of a new monastic order, whom Joachim identified as Saint Benedict . . . later on, Saint Francis of Assisi would be indentified by some of his followers as the new Messiah, as the second Christ, the bearer of the new age' (77).

The early Spirituals and their spiritual heirs in the order's later history were concerned, among other things, with what William Short has described as Franciscan 'spiritual renewal' of the order and which included a broad reform of what they viewed, following the thirteenth-century friar Ubertino de Casale, the 'unfaithful and "carnal" church'.[29] The problem was that many of the Franciscans in this heritage judged that the reform of the Church would happen not in Europe but in the mission lands. In this way, the communities that would arise as a result of the Franciscans' faithful witness to Christ through the embrace of 'lady poverty' were to have the character of a new monasticism of the kind that Joachim of Fiore predicted for the age of the Holy Spirit. In many cases, the peoples whom the sixteenth-century missionaries encountered in their travels were subjected to the same kind of analysis that the mendicants used to analyze allegedly Christian persons in their own countries. They would be evaluated based on their proximity to the example of gospel poverty (the closer the better) and on their attachment to wealth, power and other worldly trappings. All of this introduces an important question: what did the particular spirituality of this wing of the Franciscans have to do with their approach to mission? The answer comes in two parts: poverty and prophecy fulfillment, which was signaled in the Sri Lankan context but was more clearly visible in the Mexican context of the same period.

The Franciscan missionaries, encountering the native peoples of the Americas, perceived them to be a people both blessed as well as being in danger of not finding salvation. While on the one hand worshipping false gods, they also exhibited in their poverty and simplicity something strikingly close to the gospel's demands, and something that seemed to be getting further and further out of reach for the wealth- and power-hungry people under whose protection their mission advanced. As Baudot explains,

> The very characteristics of that New World, which was surprising as much for its unexpected geographical location as for its strange people were of such a providential nature that they inspired a belief that the Joachinist prophesies had begun to be realized in 1524 with the arrival in Mexico of the twelve reformed Franciscans . . . The Indians had another quality that was cherished by the Franciscans: they lived in poverty and owned nothing.[30]

So half a world away, but at the same time and in the same spiritual heritage, the Franciscan Toribio de Benavente Motolinía could see in his own land and in the land he had come to evangelize the need for a twofold purification, from idolatry (among the native peoples he encountered) and from violence and greed (among the people of his own native land). As David Orique explains,

---

29 William J. Short, OFM, *Poverty and Joy: The Franciscan Tradition* (Maryknoll, NY: Orbis Books, 1999), 69.
30 Baudot, *Utopia and History in Mexico*, 86–7.

Motolinía's understanding of the New World reflected this Franciscan eschatological legacy. He too believed that the time of tribulation had arrived with the conquest, and that the last conquest with the forces of evil was taking place. To him, God allowed this 'death agony' of suffering and hardship as punishment for sin – the sin of the Spaniards' cruelty and their worship of gold, as well as the sin of the Indigenous people's idolatrous 'paganism'.[31]

Just how much of this attitude about the need for a twofold purification from idolatry and greed carried over to the Sri Lankan contingent of the same community is difficult to know. There were certainly many clear differences. The missionaries arrived as part of a much more immediately politicized mission, and we have no such detailed ethnographic records by the Sri Lankan missionaries of the lands and peoples encountered as were developed by their counterparts in the Mexican mission.[32] At least it does not appear that the Sri Lankan mission had the same significance in terms of prophetic fulfillment and apocalyptic symbolism as its Mexican counterpart. Yet there are two aspects in terms of the common Franciscan heritage that are important to highlight.

First, the missionaries were certainly aware that the form of Christianity they brought with them, one burdened by the levels of moral compromise that made their mission possible, would strike those to whom they preached as a mixed witness. They arrived knowing that the king's conversion had been promised by his envoy as part of an agreement to gain Portuguese support for his grandson's claim to the throne. They knew also that the Portuguese king was interested in the economic advantages to be gained in this agreement, even if they discerned also a real concern to negotiate for better conditions for recent Christian converts living in Lanka. There were, so to speak, mixed motives on each side. Second, the particular theological heritage of the Sri Lankan Franciscans, from the debates about the proper meaning of gospel poverty in the life of the mendicant religious orders to the rationales for and propriety of conversions, was both well known to them and also theologically unsettled. For these points at least, we have more evidence in the Sri Lankan case. On these two topics, I submit, we can begin to see the relevance of this case for comparative theology, precisely

---

31 David T. Orique, OP, 'Journey to the Headwaters: Bartolomé de Las Casas in a Comparative Context', in *The Catholic Historical Review* (95:1, 2009), 13.

32 One influential reading for why the missionaries to the Americas took such care in collecting information about the cultures they encountered was out of a sense of testing and completing the Joachinist prophecy. Baudot again: 'There were two tasks, one urgent as the other, in the perspectives of the preparation for the approaching arrival of the Millennium. The fulfillment of the promises of the Apocalypse depended on the conversion of the Indians, but there was still a need to tie the Indians, in one way or another, to Adam's descendants and to the peoples of the Old Testament. This explains what seems at first glance to be the somewhat strange and gratuitous interest the first Franciscan missionaries of Mexico took in the history of their charges at a time when the missionaries faced so many other problems on all sides' (84). See also on this issue Anthony Pagden, *The Fall of Natural Man: The American Indian and the Origins of Comparative Ethnography* (Cambridge: Cambridge University Press, 1987).

because a comparative examination of theological ideas cannot afford to over-look how religious communities dispute the meaning of their own ideas, in argument, personal example, and in their interactions with members of other traditions.

For example, what did money and its renunciation mean in sixteenth-century Sri Lanka? And what would it mean for a Buddhist king to 'convert' to Christianity? On the first question, we have evidence that the form of life that the Franciscans displayed was both generally recognizable and slightly unusual to the welcoming ruler. As Strathern explains, Bhuvanekabahu had invited the Franciscans to his kingdom, not as they had expected to baptize him, but 'on the basis of his experience of the modest activities of the one or two Observant Franciscans in Kotte. These mendicant friars, their behavior, appearance, and function in the life, would have been strongly familiar to the Sinhalese . . . they shared with the *bhikkhus* the common language of asceticism.'[33] Of course the mere fact of similar ascetic lifestyles is not a topic with much traction in comparative theology, then or now.

But Strathern emphasizes another point about the connection between the particular Franciscan expression of asceticism and their sincere hope for the king's conversion, even after they found out that his welcome of them did not include a desire to convert.

> On one level the *piedosos* would merely have reinforced that sense of familiarity. The use of fasting was a marker of otherworldliness common to both sets of virtuosi, as was the strictly vegetarian diet, a strong symbol of spiritual cleanliness in South Asia and potentially a source of immediate respect. Even their bare feet would have served to emphasize their closeness to the *bhikkhu* role. But it soon became apparent that these ultra-Franciscans were radically unusual as well as strikingly familiar. One aspect of their behavior would have jarred almost immediately. Bhuvanekabahu offered the new mission his munificence in the shape of a considerable sum of money to support them in Colombo. In an equally grand gesture, they rejected it. They continued to reject it for five or six months until the king stopped asking. For the friars this was a perfect opportunity to display their commitment to the literal observance of the Rule of Saint Francis, to advertise their position in the debate over ascetic purity that had defined the fractious history of their order.[34]

Note certain prominent features of this encounter. First, the king gave this offering to the friars despite the misunderstanding about why they had come. The gift, to be sure, was not a payoff to compensate them for their trouble. The king admired their form of life, in a way similar to but not the same as the Buddhist

---

33 Strathern, *Kingship and Conversion in Sixteenth-Century Sri Lanka*, 86.
34 Strathern, *Kingship and Conversion in Sixteenth-Century Sri Lanka*, 86–7.

monks with whom he was more familiar. He assumed that this kind of goodwill and support could coexist with the support given to other groups in his kingdom. Second, Bhuvanekabahu continued to offer this support even after it had been initially rejected. Another account of the event suggests that after the friars declined the initial support, the king conceded to their alternate suggestion: 'he repealed the laws according to which converts lost their property when they became Christians'.[35] He seems to have done quite a bit at the beginning to welcome the strange ascetics, but what he offered did not seem to have been enough.

The historical accounts vary as to exactly what happened after these initial offerings were rejected by the Franciscans. One account written later by a Franciscan friar suggests that, following the king's initial offer of support and the order's refusal, he consented to sponsor a fifteen-day public disputation in which the learned Buddhist monks, Brahmin priests, and Franciscan friars would discuss the following questions: '(1) What is God? (2) What is heaven? (3) What is an angel? (4) What is a saint? (5) What is the devil? (6) What is virtue? (7) What are sin and vice?'[36] Sadly, the accounts do not give us any specifics about how these questions were answered or by whom, but this event was certainly not helpful enough to make the king rethink his original position. While the questions seem oddly geared to the alleged Franciscan participants, the list remains noteworthy both because of what it includes and also what it omits (most importantly, what it would mean for the king who was sponsoring the debates to convert and accept baptism – the very problem that gave rise to the dispute).

The Franciscans themselves had been involved in discussions with other missionaries about this topic: what would it mean for someone to convert and how could one be sure that one was doing so for the right reasons? What would these Franciscans have counted as evidence of conversion, were it to have happened? Robert Ricard notes that an early sixteenth-century document guiding mission work in Mexico required 'that candidates must understand and accept the following: a single omnipotent God, eternal, all-good and all-knowing, the creator of everything; the holy virgin, the immortality of the soul, the demons and their perfidies'.[37] Yet it would appear difficult to know, given the very different terms of the discourse employed by Buddhists and Christians to denote analogous ideas, what 'understand' or 'accept' could possibly mean. The available records do not, for example, show any discussion about the traditional three refuges (the Buddha, the Dhamma, and the Sangha), or even if what the Christians were asking the king to do more closely resembled the level of lower ordination in the Sangha. We have only the very intriguing comment by Bhuvanekabahu to

35 This detail comes from the late sixteenth-century account of the mission by Franciscus Gonzaga, OFM, recorded in Georg Schurhammer, SJ, *Francis Xavier: His Life, His Times*, Vol. II – India: 1541–45, trans. M. Joseph Costelloe, SJ (Rome: Jesuit Historical Institute, 1977), 423.
36 Schurhammer, *Francis Xavier.*
37 Robert Ricard, *The Spiritual Conquest of Mexico* (Berkley: University of California Press, 1966), 84 (cited in Strathern, *Kingship and Conversion in Sixteenth-Century Sri Lanka*, 115).

Father Joao when the latter had rejected his monetary support, stating that he wished 'only for your salvation and that of your people'. Bhuvanekabahu replied, 'This matter is beyond doubt altogether hard and difficult, and it needs time and deliberation. Therefore we must not proceed precipitously, but little by little. Meanwhile, hope well of me since all things have their time.'[38] The Franciscan missionaries were well aware that the real reasons for joining the Christian community could easily be shielded, whether these were for financial betterment, or elevated social status, or even despite lowered status and the loss of material resources. Indeed this debate frequently arose as a response to the phenomenon of mass baptisms, and whether adequate scrutiny of conscience about the real reasons for conversion could possibly occur in such a circumstance. So what to make of such a comment by a king who had motives to convert to secure Portugal's support and motives to hold back out of a sense of duty to the people whose tradition he protected?

This incongruity between the missionaries' expectations and the king's intentions was only partly accounted for by the difficulty in knowing what conversion could have meant for the Buddhist king. It also had to do with a lack of knowledge on the part of the Franciscans about the relationship that they were expecting the king to abandon. The relationship between king and monk in Sri Lanka had its own internal logic. As Strathern explains,

> For Bhuvanekabahu the traditional means of ensuring religious harmony had been rudely dismissed. Sinhalese kings had bestowed their patronage on a variety of Buddhist and Hindu institutions. The new faith was not then immediately perceived as repugnant or threatening . . . [But] the discalced friars now changed the frame of reference: patronage was not enough – indeed it was despised – what was needed was an exclusivist transformation of interiority.[39]

Descriptions of King Bhuvanekabahu varied from wise and thoughtful, to corrupt and lascivious, to weak and dependent on the protection of the Portuguese. As one early commentator described, 'he is blessed with the qualities of gentleness and kindness and even honor, but he is no great man, he is weak and timorous, afraid to convert for fear of alienating his subjects'.[40] He had come to power at a time when the unified government of the island had fallen apart, and different political factions allied with religious communities competing for royal influence focused attention more on commercial power and preservation of favor among those who could grant an advantage against competitors. So the words of Bhuvanekabahu are quite striking, even as they come to us from a Christian chronicler:

---

38 Perniola, *The Catholic Church in Sri Lanka*, 40.
39 Strathern, *Kingship and Conversion in Sixteenth-Century Sri Lanka*, 87.
40 Cited in Strathern, *Kingship and Conversion in Sixteenth-Century Sri Lanka*, 2.

Neither for the present king of Portugal nor for two more like him will I abandon the law in which I was born, nourished, and educated; and I assure you that I shall never accept the law of the Christians and profess it. And if anyone would force me to do so, I would rather lose my kingdom and my country than be baptized. You and your friars can offer your law to my subjects. If any wish to accept it, this will be agreeable with me and I shall prevent no one from joining you. But if they do not wish to do so, no one will be able to blame me for it.[41]

This comment is interesting because it demonstrates two sides of early Buddhist views of attachment that might have been at play. On the first side, we can consider the traditional list of four kinds of attachment or clinging: to physical pleasures (*kama*), to views (*ditthi*), to conventional rules (*sila*), and to senses of a permanent or unchanging self (*atta*). One can imagine that baptism might have been viewed as an occasion for increasing any one of these four objects of attachment. We do not know why he understood the Franciscan's request as the acceptance of a new law. Since we have no direct evidence of the extent of the king's knowledge of his tradition, we cannot be sure exactly how he would have interpreted conversion in specifically Buddhist terms. But on the second side, it is clear that the demands of his role as a Buddhist king, as a *cakkavatti* or wheel-turner of the Buddha's law, were deeply ingrained as the basic expression of his care for his land. Obeyesekere expresses well the problem for the king of the Buddha's island:

If any non-believer becomes a king of Sri Lanka by force at any time, that dynasty will not last owing to the special influence of the Buddha. Because this Lanka is rightfully those of kings who had right views [Buddhists], their rightful dynastic tenure (*kula praveniya*) will absolutely prevail. For these various reasons the kings of Sri Lanka are drawn by a natural love of mind to the Buddha and will establish the *sasana* without delay or neglect and protect the wheel of the law and the wheel of doctrine and reign so that the rightful dynastic tenure will be preserved.[42]

Moreover, the patronage of Buddhist monasteries by kings, while historically an expression of political power as well as a judgement about convincing religious arguments, also plays an important role here. As Maria Heim explains,

---

41 Schurhammer, *Francis Xavier*, 424.
42 Gananath Obeyesekere, 'On Buddhist Identity in Sri Lanka', in Lola Romanucci-Rossi and George A. de Vos (eds), *Ethnic Identity: Creation, Conflict and Accommodation* (London, 1995), 234 (cited in Strathern, 148).

The purest recipients [of gifts by kings and other lay persons] are monks and nuns who are the least eager to receive. The more ascetic and aloof from material support a monastic is, the closer he or she is to the spiritual goal, and so the gift is more fruitful for the donor . . . Ironically this leads to a curious structural tension between the donor and the receiver in that naturally the donor will want to give lavishly to such people, even though their accepting such largesse would threaten the very renunciation for which they are so highly esteemed.[43]

While the implications for comparative theology were naturally not explored in these contexts, the questions that emerge from them abound.

Would the king have applied the same logic to the morally upright Franciscans as he would have applied to his own monks? How would the king have responded if he had known about the compromises entailed in the Franciscan missions to his land or about the debates that lay beneath the Franciscan mode of life that struck him initially as worthy of praise? Would the friars have found anything useful, perhaps even cautionary, had they known more about the relationship of their lifestyle to other communities to whom the king gave support? Was there anything in the very discourse used by these sixteenth-century communities that could have made sense of the difficult comparative notion of 'exclusivist transformation of interiority' [Strathern's term for conversion] or the practice of and rationale for baptism? Would the king have treated the friars any differently had he known that the friars' interpretation of the gospel had been deeply debated at the heart of the Christian empire?

As I indicated at the beginning of this essay, this historical case cannot be a full exercise in comparative theology, even as it generates questions that point to the kind of attitude comparative theologians might adopt in thinking about mission contexts. But the example of King Bhuvanekabahu's encounter with the Franciscans illustrates how questions derived from particular mission contexts link the meaning of basic theological ideas with the behaviors through which those ideas are communicated to those receiving missionaries in their land. In this way, comparative theology must pass through ethical moments precisely when it works on theological ideas the meaning of which changes as they are lived in various historical contexts.

Mission, Hegemony, and Ethics in Comparative Theology

At the beginning of this essay, I offered the suggestion that comparative theology should not proceed without some attention to the history and location of particular interreligious interactions, which for Christian theologians means attention

---

43 Maria Heim, *Theories of the Gift in South Asia: Hindu, Buddhist and Jain Reflections on Dana* (New York and London: Routledge, 2004), 62.

to the history and theology of mission. My example of the Franciscans at King Bhuvanekabahu's court was meant to illustrate the kinds of questions that arise when we think both about the interactions at play in mission history, but also the levels of doubt, misunderstanding, and intra-religious debate that are often concealed behind these interactions. For behind every essentialism, especially but not exclusively the theological essentialisms to which many comparative theologians see their own work as a corrective, we often find persons struggling to be reconciled to their own failed histories and to gain awareness of their communities' legacies of physical and ideological violence.

So while the relevance of the events just recounted might at first appear marginal, their importance becomes clearer when we begin to think about the mission cases in light of our own certainties about what we study, why we study it, and how much of own theological questioning we are willing to fore-ground.[44] As a comparative theologian, I wish to know whether the theological ideas that I have inherited from my own tradition mean anything outside of that tradition. I cannot assume that that they do; I must hold them all as hypotheses in need of long-term testing drawn from particular biographies, culturally sensitive group histories, and the debates about these ideas within the traditions from which they are drawn. And I must always be ready for the possibility that my ideas will be meaningless or only minimally analogous in another religious context, even if the tradition that I inhabit instructs me that such ideas have universal applicability and meaningfulness. My own theological tradition shows no signs of being uniformly honest about the depths to be probed in religious discourse other than its own, although I believe it contains the resources and can form people capable of such fair-minded assessments.

Let me now draw together these observations by offering three lessons that attending to the case of the Franciscans in Sri Lanka and analogous cases might hold for comparative theology. First, for comparative theologians working from a broadly Christian framework, the Franciscan mission in Sri Lanka illustrates

---

44 I sometimes find it puzzling to know exactly what the contemporary predilection for stating the context from which comparative projects emerge has to do with the content of the *lives* that give rise to the topics comparativists study. For example, if I were to acknowledge the social and theo-logical location from which my own scholarship departs (theologically uncertain Roman Catholic white man, living in relative comfort in Northern Indiana, employed by the ecclesial ancestors of French missionaries on a parcel of land previously inhabited by the Potawatomi tribe of native peoples), each term in that phrased autobiography is an essentialism that belies the complexity of the person behind the term. Moreover, in the act of giving such a summary, I am assuming that those reading it will bring to each term a collection of ideas not all of which I would associate with that term and not all of which I express in any unified and coherent way in my own life. The problem of course is that each of my actions, indeed each of the words that I write (I write about Buddhist and Christian perspectives on moral struggle), are also a reduction of the complexity of the persons that produced them, and I must assume the same complexity in all those about whom I write. The essential question for me, as a comparative theologian, becomes how my work preserves the com-plexity and as-yet unfinished nature of all those about whom I write. At least one of the ways this happens is through the preservation of questions in the midst of and after comparisons.

how attention to the mission context of interreligious encounters begins to clarify the unsettled nature of many of the religious ideas that are often taken as the starting rather than the end points for comparative theological reflection. For example, the Franciscans who came to Sri Lanka were themselves at odds with many in their own community about the evangelical counsel of gospel poverty, even as their own way of living that counsel made them initially attractive to the Buddhist king and welcomed in his land. Yet what they were expecting of him, namely an interior conversion of heart, was something they could neither see nor communicate to him in terms that were compelling in light of his commitments to his role as a guardian of the Buddha's teaching. It is a slightly different manifestation of what Lee Yearley has termed the new virtue of 'spiritual regret'[45] – that is, to be able to look at another tradition and sincerely affirm its distinctive goods, even if one does not wish to possess those goods oneself – when comparative theologians can look at a case like the Franciscan mission to Sri Lanka and wonder why the parties to that encounter did not think it important to talk to each other about issues that seem so clearly relevant to us today. What could the notion of baptism have meant to a Buddhist king whose role was significantly affected by his conviction that he must preserve the Buddha's *dhamma*? Why did the Franciscans think that their rejection of royal sponsorship, indeed their extreme embrace of Christ's poverty, would lead the king to understand and embrace the story they brought? How was the king's way of treating the Franciscans different from his way of treating other religious communities on the island?

Second, it is sometimes difficult to foresee how studying one encounter between religious groups in one part of the world will affect how we study other religious encounters elsewhere. Yet the case of the sixteenth-century missionaries is suggestive in this way as well. The group of Franciscans that travelled to Sri Lanka was of the same spiritual heritage as those that travelled to Mexico. This heritage was, as we have seen, not without its theological challenges from other Franciscans and from the institutional Roman Catholic Church. This specific expression of Franciscan Catholicism led some of the friars in Mexico to reflect on the violent legacy that their own mission would carry, even as they viewed the 'discovery' of the people there as providential and the fulfillment of a spiritual prophecy. It led them to view the people of their mission as exhibiting much of what they hoped their own culture would embrace, even as they were convinced of the necessity of the gospel for their perfection. Yet this Franciscan heritage produced a very different result in Sri Lanka. There was an immediate recognition of the missionaries' manner of life by the Buddhist king and the renunciants with which he was familiar, even as the new 'discalced' ones were preaching an unfamiliar story that required a kind of change which other communities' stories did not require. It would be fair to say that the change they

---

45 Lee H. Yearley, 'New Religious Virtues and the Study of Religion', Fifteenth Annual University Lecture in Religion, Arizona State University, Department of Religious Studies, 1994, 15–16.

were seeking was one that even many of their own people in Portugal, who shared their religious commitments, could not bring themselves to make. These encounters were not comparative theology in any recognizable sense, but within them we can begin to discern the important yet inconclusive interplay between behaviors and beliefs which both prompts and contextualizes comparative thinking.

Or consider something as deceptively simple as whether the notion of 'mission' in Christian theology is really a settled matter. As Lawrence Cunningham has put it,

> Recalling that the word 'mission' is from the Latin word 'to send', it is of the essence of Catholic Christianity that as the Father sent the Son, so too the Son sends the Apostles and their successors to preach the Gospel to all creatures. In that sense, 'mission' is a core concept that cannot be reduced to the narrow meaning of sending professionals out to plant the Church in alien lands. Such missionary expansion, of course, is a critical part of the Church's activity, but it occurs under the impulse of the far more fundamental notion imposed on all baptized Catholics to be missionaries in the broadest sense of that term.[46]

But this theological account of mission does not signal the practical difficulties of mission rationales or activities in various places, nor does it relate easily to other warrants for interreligious conversations about the truth of one's beliefs.[47] The

---

46 Lawrence Cunningham, *An Introduction to Catholicism* (Cambridge: Cambridge University Press, 2009), 192.

47 So for example, we have the frequently cited example of Buddhism as a 'missionary religion'. Yet as Jonathan Walters has shown, with reference to the so-called 'Buddha's Great Commission' speech in the commentary on the *Buddhavamsa* (*Madhuratthavilasini*) as well as the 'historical Asokan missions' especially of his son/nephew Mahinda to Sri Lanka, the notion of mission is itself a problematic comparative category which has had the unfortunate effect of obscuring the particular ways that Buddhists had of communicating their religious ideas and behaviors to others. So for example, in analyzing the term *dhamma-duteyya* (message or errand about the Dhamma) which is frequently translated as 'mission', Walters explains: 'Of course "errand of Truth" and "mission" come very close to each other. We are certainly talking about action which is related to the communication of religious perspectives . . . The question becomes, does communication of one's religious beliefs, i.e. preaching, necessarily constitute "mission"? . . . For the Anglo-American Protestants and historians of religions, "missionary" and "non-missionary" religions (or forms of a particular religion) were distinguished by the absence or presence of "missionary spirit" . . . [which] was considered a way of being religious, an essential and driving commitment to convert others, based upon compassion, of which preaching, civilizing, scholarship, suffering and personal salvation were secondary effects . . . The definition of "missionary spirit" was so narrow that even Jesuits – who shared many of the characteristics of the Protestant missionaries (preaching to convert the world, studying native languages and cultures in order to get at the people, civilizing, discoursing missiologically, feeling a sense of calling or duty which is based on compassion for the lost) – were excluded because their particular from of mission was, given the Protestant understanding of Rome as an Evil Empire, considered closer to the world of emissaries, diplomats and spies than "missionaries".' See Jonathan S. Walters, 'Rethinking Buddhist Missions' (unpublished PhD thesis, University of Chicago, 1992), 206–7.

difficulties that confronted the Franciscan missionaries as they tried to understand the rationales for their mission were not the topic of their interreligious
conversations. Just communicating some sense of their own mission to the
people with whom they lived was difficult enough. What was going on behind
what they shared with those hearing the gospel was equally important for understanding their work, as the theological ideas themselves were in motion, the
products of not yet settled conversations. This suggests another way in which the
Sri Lankan case can pose instructive questions for contemporary comparative
theology. How do the *particularities* of one comparative theological project
matter for the particularities of another comparative theological project? At times
one is tempted to think that those unenlightened hegemonic missionaries might
have been better equipped to answer such questions than we are today.

The third lesson pertains to the struggle of persons in any religious group to
live up to their own highest ideals. Violent tendencies, some more overt and
physical and others more subtle but still real, pervade virtually all forms of religious life and expression. One way of thinking about hegemony in comparative
theology would be to say that whoever determines the questions asked has,
through the dominance of their own religious discourse, already over-determined
the answers that might arise in conversation. In a related way, the simple numer-
ical dominance of Christian theologians in comparative theology suggests a
kind of hegemony of persons, well-intentioned perhaps, but stifling and shape-
imposing nonetheless. What I think the foregoing case suggests is that attention
to the fragmentary artifacts, what David Tracy would call the 'shards', of comparative theology in mission history produces a much different focus point when
we ask about the presence of hegemony in comparative theology. I want to
speak about this lesson as developing sensitivities to the hegemonies within us.

Hegemony denotes rule and control of one party by another. When we use
this term in reference to theological study, it frequently means to control the discussion through the employment of a dominant discourse, or to cite those in
particular traditions whose voices carry weight in their eclipse of other voices
whose speech has been systematically and continuously blocked. So it is in
response to such modes of theology that Michelle Voss Roberts in her essay for
this volume identifies certain liberating currents at work in some recent comparative theology. She suggests, developing the language of Collins, that 'Comparativists can extend their commitment to the particular by considering the
"outsider within".'[48] While I would want to affirm this focus point in comparative studies more broadly, I also suggest that there is another voice that has not
often been heard that exists within dominant theological discourses as a faint
echo, a kind of 'insider without'. This is the voice within dominant theological
discourses that wants to retain a moral vigilance against its own totalizing
impulses to protect a more patient, honestly critical, yet humble moment. It is

---

48 Voss Roberts, this volume, p. 115.

the element of cautious theological speech that comes with reviewing the history of one's writings and actions on behalf of a half-understood God. Such a form of theology recognizes that in addition to (and within) the hegemonic tendencies of groups or individuals with positions of privilege, there are hegemonies within individuals, border skirmishes between mind and heart that cannot and will never be entirely eliminated. What I have been suggesting is that attention to mission contexts, which are much more complex and diverse than the example I have offered here, may be a fruitful place to look for the constructive uses of these hegemonies within.

I continually find myself wondering whether those who are drawn to comparative theology despite its pretentions and pitfalls come to it because they recognize something like a common calling. I suggested in the first section of this paper that comparative theology may exhibit a distinctive spirituality or tone of reflection that is both intellectually reserved and historically gradual. I think it may also be characterized by a kind of sorrow and solidarity that comes with attention to the ease and frequency with which even the most well-intentioned and intellectually gifted religious persons want to settle matters well before there is any need to find answers.

This spirituality, however one might want to name it, seems also coupled with a strong moral impulse. And thus I want to suggest, by way of conclusion, that it might be helpful if we were to think of ethics as a moment at which to begin and to which we should return within the longer trajectories of our comparative theological lives – the dynamic of passing through ethical moments. Here I use the term 'ethics' not as a description of a particular religious tradition's laws, values and patterns of social order but, as many contemporary scholars have put it, as critical reflection on modes of life. Such a view of ethics as applied to comparative theology means that examining a particular theological concept, historically situated in each tradition in which it is considered, should begin with or consider early on what difference theological ideas have made to how people treat others in the context of practical encounters. Have particular ideas been occasions for violence? Has the violence been occasioned by the ideas themselves or the occlusion of these ideas by what are perceived to be necessary moral compromises? Have members of religious groups who have been in dialogue with each other shown some caution regarding the moral ambivalence of their own comments and that which remains unsaid in the process of together-reading towards truth?

5

Comparative Theology and the Status of Judaism: Hegemony and Reversals

DANIEL JOSLYN-SIEMIATKOSKI

Judaism is a submerged tradition within the writings and practices of comparative theology. When comparative theology is written (predominantly by Christian theologians), Judaism is rarely a tradition that is engaged. When Judaism is considered, often two things happen: either it is studied within a panoply of other systems of belief and practice or only its scriptural and philosophical traditions are written about while the heritage of rabbinic Judaism remains in the background. This essay will examine the constellation of discourses concerning Judaism within the current field of comparative theology and propose that the Christian orientation of most comparative theology scholars has resulted in a latent hegemonic view of Judaism in which a reflexive, subconscious form of supersessionism has operated. As a result, there has not yet been produced a work of comparative theology that engages in the depth of the Jewish tradition and performs the work of 'reread[ing] one's home theological tradition . . . after a serious engagement in the reading of another tradition'.[1] This essay will conclude with an attempt to model such a re-reading by an analysis of the concept of the Torah in a rabbinic Jewish text, Mishnah *Avot*.

I approach the study of comparative theology as a male Euro-American Episcopalian historian of Christianity involved in the study of pre-modern Jewish–Christian relations. Coming out of this historical study is a commitment to contribute to the construction of a non-supersessionist post-Holocaust Christian theology. I employ a comparative theology method flowing from Francis X. Clooney's approach because of the seriousness with which this method takes both the reading of traditions other than one's own and the commitment to

---

1 Francis X. Clooney, SJ, *Theology after Vedanta: An Experiment in Comparative Theology* (Albany: State University of New York Press, 1993), 3.2; Edith Wyschogrod, *An Ethics of Remembering: History, Heterology, and the Nameless Others* (Chicago: University of Chicago Press, 1998), 8.

re-reading one's own tradition afterwards. Studying the history of Jewish–Christian relations has caused me to realize that theology has been inextricably bound up with Christian oppression of Jews. As an act of repentance and forgiveness, I seek to re-work forms of Christian theology impinging upon Jewish subjects. In this way I identify myself as both a comparative theologian and a historian who 'is driven by the urgency of a promise to the dead to tell the truth about them, a promise that is prior to her account of the facts'.[2]

Hegemony and Jewish–Christian Relations: The Problem of Supersessionism

Historically, there has been a hegemonic Christian attitude towards Jews and Judaism. This attitude, born out of initial contestations and controversies in the early centuries of the Common Era, included the incorporation of anti-Judaism into Christian theology. Anti-Jewish theological positions intentionally marginalized Judaism as a lived expression of belief and culture rooted in an eternal covenant between the people of Israel and God. Anti-Jewish Christian theology is at its core supersessionist. That is, it espouses the belief that the Church has replaced Israel as God's chosen people.[3] There are three key components in classical views of supersessionism. First is the rejection of the Jews as possessors of a continuing covenant with God. The second component holds that with the coming of Christ and the institution of the Church, humanity is able to fulfill its longings for relationship with God. As a result, the historical people of the Israel of the Old Testament are no longer necessary for the implementation of God's plan of salvation. Third, supersessionist teachings hold that the Jews have rejected Jesus of Nazareth as the Messiah and actively participated in his crucifixion. Following on this, God has ended the covenant with the historical people of Israel. According to this line of thought, the abrogation of the covenant by God is evidenced by the destruction of the Temple in 70 CE by the Roman Empire and the subsequent loss of the land of Israel.

Supersessionist theology as a body of hegemonic discourses created a distorted Christian view of the lived experiences and beliefs of Jews and Judaism. Such discourses contributed to and perpetuated Christian violence directed towards Jews, physical and ideological, and helped establish the necessary conditions for the events of the Holocaust.[4] Accompanying these negative effects, supersession-

---

2 Edith Wyschogrod, *An Ethics of Remembering: History, Heterology, and the Nameless Others* (Chicago: University of Chicago Press, 1998), 8.

3 For this explication of the definition and theological categories of supersessionist thought outlined in the paper, I am indebted to definitions provided by Philip A. Cunningham of St Joseph's University, Philadelphia, PA.

4 On the relationship between the rise of National Socialism, the Holocaust, and the Christian churches, see Susannah Heschel, *Christian Theologians and the Bible in Nazi Germany* (Princeton, NJ: Princeton University Press, 2008); Richard Steigman-Gall, *The Holy Reich: Nazi Conceptions of Christianity, 1919–1945* (Cambridge: Cambridge University Press, 2003); Robert P. Ericksen and Susannah Heschel (eds), *Betrayal: German Churches and the Holocaust* (Minneapolis, MN: Fortress Press, 1999).

ist thought regarding Jewish life also distorted Christian theology. Beginning in the second century and continuing to the contemporary period, significant numbers of Christians have either been taught supersessionism actively or ingested it passively through the medium of traditional Christian authors and teachings.[5] A significant result of a supersessionist Christian theology of Judaism was an inability to account for developments in Jewish life and culture after the biblical period. Well into the medieval period, Christian theologians frequently did not grasp that Judaism continued to develop as a vibrant religious tradition; rather, contemporaneous Jews were taken to be representative of biblical Jews. When medieval Christians did 'discover' the writings of rabbinic Judaism, such as the Talmud and *midrash*, they were taken as perversions of the scriptural texts, containing blasphemies about Jesus and Mary and so epitomes of the worst of 'pharisaical' Judaism. Christian theological considerations of normative forms of Judaism emerging out of rabbinic traditions continued to emphasize the legalistic and 'pharisaical' dimensions of this living tradition.[6] The overall effect of Christian supersessionist theologies of Judaism was to create a series of hegemonic discourses about Judaism that replicated themselves within Christian theological circles well into the twentieth century.

The hegemonic dimensions of supersessionist thought are further illuminated in Edward Said's concept of Orientalism. Said's analysis of Orientalism in the work of the same title places the Oriental, specifically the Arab, as an object of fascination and manipulation for western intellectuals and state powers. Said defines Orientalism as a

> . . . *distribution* of geopolitical awareness into aesthetic, scholarly, economic, sociological, historical, and philological texts . . . it is, above all, a discourse that is by no means in direct, corresponding relationship with political power in the raw, but rather is produced and exists in uneven exchange with various kinds of power, shaped to a degree by the exchange with power political (as with colonial or imperial establishment), power intellectual (as with reigning sciences like comparative linguistics or anatomy, or any of the modern policy sciences), power cultural (as with orthodoxies and canons of taste, texts, values), power moral (as with ideas about what 'we' do and what 'they' cannot do or understand as 'we' do).[7]

---

5 See, for example, Marcel Simon, *Verus Israel: A Study of the Relation Between Christians and Jews in the Roman Empire (135–425)*, trans. H. McKeating (New York: Oxford University Press, 1986); Leon Poliakov, *The History of Anti-Semitisim*, trans. R. Howard et al., 4 vols (New York: Vanguard Press, 1965–1985); Edwin H. Flannery, *The Anguish of the Jews: Twenty-three Centuries of Anti-Semitism* (New York: Macmillan, 1965).

6 On the premodern developments of these ideas, see Jeremy Cohen, *Living Letters of the Law: Ideas of the Jew in Medieval Christianity* (Berkeley: University of California Press, 1999).

7 Edward W. Said, *Orientalism* (New York: Vintage Books, 1994), 12.

The operation of the forms of power Said identifies in this quote (powers political, intellectual, cultural, and moral) has left an imprimatur upon the global scene. Certainly the effects of these forms of power have worked their way into the current geopolitical, cultural, economic, and religious relations that define contemporary struggles against marginalization visited upon the developing world. But the dynamics of these power relations in their political, intellectual, cultural, and moral iterations are not restricted to Orientalism as Said defines it. These power relations also exist in Christian supersessionism.

Said argues that Orientalism has roots in medieval Christian scholars who objectified Islam and Muslims. Quoting the work of R. W. Southern, Said marks the beginning of Orientalism as a field of study with a decree of the council of Vienne in 1312 that created chairs for the study of Arabic, Greek, Hebrew, and Syriac at the universities of Paris, Oxford, Bologna, Avignon, and Salamanca.[8] Medieval Orientalism was deployed to manage western Christian anxieties about the Orient, and Islam in particular. But the study of Islam and the Orient was not to learn about something outside of Christendom on its own terms but rather to reinforce the narcissistic self-image of Christian elites. Thus the Orient and its inhabitants could never be their own, in western terms, but only ever the unchangeable Other constructed for western Christian consumption.[9]

Said's definition of Orientalism's origins within medieval European Christianity ignores that what was done to Islamic and Arab subjects in this process had already happened to Jews. Supersessionism is the elder brother of Said's Orientalism. The image of Jews and Judaism was constructed by the foundational ecclesiastical thinker and leaders of pre-modern Christianity with the result that the Jews emerged as the fundamental Other by which Christian intellectuals constructed the Church as the elect people of God, the *Verus Israel*. The powers political, intellectual, cultural, and moral that created the Orientalist context were already also active within supersessionism. Thus medieval Jews were subject to power political in their dependence on charters and the protection of bishops in order to reside in Christian cities.[10] They were subjected to power intellectual in Christian theological constructions of Judaism as a fossilized religion of the Bible lacking any contemporary vitality and existing under the wrath of God as a sign to the world.[11] Jews were under the sway of power cultural in the artistic renderings of Jews as monstrous and the personification of the Synagogue as blind in medieval art.[12] And Jews were subject to power moral in

---

8 Said, *Orientalism*, 50. Said cites R. W. Southern, *Western Views of Islam in the Middle Ages* (Cambridge, MA: Harvard University Press, 1962), 72.

9 Said, *Orientalism*, 59–61.

10 For documents on this set of relationships in German lands, see I. Elbogen et al. (eds), *Germania Judaica*, 3 vols (Tübingen: J. C. B. Mohr, 1963–2003).

11 See Cohen, *Living Letters of the Law*.

12 See Heinz Schreckenberg, 'Die christlichen Adversus-Judaeos-Texte (11.–13. Jh.): mit einer Ikonographie des Judenthemas bis zum 4. Laterankonzil' (Frankfurt am Main: Peter Lang, 1991).

restrictive legislation concerning Jews and slanders about Jewish host desecration and murder of Christian children in hagiographies and sermons.[13]

Considering this background for the purposes of examining the status of Judaism within the discipline of comparative theology means that the predominantly Christian practitioners of this theological method ought to be aware of the historical and ideological dynamics involved in (not) considering Judaism when doing theology comparatively. Just as Orientalist discourses made the Oriental Other visible when it suited western interests and invisible when it did not, so the supersessionist construction of the Jewish Other has been perpetuated for so long in Christian thought and life that even comparative theology scholars fall prone to producing Jews when it fits their needs and renders them and their tradition invisible when it does not. Supersessionism has been so enmeshed in Christian discourses for so long that even the most well-intentioned theologians committed to the thriving of all peoples have fallen prone to it. Thus it has been shown that liberation theologians in diverse contexts have engaged in supersessionist discourses, and feminist theologians have replicated iterations of this theology.[14] These facts do not mean that these theological approaches ought to be abandoned or their commitments repudiated but rather that they should be re-read in light of a deep engagement with the Jewish tradition. In a similar way, comparative theology ought to be re-read with an eye to identifying and reversing hegemonic supersessionist discourses where they occur and encouraging expressions of non-supersessionist alternatives.

Although many forms of traditional Christian thought have manifested supersessionist attitudes towards Judaism, the rhetoric of superiority and the replacement of other traditions with Christian belief has a long history in the encounter of (especially) missionary brands of Christianity with non-Christian communities. Thus, the logic of supersessionism manifested in the treatment of and rhetoric about Jews within Christendom was rearticulated in the Christian missionary encounter with local cultures outside of Europe. While this essay focuses on the place of Judaism in comparative theology produced by Christian practitioners, the after-effects of dynamics similar to supersessionism can be found in other forms of comparative theology.[15] Furthermore, the Christian relationship to a Jewish near 'Other' need not be a unique example. Investigations might reveal similar dynamics in Hindu relationships with Jainism and Buddhism, for example. A desirable element in the development of comparative theology is to

---

13 See Miri Rubin, *Gentile Tales: The Narrative Assault on Late Medieval Jews* (New Haven: Yale University Press, 1999).

14 On a critique of Latin American liberation theology, see John Pawlikowski, *Christ in the Light of the Christian–Jewish Dialogue* (New York, Paulist Press, 1982), 59–73. For a critique of Asian liberation theology, see Peter C. Phan, *Being Religious Interreligiously* (Maryknoll, NY: Orbis, 2004), 163–71. A provocative roundtable discussion of the problem of supersessionism in Christian feminist theology can be found in the *Journal of Feminist Studies in Religion* (20:1, 2004), 91–132.

15 For an example of this dynamic, see Richard King, *Orientalism and Religion: Postcolonial Theory, India and 'the Mystic East'* (New York: Routledge, 1999).

produce more studies that destabilize the privileged status of Christianity and so, for instance, include comparative theologians who reflect upon Islam and Buddhism or Taoism and traditional African religions.[16]

Repairing Jewish–Christian Relations: *Nostra Aetate* and Other Efforts

The question of the status of Judaism within comparative theology evolved out of the engagement of Christian churches with the crisis of Jewish–Christian relations in the decades following the Holocaust. Although a wide range of Christian communities engaged with this question, the Roman Catholic Church has been exemplary regarding the extent and depth of its theological reflections and ecclesial mandates. This work of repairing and rethinking Catholic–Jewish relations began with the seminal 1965 *Declaration on the Relation of the Church to Non-Christian Relations*, also known as *Nostra Aetate*, issued at the Second Vatican Council. This document placed theological reflection on the relationship between Christianity and other religions as part of the intellectual and social activity of the Roman Catholic Church and encouraged similar actions in other Christian bodies.

Nostra Aetate set the stage for serious engagement with other traditions within the field of Roman Catholic scholarship. Regarding Judaism, the fourth section of *Nostra Aetate* addressed the relationship between the Church and the Jewish people and raised the problem of supersessionism.[17] The significance of this section of *Nostra Aetate* rests in four key teachings on Jews and Judaism. First, *Nostra Aetate* emphasized a spiritual link between Jews and Christians rooted in the connection between Christians and Jews in the figure of Abraham. This notion of an indissoluble spiritual link emerged as a consistent idea in later Roman Catholic statements on Jewish–Christian relations.[18] Second, *Nostra*

---

16 I am grateful to Kristin Beise Kiblinger and Jeffery D. Long for their comments on these points. The past decade has seen an increase in comparative work between Hinduism and Judaism. See, for example, Barbara A. Holdrege, *Veda and Torah: Transcending the Textuality of Scripture* (Albany: State University of New York Press, 1996) and the work of the Comparative Studies in Hinduisms and Judaisms Group of the American Academy of Religion.

17 Austin Flannery (ed.), *Declaration on the Relation of the Church to Non-Christian Relations* in *Vatican II: The Conciliar and Post-Conciliar Documents*, Vol. 1 (Collegeville, MN: Liturgical Press, 1984), 738–42. Some other statements on Jewish–Christian relations were released earlier, notably the 1947 'Address to the Churches' by the International Council of Christians and Jews in Seelisberg, Switzerland. But *Nostra Aetate* inaugurated a wave of critical Christian reflections on the relationship between Judaism and Christianity. On the history of the development of *Nostra Aetate* as originally a document dealing solely with Judaism to one addressing non-Christian religions in general, see Philip A. Cunningham, Norbert J. Hofmann, and Joseph Sievers (eds), 'Drafts Leading to the Conciliar Declaration *Nostra Aetate*', in *Catholic Church and the Jewish People: Recent Reflections from Rome* (New York: Fordham University Press, 2007), 191–200.

18 See, for example, two separate statements from the Pontifical Commission for Religious Relations with the Jews: 'Guidelines and Suggestions for Implementing the Conciliar Declaration *Nostra Aetate*, No. 4' (1974) and 'We Remember: A Reflection on the *Shoah*' (1998).

Aetate specifically taught, citing Romans 9:4–5, that Jews continue to possess a covenant with God. At the same time, the declaration expressed the eschatological hope that Jews and Christians alike would eventually come together as one body. A third key teaching from *Nostra Aetate* is the assertion of the Jewish identity of Jesus and the earliest generation of the Church. Finally, *Nostra Aetate* denounced the blood guilt and deicide charges which historically had been leveled against Jews and resulted in episodic violence. Although the Gospels related that some Jewish authorities were implicated in the arrest and crucifixion of Jesus, *Nostra Aetate* clearly taught that the scriptural witness belied any blanket assertion of Jewish guilt. Furthermore, the document repudiated all forms of persecution against Jews.

Nostra Aetate was a watershed document that led to the production of statements by many Christian church bodies on the status of Judaism.[19] The teachings on the proper relationship between Jews and Christians initiated at the Second Vatican Council has resulted in multiple statements on Jews and Judaism from various Vatican congregations and commissions, to say nothing of the range of declarations and documents from national bishops' councils. As a body, the statements of the past 45 years emanating from the Vatican have the weight of magisterial teaching. This brief survey tells us how one particular Christian ecclesial body has taken the initial steps of incorporating a more positive view of Jews and Judaism into its official teachings on other religions; it also raises the subsequent question of how individual Christian theologians grappling with the fact of religious pluralism have considered (or not) the status of Judaism.

Along with official statements on Jews and Judaism by Christians from a wide range of churches, many individual Christians also engaged in dialogue with Jews and wrote on the need to evaluate Judaism in theologically affirmative modes. Biblical scholars, theologians, and historians have made significant strides in fostering positive Jewish–Christians relations.[20] These Christians have helpfully moved Christian thought and practice away from supersessionist modalities. Yet they have rarely engaged in depth with traditional Jewish texts as a resource for theological reflection.[21] That is, theological engagement with Jewish sources and concepts is episodic and specific to particular contexts for dialogue. But rarely is the breadth of the Jewish tradition engaged with as a resource even for

---

19 For a broad collection of statements on Jewish–Christian relations, see Boston College Center for Christian–Jewish Learning, 'Documents, Declarations and Speeches' accessed at http://www.bc.edu/research/cjl/cjrelations/resources/documents.html. Accessed 3 February 2009.

20 See, for example, the work of Mary Boys, A. Roy Eckardt, Christoph Münz, John Pawlikowski, Marcel Simon, R. Kendall Soulen, Krister Stendahl, Paul van Buren, Clark Williamson.

21 There are certainly examples of Christians and Jews reflecting together on common themes like redemption, revelation, covenant, Israel, and so forth in works like Tikva Frymer-Kensky, et al. (eds), *Christianity in Jewish Terms* (Boulder: Westview Press, 2000); and Eugene B. Korn and John Pawlikowski (eds), *Two Faiths, One Covenant? Jewish and Christian Identity in the Presence of the Other* (Lanham: Rowman & Littlefield, 2005).

Christians seeking to undo supersessionist modes in Christianity. Comparative theology holds the promise for providing such an avenue of inquiry, but in this field engagement with Judaism has been at times problematic.

Methodological Proposals and Jewish Absence

In some of the most seminal works on comparative theological method the presence of Jews and Judaism barely registers. In some cases, this absence is neither surprising nor necessarily a point of contention. Briefly considering works by Francis X. Clooney, James L. Fredericks, and Robert Cummings Neville illustrates this. One does not read Clooney's *Theology after Vedanta* wondering about his take on Judaism precisely because he makes clear that his experiment in comparative theology is between his own practice of Roman Catholicism and his study of Advaita Vedanta. Clooney makes it clear that he is engaged in mapping out a comparative theological method that would encourage an entire re-thinking of one's home tradition after a deep and sustained encounter with a single other tradition.[22] Given his methodological focus and the open-ended nature of his approach, it is easy for one to imagine how to place an encounter with Judaism into the model he provided in his own study of Advaita Vedanta. Indeed, his approach suggests that a serious engagement with Judaism by Christians would inform attitudes towards Hinduism. In *Behind the Masks of God*, Neville engages as a Christian theologian with specific religious traditions, here forms of Buddhism and Confucianism, around the theological concepts of creation and the nature of divinity.[23] Neville makes repeated references to the 'Judeo-Christian tradition' in his work, but it is clear that he has in mind the Hebrew Scriptures and New Testament in this phrase. As a Christian, Neville is concerned with a discrete scriptural tradition that Christianity in part shares with Judaism, but he does not consider any post-biblical elements of the Jewish tradition.[24] 'Judeo-Christian tradition' is arguably a supersessionist term in that it reduces the Jewish tradition to those scriptural texts it shares with Christianity, thus implying that Judaism ends with the rise of Christianity. While Neville likely meant no malice by the use of this term, it illustrates the depths to which latent supersessionism has penetrated Christian theological discourses. Finally, James Fredericks in *Faith among Faiths* offers a critique of the pluralist school in the field of Christian theology of religions and offers comparative theology as a means of moving beyond the pluralist position. Much like Clooney, Fredericks presents comparative theology as a practice of reading texts from differing traditions in concert. As a means of illustration he compares

---

22 Clooney, *Theology after Vedanta*, 153.
23 Robert Cummings Neville, *Behind the Masks of God: An Essay Toward Comparative Theology* (Albany: State University of New York Press, 1991).
24 See, for example, Neville, *Behind the Masks of God*, 19.

Gospel passages with texts from Buddhist and Hindu traditions, though there are only passing mentions of Judaism as one of many world religions.[25]

In considering these three books on comparative theology and their method-ological approaches, what is most striking is that each author chose to engage with religious traditions that originated in Asian countries, particularly India, China, and Japan. Each author had commitments from his own life and practice (which they have indicated in the introductions to these books or elsewhere) that indicate why they have chosen to engage with these specific traditions. As a scholar with my own personal commitment to a deep study of Judaism, I am struck by the fact that most (though certainly not all) comparative theologians have decided to engage with religious traditions that are rooted in Asian con-texts. As a result of these choices, especially by the first wave of comparative theologians, the lived reality of Judaism (and often Islam) has typically been absent from methodological considerations in the development of this discipline. One may rightly ask how what is studied and privileged (whether it is specific religious traditions, textuality over orality, or male-originated over female-originated traditions) influences one's methodology. In significant ways, the dis-cipline of comparative theology (as practiced predominantly by Christians) has framed its methodology not with the encounter of monotheistic traditions but rather with the encounter of religions originating from Asian countries. These are traditions that possess a clear body of teaching (in some cases, as with the Vedas, transcribed by westerners) yet are maximally 'Other' compared to the near 'Other' of Judaism.[26]

I want to be clear that the choosing of a particular tradition with which to engage in comparative reflection is not being impugned, but I want to question why Judaism has not been taken up as a tradition with which to grapple when constructing methodological approaches. Aside from the personal commitments that have led theologians to engage with the traditions they have chosen, it ought to be pointed out that an effect of supersessionism, even in latent forms, is to view Judaism as a precursor to Christianity and not sufficiently differentiated from it. In other words, Judaism is the near 'Other' that is not acknowledged as a fully distinct religious tradition and so does not generate the same theological questions as a consideration of Buddhism or Taoism might. Hence Neville writes about the Judeo–Christian tradition but never cites anything beyond the Christian Bible. My argument here is not that Neville is a supersessionist (nor any of the other authors considered in this essay) but rather that the subconscious effects of hegemonic supersessionism over millennia of Christian theology have leached into the development of a comparative theology methodology.

---

25 James L. Fredericks, *Faith among Faiths* (Mahwah, NJ: Paulist Press, 1999).

26 Islam also is a special case from traditions originating in South and East Asian contexts. Like Judaism it is closer to Christianity in its traditions and doctrines, but its development and relation-ship with Christianity is distinct from Judaism in important ways. Certainly more work is also needed in the area of Islam within the field of comparative theology.

Comfortable Encounters: Christian Comparative Approaches to Jewish Scriptural and Philosophical Texts

Comparative theological works written by Christians who do consider Jewish traditions tend to concentrate on scriptural texts and philosophers (specifically Maimonides) familiar to Christians. As a result, these works do not deal in depth with the core of the post-biblical Jewish tradition found in rabbinic sources. The result is a comparative look at Judaism that is impoverished by failing to consider the breadth of traditional teachings. By way of example, this section will consider the work of the comparative theologian Keith Ward.

The tendency to overlook contributions from rabbinic Judaism is significant in light of the supersessionist tendencies of Christian theology. Rabbinic Judaism provided the foundation for virtually every subsequent form of Judaism and as such holds a normative status within Jewish discourses.[27] It is important to emphasize that Judaism did not develop directly from the Israelite religion documented in the Bible but was in significant ways created through the process of rabbinic interpretation of the Torah. However, Christian supersessionist discourses tend to marginalize the contributions of rabbinic Judaism by identifying it as the direct successors of the Pharisees and hence the embodiment of the legalism that led to the rejection of Jesus and his death. In less extreme cases there has been a subtle dismissal of rabbinic Judaism as legalistic, particularistic, and inscrutable in its attention to minutiae. Thus Judaism has been understood either as a direct continuation of the Israelite tradition, with little appreciation for the depth and complexity provided by the rabbis, or a corruption of God's original call to Israel by the narrow legalism of these same rabbis. Both views have led to distorted assumptions in Christian discourses about the nature of Judaism. In turn, this has meant Christians have comfortably equated Judaism with under-developed images not recognizable to the experiences of Jews.

The British theologian and Anglican priest Keith Ward has composed several books of comparative theology in which he engages in serial analyses of religious topics in major world religions (typically Hinduism, Buddhism, Judaism, Christianity, and Islam). When he discusses Judaism in his writings, Ward at times appears to establish a hierarchy where he prefers the philosophical clarity in Maimonides and the moral exhortations of the Israelite prophets over the particularistic claims of the Torah upon the people of Israel. For example, in his early work *Images of Eternity*, when considering the meaning of the symbolic imagery of God in the Hebrew Scriptures, Ward opines that, 'the biblical writers make no attempt at all to answer this question. In particular, they do not offer a superior, more abstract philosophical concept which discloses a reality hidden

---

27 Exceptions to this do exist. For example, Karaite Jews up through the eighteenth century contested rabbinic authority though they modulated their stance in the modern period.

behind these very personalistic symbols for the devout.'[28] Ward also throws jabs at the Israelites' supposedly unsophisticated worldview when discussing biblical injunctions about idolatry: 'My own view is that the Hebrews were rather unfair to idolaters; fairness in religion was never one of their more notable virtues.'[29] In these dismissive takes on the scriptural sources of Judaism, Ward has brought into the comparative process attitudes regarding biblical precedents of Judaism that bear traces of latent supersessionism. Because of Ward's reflexive equation of Judaism with Israelite practices without introducing rabbinic interpretations of the relevant scriptural passages, Ward has, unwittingly or not, given the impression that Judaism is the heir to a bigoted tradition. Rather than investigate how rabbinic Judaism dealt with the category of idolatry, Ward dismisses the category out of hand.[30]

In later works, Ward is not quite so dismissive of the Jewish tradition, though he tends to continue to focus on scriptural traditions and modern thinkers to illuminate Jewish perspectives on revelation, creation, human nature, and community. Ward's scholarship in these works is marked by a progressive entry into the contours of Jewish thought as undergirded by rabbinic Judaism. For example, in his early work from 1987, *Images of Eternity*, he writes about the philosophical views of Maimonides. Throughout this chapter his three points of reference are the Hebrew prophets and their images of the divine, Aristotelianism, and Maimonides' own views. Nowhere does Ward deal with the rabbinic tradition that he rightly notes Maimonides synthesized with Aristotelian philosophy.[31] Similarly, in Ward's writing on Judaism in his 1994 *Religion and Revelation* and 1996 *Religion and Creation* he replicates a latent supersessionism by focusing almost exclusively on the Hebrew Scriptures as representative of Judaism. Moreover he falls into the tendency of speaking of the Hebrew tradition as a prelude for the development of Christian concepts while not fully investigating the post-biblical development of Jewish thought, especially in rabbinic circles.[32] However, as his comparative program progresses in later works like his 1998 *Religion and Human Nature* and 2000 *Religion and Human Community*, Ward begins to expand the Jewish sources he investigates. While still predominantly concerned with scriptural texts, Ward also turns to rabbinic texts to flesh out his understanding of selected teachings about the Messiah and Israel.[33] The unevenness of

---

28 Keith Ward, *Images of Eternity: Concepts of God in Five Religious Traditions* (London: Darton, Longman and Todd, 1987), 86.

29 Ward, *Images of Eternity*, 84.

30 For an illustration of how categories of non-Jews were conceptualized and related to in social terms in rabbinic thought, see David Novak, *Jewish–Christian Dialogue: A Jewish Justification* (Oxford: Oxford University Press, 1989), 26–56.

31 Ward, *Images of Eternity*, 99–116.

32 Keith Ward, *Religion and Revelation: A Theology of Revelation in the World's Religions* (Oxford: Clarendon Press, 1996), 193–204.

33 Keith Ward, *Religion and Human Nature* (Oxford: Clarendon Press, 1998), 255–60; *idem, Religion and Community* (Oxford: Clarendon Press, 1998), 9–30.

Ward's approach to Jewish sources in his works reveals a developing appreciation of the positive contributions of the rabbinic tradition towards a deeper understanding of Judaism by this Christian comparative theologian.

Reading the works of Keith Ward with an understanding of how rabbinic Judaism has been marginalized in Christian discourses, one applauds the efforts to take Jewish texts seriously while also noticing the deficiencies in attending to the rabbinic texts that form the basis of Jewish life and thought. But one also wonders what exactly Ward achieved in his comparative look at Jewish texts. Ward sought out common threads in the texts he investigated, asking what world religions have thought about subjects like revelation and human nature. In his inquiries into common themes, the turn to Judaism led him to engage primarily with texts like scripture and Maimonides that are most familiar to him as a Christian while delaying the investigation into those Jewish texts, like rabbinic writings, that would more readily indicate Jewish differences from a Christian worldview.

Approaching the Comparative Moment

Other works exist that do begin to approach a comparative moment with regard to the Jewish tradition. By a 'comparative moment' I mean a consideration of the Jewish tradition that both consciously seeks to shed supersessionist stances towards Judaism and lays the foundation for the re-reading of one's home tradition as a result of engaging with Jewish sources. The two authors considered in this section, Anthony Saldarini and Peter Phan, are, strictly speaking, not comparative theologians but a biblical scholar and a theologian of religion, respectively. Nonetheless, their approach to Judaism as Christian thinkers is instructive.

The first example is a set of three essays by the late Anthony Saldarini for volumes in the Comparative Religious Ideas Project edited by Robert Neville. In these essays, Saldarini considered the broadly defined themes of each of these volumes on the human condition, ultimate reality, and religious truth.[34] In these essays, at times assisted by Joseph Kanofsky, Saldarini investigated these broadly defined categories within traditional Jewish thought, beginning with biblical views then progressing through rabbinic and medieval perspectives before finally considering modern Jewish thought on the topics. The significance of these essays is that Saldarini, as a Roman Catholic scholar trained in the thought of

---

34 Anthony J. Saldarini with Joseph Kanofsky, 'Religious Dimensions of the Human Condition in Judaism: Wrestling with God in an Imperfect World', in Robert Cummings Neville (ed.), *The Human Condition* (Albany: State University of New York Press, 2001), 101–32; *idem*, 'To Practice Together Truth and Humility, Justice and Law, Love of Merciful Kindness and Merciful Behavior', in Robert Cummings Neville (ed.), *Religious Truth* (Albany: State University of New York Press, 2001), 83–107; Anthony J. Saldarini, 'Ultimate Realities: Judaism: God as a Many-sided Ultimate Reality in Traditional Judaism', in Robert Cummings Neville (ed.), *Ultimate Realities* (Albany: State University of New York Press, 2001), 37–59.

Second Temple and early rabbinic Judaism, succeeded in effectively communicating the breadth and depth of the Jewish tradition on these themes. He rendered topics on the nature of ultimate reality, religious truth, and human nature into Jewish idioms, not translating these terms into their more generic philosophical and theological cognates. Saldarini distinguished himself as a sympathetic Christian reader of traditional Judaism, embodying as a Roman Catholic scholar the shifts of his own church since the Second Vatican Council regarding authentic engagement with the Jewish tradition.

But because he did not employ a comparative theological method, Saldarini's sympathetic reading of the traditional Jewish texts does not lead to a re-reading of his home tradition of Roman Catholicism. Rather, the contributions of the various essays in these three volumes are drawn together by Robert Neville and Wesley Wildman in essays that seek to compare and contrast the broad themes of religious truth, human nature, and ultimate reality from a range of textually based religious traditions. The result is a set of meta-analyses of these textually located concepts that convey little sense of how the practitioners or thinkers of any one tradition might be informed by the careful study of any of these other traditions. How, for example, was Saldarini himself shaped as a Christian by engaging in his study of these themes in Jewish texts? A truly comparative moment does not arise in the volumes comprising the Comparative Religious Ideas Project, but the methodology of the individual chapters does provide a template for reading outside one's home tradition.

Peter Phan's work offers an example of a contemporary Roman Catholic theologian of religion who has reflected on the significance of Judaism for his own home tradition of Asian (Catholic) Christianity. In *Being Religious Interreligiously*, Phan tries to take into account the insights from post-Holocaust Jewish theology in the construction of an Asian liberation theology.[35] This move represents a second step after Phan's initial accounting of contemporary Catholic teachings about Judaism and his critique of supersessionist thought in some Asian theologians.[36] In seeking to embrace a non-supersessionist Christian theology of Judaism, Phan discovers in Holocaust theology another articulation of the tension between belief in the divine and the reality of human suffering that he also discovers in Asian theology. The significance of Phan's project rests in the fact that he sees Judaism as a resource for his own theology and he explicitly frames his engagement with Jewish sources as an effort to overcome the hegemony of traditional Christian supersessionist discourses.

Phan's work is a hopeful sign for the continued emergence of non-supersessionist Christian theologies. His insights could easily be moved towards a truly comparative moment. Phan helpfully provides a parallel analysis of Holocaust theology and Asian liberation with an emphasis on putting certain concepts from the former into the language of the latter. Hence the question of the suffering of

---

35 Phan, *Being Religious Interreligiously*, 171–85.
36 Phan, *Being Religious Interreligiously*, 137–71.

the Jewish people moves into a discussion of the concept of *han* from Korean *minjung* theology. Observing that Phan interprets Holocaust theology into Christian liberation theology terms, one could then take the next step by asking how his home tradition itself is informed and transformed by engaging with Holocaust theology. Phan provides an important model for dealing seriously with Jewish theological resources that can be transposed to a comparative theology methodological framework.

Another Attempt at Reversing Hegemony: Reading Mishnah *Avot* on Torah

The preceding survey of writings from key figures in the developing field of comparative theology reveals the tenuous status of Judaism within it. In the development of methodological frameworks of comparative theology by pre-dominantly Christian theologians, Judaism has not been one of the privileged traditions that these theologians have thought with. Among those theologians who have engaged Jewish texts thematically, the texts that form the basis for traditional Judaism and its successors have not been engaged with to the same degree as more familiar texts from the Hebrew Scriptures and the philosophical writings of Maimonides. This stands in contrast to the practice of comparative theologians dealing with other traditions who study commentarial traditions in depth.[37] Even when rabbinic texts or other writings less familiar to Christian audiences are considered, rarely does one discover a truly comparative moment when the Christian home tradition is re-read after sustained encounters with Jewish texts. This state of affairs is not unique to comparative theology texts as produced by Christians but is representative across contemporary Christian theology. Even among Christian authors explicitly engaged in re-thinking Christian discourses in light of the Holocaust, rarely is the Jewish tradition itself engaged with as a resource for the doing of theology. Christians seeking to over-turn the hegemonic influence of supersessionist discourses that run so deeply in the broad traditions of Christianity ought to also inquire how the study of the foundational texts of rabbinic Judaism is useful.

Here I am moving past Clooney's suggestion that the comparative theology enterprise include the patient deferral of truth claims.[38] This is because of the particular moral claim that the history of Christian anti-Judaism presents to me as both a historian and a comparative theologian. Comparative theology is an especially useful means by which Christian theology can move beyond the hegemonic discourses of supersessionism by turning towards Jewish sources. By attending to those sources of traditional Judaism that historically had been marginalized and denigrated within the Christian tradition, there can be a cre-

---

37 See for example Clooney, *Theology after Vedanta*; and Daniel P. Sheridan, *Loving God: Krishna and Christ: A Christian Commentary on the Narada Sutras* (Leuven: Peeters, 2007)
38 Clooney, *Theology after Vedanta*, 188.

ation of a non-supersessionist theology that is informed not only by internal Christian stances but by Jewish ones as well. By engaging with traditional Jewish texts in the realm of *halakhah* or *midrash*, the Christian is confronted by the LLdifferentness of Judaism and is thus forced to rethink assumptions about both Judaism and one's home tradition.

This essay will conclude with an effort to briefly model how a comparative reading of a rabbinic text can lead towards a non-supersessionist Christian theology. The text I have chosen to investigate is Mishnah *Avot* (or 'Fathers'), also known as *Pirke Avot* ('Chapters of the Fathers'). This text is one of the 63 tractates of the Mishnah, a codification of oral teachings mostly from the first and second centuries of the Common Era and redacted around 200 CE. The Mishnah in turn served as the foundation for much of the subsequent rabbinic tradition; it is the Mishnah that the Talmud offers commentary upon. Although *Avot* might have only been added to the Mishnah around 300 CE, this tractate is an important early witness to rabbinic thought and values as a collection of sayings, often couched in ethical terms, by the earliest generations of the rabbis and proto-rabbinic sages.[39]

A central theme in *Avot* is the centrality of the Torah for Jewish identity and the creation of rabbinic authority. This theme is sounded in the first saying of *Avot*:

> At Sinai Moses received the Torah and handed it over to Joshua who handed it over to the elders who handed it over to the prophets who in turn handed it over to the men of the Great Assembly. The latter said three things: Be deliberate in judgement, raise up many disciples, and make a fence around the Torah. (*Avot* 1.1)[40]

On the surface, the first half of this passage could be read as simply an account of the giving of the written Torah at Sinai. But one must pay attention to the detailing of a chain of transmission from Moses to Joshua to the elders during the time of Joshua to the prophets to the men of the Great Assembly. The phrase 'men of the Great Assembly' is especially important for understanding this saying. This phrase refers to the leaders during the post-exilic period of life in the land of Israel. In rabbinic self-understanding, these men of the Great Assembly preserved the traditions of Israel and so were the precursors of the rabbis themselves as well as the efforts at the preservation of Jewish practice and identity.

The emphasis on the transmission of the Torah in this opening passage of *Avot* points to the importance of an oral transmission of the teachings of the Torah.

---

39 On the development of the Mishnah, see H. L. Strack and Günter Stemberger, *Introduction to the Talmud and Midrash*, ed. and trans. Markus Bockmuehl (Minneapolis, MN: Fortress Press, 1992), 108–48.

40 *Pirke Avot: A Modern Commentary on Jewish Ethics*, ed. and trans. Leonard Kravitz and Kerry M. Olitzky (New York: UAHC Press, 1993).

The oral transmission of the Torah expressed how the instructions of the written Torah were to be fulfilled in the daily rhythms of life. According to the rabbis, both the written and oral Torah were given at Sinai to Moses and they themselves were the heirs and instructors of both. Wherever the written Torah was studied and taught among the people of Israel, beginning with Moses down to the rabbis, so was the oral Torah studied and taught. This view is summed up by the medieval Spanish teacher Rabbenu Yonah (or Jonah ben Abraham of Gerona, d. 1263) who commented on *Avot* 1.1 that:

> It is written, 'And I will give you the tablets of stone, and the law and the commandment' (Exodus 24:12): 'the law' refers to the Written Torah; 'the commandment' refers to the Oral Torah. Thus all the commandments were given to Moses at Sinai along with their interpretations: what was written down is called the Written Torah, the interpretation is called the Oral Torah.[41]

Rabbenu Yonah interpreted this passage from *Avot* to mean that the giving of the Torah and the ongoing process of rabbinic commentary on it in the form of the oral Torah are central to Jewish self-understanding. The rabbis based their claim to authority on the concept that they were the heirs and guardians of the Torah.[42]

The concept of the Torah as a living text is illuminated by the exhortation at the end of *Avot* 1.1 to 'make a fence around the Torah'. In other words, the insights into the meaning of the written Torah interpreted within the oral Torah must be preserved even as the needs of the Jewish community develop. Through the concept of making a fence around the Torah, the rabbis expanded the observances of Torah to ensure that it was not transgressed.[43] For example, Exodus 12:15 prohibits the eating of leaven from the first day of Passover. Since in the rabbinic period a day was understood to begin at evening, it was feared that some might flout the spirit of the command by eating leavened products right up to the moment of nightfall. As a result, the prohibition was moved to mid-afternoon, as the Mishnah attests. The Babylonian Talmud moved the prohibition on eating leaven up to 10 o'clock in the morning in order to further protect the original command in the Torah.[44]

In rabbinic understanding, this concept of a fence around Torah signified the importance of preserving the integrity of divine revelation, thus ensuring it would always exist for humans to access.[45] The fulfillment of Torah and the

---

41 *The Living Talmud: The Wisdom of the Fathers and Its Classical Commentaries*, trans. Judah Goldin (New York: New American Library of World Literature, 1957), 43.

42 On the development of the concept of Oral Torah, see David Kraemer, *The Mind of the Talmud* (Oxford: Oxford University Press, 1990), 115–18.

43 Kravitz and Olitzky, *Pirke Avot*, 2.

44 Kravitz and Olitzky, *Pirke Avot*, 13; Mishnah, *Pesachim* 10.1; Babylonian Talmud, *Pesachim* 1.4.

45 *Pirke Aboth*, ed. and trans. R. Travers Herford (New York: Bloch Publishing, 1925), 21.

observance of the fences built around it were not perceived as a burden. As *Avot de-Rabbi Nathan* A, an early third-century commentary on Mishnah *Avot*, teaches that, 'whosoever studies Torah is free'.[46] In this light, one can understand why this same early commentary taught that keeping seemingly insignificant commands was important. 'These minor commandments, tender as lilies, when Israel puts them into practice, lead them to the life of the world to come.'[47] The fence around Torah is best envisioned not as a stone wall but as stakes that can be moved and adjusted as each generation needs it. Keeping the Torah with intentionality to the utmost of one's ability, even in the smallest of ways, sets one upon the path of redemption. Observing the fences of the Torah is an expression of piety and love for the gift of the Torah given at Sinai.

This interpretation of the significance of the Torah given at Sinai and the attitude towards keeping it differs markedly from traditional Christian understandings of the Law. The very word 'Law' (derived from the Greek *nomos*) captures a different sense than Torah, which is best interpreted as 'instruction'. The Christian tradition has predominantly interpreted the giving of the Torah at Sinai as a disciplinary measure. For instance, Paul's words in the Letter to the Galatians have been interpreted in this way: 'Now before faith came, we were imprisoned and guarded under the law until faith would be revealed. Therefore the law was our disciplinarian until Christ came, so that we might be justified by faith' (Galatians 3:23–24, NRSV). Paul understood the Law to function positively as a protective custodian watching over Israel's spiritual development but still temporary in nature until the coming of Jesus Christ.[48] When considering the period from the giving of the Law at Sinai to the coming of Christ, Paul repeatedly associates it with punishment for a wayward Israel and a sign of Israel's disobedience (2 Corinthians 3:4–18; Galatians 4:21–31; Romans 5:12–14). Although Paul affirms that the Law was good in so far as it was given to regulate the life of Israel (Romans 7:10, 10:5), this is a secondary feature of God's covenant relationship with Israel that demands the response of faith.[49]

Christians historically took the Pauline perspective on the Law and emphasized the punitive and temporary nature of the Law while marginalizing the notion of the Law as life-giving or having a positive value after the coming of Christ that is also a feature of Pauline thought. Two second-century works feature this shift. In the *Epistle to Barnabas* great emphasis is given to Moses' shattering of the first tablets of the Law after the episode of the Golden Calf in

---

46 *Avot de-Rabbi Nathan* A, 2. This translation is from *The Fathers According to Rabbi Nathan*, trans. Judah Goldin (New Haven: Yale University Press, 1955), 20. There are two versions of this commentary, designated as A and B. All of the references in this essay are to A.

47 *Avot de-Rabbi Nathan*, 2, 18.

48 James D. G. Dunn, *The Theology of Paul the Apostle* (Grand Rapids, MI: William B. Eerdmans, 1998), 138–42.

49 Dunn, *The Theology of Paul*, 149–55.

Exodus 32. The original tablets were understood by the author to contain the
Ten Commandments, life-giving instructions for Israel. But the second set of
tablets Moses received to replace the first contained the restrictive laws of purity
and ritual that were meant to keep Israel in check as a punishment for its tendency towards idolatry.[50] The Christian apologist Justin Martyr similarly argues
with his fictive Jewish interlocutor in *Dialogue with Trypho* that the ceremonial
laws were given to Israel in order to restrain idolatrous impulses.[51] In both texts
the coming of Jesus Christ signals a release from the punitive bonds of the Law.

These attitudes towards the futility of the Law and the uselessness of Jewish
observance of it have been features of supersessionist theology for millennia.
However, encountering traditional Jewish understandings of the meaning of the
giving of Torah challenges these understandings. Specifically, the concept of
making a fence around Torah derives from rabbinic commentaries; similarly,
adding to the requirements of Torah observance, as something that for Jews
merits the world to come, is profoundly challenging to Christian theology,
especially in an Augustinian–Lutheran trajectory, that opposes the binding
nature of the Law to the freeing, gracious gospel of Jesus Christ.

In observing this tension one is led to the question of the nature of Jesus' own
Torah observance. Impelled by this passage from *Avot*, one is reminded of evi-
dence from the Gospels that undermines a supersessionist interpretation of the
Law and the binary categories of Law and Gospel. Jesus' attitude towards the
Torah is best reflected in the Sermon on the Mount recorded in Matthew
5:17–19:

> Do not think that I have come to abolish the law or the prophets; I have come
> not to abolish but to fulfill. For truly I tell you, until heaven and earth pass
> away, not one letter, not one stroke of a letter, will pass from the law until all
> is accomplished. Therefore, whoever breaks one of the least of these com-
> mandments, and teaches others to do the same, will be called least in the
> kingdom of heaven; but whoever does them and teaches them will be called
> great in the kingdom of heaven.

Here Jesus' teaching echoes the emphasis on the value of Torah in *Avot*; both
the teachings of Jesus and those of the rabbis in *Avot* express the intention of
upholding Torah even in the process of forming new communities around their
leadership.

Traditional interpretations of the Sermon on the Mount have emphasized the
revolutionary nature of Jesus' teachings and the supposed sharp departure he

---

50 Pierre Prigent (ed.), *Epistle of Barnabas*, Sources Chretiennes 172 (Paris: Cerf, 1971), 4.6–8.
51 Justin Martyr, in *Dialogus cum Tryphone*, ed. Miroslav Marcovich, Patristische Texte und
Studien 47 (Berlin and New York: Walter de Gruyter), 22.

took from contemporary Jewish teachings.[52] But more recent scholarship has interpreted this discourse as indicative of Jesus' own deep connections and regard for the Torah. Jesus' teachings here on topics such as divorce or the Sabbath are not a rejection of Torah but part of a debate among those committed to the Torah in proto-rabbinic circles.[53] Moving away from a depiction of Jesus as one who overturns the Law to his depiction as a keeper of the Torah would require Christians to come to terms with an understanding of the Torah as the ground and inspiration of Jesus' own life and ministry.[54]

Thinking in a comparative fashion about the meaning of the Torah given at Sinai in light of the person of Jesus Christ also raises significant issues concerning Christological doctrines. If Jesus submitted himself to the teaching of Torah, how does this square with a Chalcedonian understanding of Jesus Christ as one person with a fully human nature and a fully divine nature? If Jesus Christ is the Word of God incarnate, how did he submit himself to God's word in Torah? Was the Second Person of the Trinity, the Son and the Logos, the active agent of revelation at Sinai? If so, then was Jesus Christ obedient to the Torah that he himself revealed? In these questions, we see how deeply re-reading one's home tradition in the light of another, even a 'near' Other like Judaism, does lead to serious reflection upon deeply held and foundational beliefs.

Conclusion

This essay has considered questions of hegemony in relation to Judaism both in terms of supersessionist discourses that have marginalized lived expressions of Judaism in broad traditions of Christian theology and in terms of the tenuous status of Judaism in the developing field of (Christian) comparative theology. Jewish traditions and texts have not been engaged with in the same degree as those from other traditions, particularly ones that find their roots in Asian contexts. And when Judaism is engaged with, often those texts from the rabbinic tradition that form the basis for traditional expressions of Judaism are passed over in favor of seemingly more familiar or accessible texts. I have attempted to

---

52 A typical example is from one of the most prominent New Testament scholars of the twentieth century, Joachim Jeremias, who claimed that Jesus specifically taught in opposition to rabbinic instructions on the Law. See Joachim Jeremias, *New Testament Theology*, trans. John Bowden (New York, Scribner, 1971), 208.

53 See especially Philip Sigal, *The Halakhah of Jesus of Nazareth According to the Gospel of Matthew* (Atlanta: Society of Biblical Literature, 2007); and Anthony J. Saldarini, *Matthew's Christian–Jewish Community* (Chicago: University of Chicago Press, 1994). Sigal in particular makes a strong argument for placing Jesus of Nazareth as a sage and prophet in proto-rabbinic circles by contextualizing the Gospel of Matthew within the earliest strata of the Mishnah and Tosefta while emphasizing the distinction between the proto-rabbinic movement as a whole and the party of the Pharisees represented in the New Testament.

54 A similar re-evaluation of Paul's understanding of the Law has developed in recent decades, especially as found in his letters to the Romans and the Galatians.

illustrate what a comparative reading of a traditional rabbinic text might look like. Such practices of reading Jewish texts and practices closely as a Christian require both the conscious removal of supersessionist lenses and the imaginative willingness to attend to the 'near' Other found in Judaism for a richer understanding of Christianity. The practice of attending to such 'near' Others is one that can be replicated in other comparative studies and indeed looks to the use of comparative theology beyond the boundaries of its traditionally Christian practitioners.

6

Gendering Comparative Theology

MICHELLE VOSS ROBERTS

When the new mendicant orders, the Franciscans and Dominicans, exploded onto the scene in thirteenth-century Europe, women like Clare of Assisi expected that they too would be permitted to undertake a religious life outside the cloister. The women's branches of these orders, however, were required to accept enclosure and prevented from embracing absolute poverty. In another attempt to follow the apostolic ideals of this movement, laywomen known as beguines blazed their own path of celibacy, poverty, and service until this, too, was officially forbidden in the fourteenth century. Mechthild of Magdeburg describes the difficult inception of her beguine life: 'I had had the desire to be despised through no fault of my own. Then for the sake of God's love, I moved to a town where no one was my friend except for one person' (FL IV.2).[1]

By the fourteenth century, the Trika school of Kashmir Saivism had integrated meditation into the householder life and thus distinguished itself from earlier Vedic traditions oriented toward renunciation and asceticism.[2] The poet-saint Lalleswari thus taught that 'even as householders' and 'while conducting worldly activities' one can remain awake to one's true spiritual identity (Odin #130, #71).[3] Even so, her devotion put her at odds with her family. Her mother-in-law starved her and impugned her fidelity. After an incident in which her jealous husband angrily struck and shattered the water jar she had carried back from her meditations at the river, Lalleswari renounced her home.

---

1 All references to Mechthild's text are from Mechthild of Magdeburg, *The Flowing Light of the Godhead* (FL), trans. Frank J. Tobin (Mahwah, NJ: Paulist Press, 1998). Tobin's translation follows Hans Neumann's critical edition of the Middle High German, *Das fliessende Licht der Gottheit*, 2 vols (Munich: Artemis, 1990, 1993).
2 Gavin Flood, 'The Saiva Traditions', in Gavin Flood (ed.), *The Blackwell Companion to Hinduism* (Oxford: Blackwell Publishing, 2003), 213.
3 In this essay I follow the translations of Jaishree Kak Odin, *To the Other Shore: Lalla's Life and Poetry* (New Delhi: Vitasta, 1999) but refer to other versions when differences in translation become significant.

As unconnected as these two scenarios may be historically, they both illustrate how women become marginal subjects when the highest religious paths in their traditions are designed for men. Elsewhere, I have considered what the specificity of the two women's lives and thought can offer to a constructive feminist and Christian theology.[4] Here, I focus on the broader patterns that emerge when we study them comparatively in light of Patricia Hill Collins's category of the 'outsider within'. As African-Americans in the United States possess 'formal citizenship rights' without always enjoying 'substantive citizenship rights',[5] women may officially belong to Christian, Muslim, Hindu, Buddhist, or Jain communities but not be admitted into the practices and canons of these traditions to the same extent as men.[6] The ambiguous status of women as 'outsiders within' leaves them bereft of the *adhikara* (competence or privilege) to participate in the practices that properly define theology.

Comparative theologians, including many in this volume, have begun to engage in postcolonial and post-Holocaust scrutiny of the hegemony of Christian norms. I consider the related hegemony of gender in comparative theology and trace some emblematic treatments of 'the feminine' in the discipline. I then return to the 'outsider within' and the lessons Mechthild and Lalleswari hold for comparative theologians. I propose that attention to the 'outsider within' will enable a feminist comparative theology to open up new subjects, genres, and goals for the discipline.

The Problem of Essentialism

In light of postcolonial scholarship on western and Christian hegemony, comparative theologians have largely abandoned the impulse to attribute essential natures to particular religions for close readings of indigenous voices. Feminist theory and theology similarly eschew essentialization on another front, as they topple patriarchal stereotypes through women's perspectives. Richard King reflects on the overlap between feminist and postcolonial concerns: 'It would seem that the patriarchal discourses that have excluded the "feminine" and the female from the realms of rationality, subjectivity and authority have also been used to exclude the non-western world from the same spheres of influence.'[7] A shared concern with essentialism challenges both feminist and comparative approaches to theology.

---

4 Michelle Voss Roberts, *Dualities: A Theology of Difference* (Louisville: Westminster John Knox, 2010).

5 Patricia Hill Collins, *Black Feminist Thought: Knowledge, Consciousness, and the Politics of Empowerment* (Boston: Unwin Hyman, 1990), 5.

6 Padmanabh S. Jaini has explored the striking example of the exclusion of Digambara ('sky-clad') Jain women from the full ascetic practice of nudity, and thus from liberation from rebirth, in *Gender and Salvation: Jaina Debates on the Spiritual Liberation of Women* (Delhi: Munshiram Monoharlal, 1991).

7 Richard King, *Orientalism and Religion: Postcolonial Theory, India and 'the Mystic East'* (New York: Routledge, 1999), 114.

Feminist theologians have not always avoided the pitfalls of essentialism. The history of feminist movements in the west has been one of increasing orientation to the question of difference in response to the presumption of white, educated, heterosexual, able-bodied, middle-class voices to speak on behalf of a monolithic 'woman'. This concern is heightened in the postcolonial context, as women in the west appropriate eastern religious resources and decry oppression across the globe. Rachel McDermott discerns an 'Orientalist posture in a new guise' in New Age uses of Hindu goddesses;[8] and Chandra Mohanty notes a tendency of western feminists to essentialize their 'oppressed third world sisters'.[9] My own position within feminism, as a woman who inhabits the privileged categories just listed, demands particular vigilance on such issues of difference. I attend in particular to *religious* diversity, a kind of difference that has featured less prominently than others to date in feminist theology.[10]

The postcolonial discourse that informs the most recent contributions of comparative theology has had its own blind spots. Edward Said's documentation in *Orientalism* of the rhetorical 'feminization' used to demoralize the colonized Other might have alerted scholars to the collusion of colonial and patriarchal logic in Orientalist thought. Jane Miller observes that rather than overcome the latent sexism in their work, however, postcolonial critiques of Orientalism have tended to elide actual women.

If women are ambiguously present within the discourses of Orientalism, they are just as ambiguously present within the discourses developed to expose and to oppose Orientalism. Their presence in both is as forms of coinage, exchange value offered or stolen or forbidden, tokens of men's power and wealth or lack of them. The sexual use and productiveness of women are allowed to seem equivalent to their actual presence and their consciousness.[11]

Miller's comments highlight how critiques like Said's reify woman as a symbol and pay very little attention to women's lives and voices. In short, the colonized may no longer be 'women', but women are still colonized.

---

8 Rachel Fell McDermott, 'New Age Hinduism, New Age Orientalism, and the Second-Generation South Asian', in *Journal of the American Academy of Religion* (68:4, 2004), 726.

9 Chandra Talpade Mohanty, 'Under Western Eyes: Feminist Scholarship and Colonial Discourses', in Chandra Talpade Mohanty, Ann Russo and Lourdes Torres (eds), *Third World Women and the Politics of Feminism* (Bloomington: Indiana University Press, 1991). Mary Daly's analysis of *sati* has become emblematic of the problems of representation in post-colonial discourse. See Renuka Sharma and Purushottama Bilimoria, 'Where Silence Burns: Sati (Suttee) in India, Mary Daly's Gynocritique, and Resistant Spirituality', in Sarah Lucia Hoagland and Marilyn Frye (eds), *Feminist Interpretations of Mary Daly* (University Park, Pennsylvania: The Pennsylvania State University Press, 2000).

10 Rita Gross articulates the need for the inclusion of religious diversity in Rita M. Gross, 'Feminist Theology as Theology of Religions', in *Feminist Theology* (26, 2001), 86.

11 Jane Miller, *Seductions: Studies in Reading and Culture* (Cambridge, MA: Harvard University Press, 1991), 122. See Reina Lewis, *Gendering Orientalism: Race, Feminity and Representation* (New York: Routledge, 1996) for an example of how this scholarly oversight is beginning to be rectified.

Comparative Theology and 'The Feminine'

Brief examples from the works of Bede Griffiths, Aloysius Pieris, and Francis X. Clooney may serve to delineate the trajectory of 'the feminine' in comparative theology. As with the postcolonial studies cited above, comparative theologies of Christianity and the religions of Southwest Asia illustrate a gradual shift from the feminine as a symbol to gender as a locus of particular material differences. Here, too, women's voices are slow to emerge.

In the work of Bede Griffiths, British Benedictine friar and guru at the Shantivanam Ashram in Tamil Nadu, the essentialization of woman and of the east go hand in hand. Worried about the effects of modernity upon western Christianity, he seeks the 'the other half of [his] soul' in the east, where 'people live not from the conscious mind but from the unconscious, from the body not from the mind'.[12] The east is the intuitive, feminine partner in a marriage that will restore wholeness to a Christianity mired in the modern, rational, and scientific west. He cites 'the suppression of women in the Church' as 'but one of the many signs of this masculine domination', but he does not then flesh out the connection between the feminine as symbol and the material conditions of women in India.[13] One of the problems with the positive symbolic role of the feminine, then, is its inability to account for patriarchy in the more 'feminine' religions of the east.

Aloysius Pieris, a Sri Lankan Jesuit theologian, similarly seeks a subconscious, bodily, and mystical dimension that is missing in a more rational, intellectual religious orientation.[14] He proposes a union between two gendered tendencies, a humble female impulse toward *agape* and a male movement toward *gnosis*. Pieris cites feminism as an essential and permanent critique of religious ideology that calls us to rediscover 'our agapeic potentialities, by a massive reactivation of this atrophied part of our being, that is to say, by allowing the woman in all of us to be born again'.[15] In contrast to Griffiths, the east is not the panacea for what ails the masculine west, for the impulses toward *gnosis* and *agape* can be found in both Buddhism and Christianity. For him, the two religions share a common message but with differing emphases: in a reversal of Griffiths' gender symbolism, 'Buddhist gnosis' serves as the masculine counterpart to the more feminine 'Christian agape'.[16] These principles work together toward self-transcendence. Though sensitive to the problems of essentializing east and west, Pieris continues to essentialize the masculine and the feminine.

---

12 Bede Griffiths, *The Marriage of East and West* (Springfield, IL: Templegate, 1982), 8.
13 Griffiths, *The Marriage of East and West*, 199.
14 Aloysius Pieris, *Fire and Water: Basic Issues in Asian Buddhism and Christianity* (Maryknoll, NY: Orbis Books, 1996), 12–19.
15 Pieris, *Fire and Water*, 55.
16 Pieris, *Fire and Water*, 59.

Feminists are likely to concur with Pieris's goal of full humanity as well as his immense sympathy for liberation theologies (to which I return below). Pieris is aware of feminist theological critiques of self-denial and transcendence,[17] but he worries that feminisms based on 'winning lost rights or repairing past damages [or an] individualist liberalism based on personal dignity and worth' neglect the spiritual liberation that comes from 'the larger perspective of self-transcendence'.[18] Because he maintains that abuse of the ideal, not the ideal of transcendence itself, is to blame,[19] women's material concerns and their desire for justice tend to drop from view in his comparative work.

Griffiths and Pieris share the romantic notion, common to much of the rhetoric in their Catholic and Asian contexts, that 'the feminine' is an essence complementary to 'the masculine' and that these principles must be united in religion. Some feminist ethicists have claimed that undervalued feminine qualities such as connectivity and care are of equal or superior importance to masculine values, and comparative theologians approximate this model when they designate a complementary gender binary that retrieves what has been neglected.[20] Yet feminist theory has also been quite wary of gender essentialism, which falls short beside the embodied experience of women who differ from one another in a multitude of ways. Essentialist notions of gender not only exclude women who fail to live up to the feminine ideal; they also perpetuate restrictive social models with the notion that biology is destiny.[21]

Francis Clooney eschews generalizations about traditions in favor of careful side-by-side readings of particular texts, a method that opens the door to considering the diversity within religious traditions, including their gender diversity. His book, *Divine Mother, Blessed Mother: Hindu Goddesses and the Virgin Mary*, engages contemporary feminist theory to question traditional Christian models of male divinity. He thus argues that 'exclusion of female experiences and images' in theology leaves 'a diminished set of experiences to draw upon in addressing God'.[22] For some, this statement might send up flags warning of

---

17 The classic critique can be found in Valerie Saiving, 'The Human Situation: A Feminine View', in Carol P. Christ and Judith Plaskow (eds), *Womanspirit Rising: A Feminist Reader in Religion* (New York: Harper & Row, 1979).

18 Pieris, *Fire and Water*, 57. Pieris's concerns with the western origin of the rights-based model he repudiates indicate a greater affinity for second-wave, or 'gender' feminism, which analyzes how differences between men and women structure relations, than the earlier, first-wave concerns with equal access to jobs, wages, and the vote. Since the 1980s, a third wave has paid increasing attention to women's differences.

19 Pieris, *Fire and Water*, 58.

20 See, for example, Nell Noddings, *Caring: A Feminine Approach to Ethics and Moral Education* (Berkeley: University of California Press, 1984); and Carol Gilligan, *In a Different Voice: Psychological Theory and Women's Development* (Cambridge, MA: Harvard University Press, 1982).

21 For one such critique, see Elizabeth Spelman, *Inessential Women: Problems of Exclusion in Feminist Thought* (Boston: Beacon Press, 1998).

22 Francis Xavier Clooney, *Divine Mother, Blessed Mother: Hindu Goddesses and the Virgin Mary* (Oxford: Oxford University Press, 2005), 4.

re-warmed essentialist notions of women's experience, especially when focused on the figure of the Virgin Mary;[23] but Clooney endeavors to attend to the particular, embodied aspects of devotion. His approach thus accords with contemporary feminists who problematize 'woman' as a homogeneous category by insisting that race, ethnicity, nation, class, caste, sexuality, religion, ability, age, and other markers condition women's experience. Bodies matter, and the encounter with Hindu goddesses encourages Christians to contemplate a feminine and material divine. As Clooney acknowledges, the project is limited because the texts he reads on female divinity are all male-authored; yet this work is significant because gender theory has begun to make an impact in the field.[24]

Feminist and comparative theologies find common ground with a shared interest in the particular. Clooney calls comparative theology to ever more particular sites of comparison, a method with the potential to combat gender essentialisms as it has already done for cultural and religious essentialisms. As the 2006 Statement for the Comparative Theology Group for the AAR suggests, women's texts, theologies, and practices deserve attention as part of a focus on the particular.

> [A] Comparative Theology Group will also be a forum in which attention to cultural and religious differences makes us notice and problematize standard historical priorities, and to bring to the fore concerns regarding gender, race/ethnicity, and socio-economic status. We will examine questions such as the kinds of theology produced by women and the institutional structures that have facilitated and/or hindered such production in a variety of world religious traditions. (Statement III.2.a)[25]

Gender analysis has been slow to emerge in comparative theology, but the content and methods of feminist theology will both help the discipline to be true to its postcolonial project and uncover new sites of comparison.

---

23 Elizabeth Johnson worries that theologians who make Mary the feminine face of God 1) set up unrealistic ideals (the paradox of virgin and mother); 2) stereotype women in terms of mothering, nurturing, and bodies in a way that limits their options; 3) fail to listen to women's diverse self-definitions; and 4) neglect the symbolic nature of theological language by attributing a 'feminine dimension' to God. Elizabeth A. Johnson, *She Who Is: The Mystery of God in Feminist Theological Discourse* (New York: Crossroad, 1996), 52–4. For more on this, see Elizabeth A. Johnson, *Truly Our Sister: A Theology of Mary in the Communion of Saints* (New York: Continuum, 2003).

24 He writes, 'All this textual work must of course also be accompanied by accounts of experience, particularly women's narratives of the divine.' Clooney, *Divine Mother, Blessed Mother*, 233.

25 Comparative Theology Group. 'Statement for the Comparative Theology Group for the AAR'. http://www.aarweb.org/upfiles/PUCS2007/AARPU145/CTGroupAAR.doc. (Last accessed 4 March 2010.)

Insiders, and the 'Outsider Within'

Despite professed interest in particularity, the self-definition of comparative theology may be partly to blame for the absence of women's voices and texts thus far. According to the 2006 Statement, comparative theologians study the relationships between truth claims of 'insiders' of different religious traditions and the meaning of these relationships for 'how comparative theologians present and argue for the truth of their own traditions' (I.2). Comparative theologians reflect upon the insider viewpoints of multiple traditions in order to speak again as insiders in their own traditions. Comparative theologians, then, are insiders speaking for and about other insiders. The strength of the Statement is that it deals honestly with the fact that theologians have particular theological starting points. It renounces colonialist appropriations of 'other' religious traditions that may have characterized earlier approaches to the discipline. But I suggest that, because of the ways in which women and other marginalized subjects often remain outsiders despite being 'within' a tradition, the Statement's emphasis on 'insiders' has unintended and undesirable consequences. We must reconsider what this definition – insiders speaking for and about insiders – means in light of the tendency to exclude voices on the margins of religious traditions.

Comparativists can extend their commitment to the particular by considering the 'outsider within'. The critical purchase of Patricia Hill Collins's 'outsider within' formulation is its concentration on 'real differences of power . . . on the margins within intersecting systems'.[26] Feminist and other liberation theologians lift up persons on the margins of discourse and the underside of power relations, whether biologically male or female. To speak from a marginalized subject position calls into question the structure of theology as an insider discourse and draws attention to the power operating within religious traditions.

'Woman', then, is a subject on the margins of religious traditions whose subject position is worth exploring in comparative perspective because of the ways she challenges our definitions of traditions and of theology. For example, when we deem only élite figures like Patanjali, Sankara, and Ramanuja as Indian subjects worthy of study, and then pair them with other such élites like Benedict of Nursia, Thomas Aquinas, and Bernard of Clairvaux, we give the impression that these authors are more broadly representative than is actually the case. The recognition of the diversity of traditions sometimes conflicts with the necessity of defending our choice of interlocutors. Peter Feldmeier, for instance, introduces Saint John of the Cross and Bhadantacariya Buddhaghosa as 'two classical representatives of the Christian and Buddhist traditions'. He continues,

---

26 Collins, *Black Feminist Thought*, 8.

> While these two representatives cannot speak for the whole of either the
> Christian or the Theravada Buddhist tradition, *they do represent themes, practices,
> and theological commitments that are broadly agreed upon in their spiritual traditions.*[27]

The ambivalence of this statement indicates that assertions of theologians' representative capacity are always unstable, yet scholars rarely attempt to claim that
women's thought and practice represent their traditions as a whole. Women's
difference from androcentric norms implies deviance and inauthenticity; the
same does not go for men's difference from women or from one another. The
solution to this bias is not to prove women's value by virtue of how 'traditional'
they are. Nor should we expect male theologians to be ambassadors for their
entire religion or milieu, or apologize for the ways in which they are not. If
comparativists are interested in difference, then internal diversity in religions
should not determine who is and is not worthy of comparison. Removing the
'traditional enough' bar opens the door to voices still deemed unimportant by
failing to mirror aspects that have defined 'the tradition' as such.[28]

I have suggested that comparative theologians should attend to gender as one
of many facets of the 'outsiders within' the traditions we compare. Doing so can
also help us interrogate what kinds of 'insiders' we are as comparative theologians. In other words, comparative theologians can *study* women as 'outsiders
within' religious traditions; but we may also *be* 'outsiders within'. Collins blurs
the boundaries between positions by maintaining that 'outsiders within' are
'people who no longer belong to any one group'.[29] The 2006 Statement recognizes that comparative theologians are sometimes 'insiders' to multiple groups:

> We are also aware that the emerging study of 'multiple religious belonging'
> and 'religious hybridity' is also reflected in the choices of members of the
> Academy, who by personal choice and academic commitments maintain
> loyalties not easily contained within just a single religious tradition or under
> the appellation of 'the study of religion'. (Statement I.4)

---

27 My emphasis. Peter Feldmeier, *Christianity Looks East: Comparing the Spiritualities of John of the
Cross and Buddhaghosa* (New York: Paulist Press, 2006), 6; cf. 117–18.

28 Jeannine Hill Fletcher elucidates how even labels such as 'Christian' exacerbate the problem of
representation: 'This process of categorization is defended as a practical necessity: in order to discuss
different religions, particularities are subsumed under a limited set of distinctions. But this categorization classifies persons on the basis of a singular identity feature. In order to define Christian
identity vis-à-vis other religious identities, one must isolate that feature which will constitute membership in the category "Christian" . . . That is, by defining "Christians" as an internally coherent
group, this categorization misses the distinctiveness of actual Christians in lived situations.' Jeannine
Hill Fletcher, *Monopoly on Salvation? A Feminist Approach to Religious Pluralism* (New York: Continuum, 2005), 78.

29 Collins, *Black Feminist Thought*, 5. For example, she describes how African American women
'belong' uneasily in the categories of 'American', 'Black', and 'female'. Their knowledge differs
from that of dominant culture and from groups whose 'oppositional knowledges' develop in
response to only one type of oppression (8).

Feminism is just such a loyalty that is 'not easily contained': as a spiritual tradition and community, it marks a unique sort of insider position. The feminist comparative theologian belongs less clearly to a single theological tradition than theologians whose primary commitment is, say, to Christianity or Islam, although she or he may also belong to one or more of those traditions as well. A feminist stance is interreligious and comparative. As in my own dual participation in Presbyterian Christianity and the practice of Yoga, feminists extend a hermeneutic of suspicion toward all orthodoxies even as they search out liberating moments in many traditions.

The introduction of feminist theology to the comparative endeavor can help comparativists be true to their word. It suggests that we will allow the texts and practices of women and other marginal subjects to become more prominent in our work, that we will excuse ourselves from the preoccupation of representing entire traditions, and that we will become more aware of how our own commitments cross religious boundaries. What will we learn when we turn to women as outsiders within theological traditions? I would like to suggest, by way of a comparative case study of Mechthild of Magdeburg and Lalleswari of Kashmir, that the next phase of comparative work will need to deal with challenges relating to theological genre, androcentric hagiography, and liberative vision.

Generic Complications

Women's wisdom often appears in devotional, poetic, and oral forms that do not conduce to the standards of the formal religious or philosophical training afforded to men. What Kwok Pui-lan writes of the voices of colonized women rings true for women in many of the world's religions:

> Even if they have 'spoken', their speech acts are expressed not only in words but also in forms (storytelling, songs, poems, dances, and quilting, etc.) that the academic and cultural establishments either could not understand or deemed insignificant. These knowledges have been ruled out as nondata: too fragmented, or insufficiently documented for serious inquiry.[30]

Mechthild writes poetry, visions, prophecies, instructions, and liturgy; and while she is aware of the theological scruples of her critics, she could hardly enter into a Latin scholastic disputation. Lalleswari does not write. Her verse-like aphorisms, called *vaakh*s, were preserved in oral memory for centuries before any written record of them existed. She demonstrates practical knowledge of the Sanskrit Yoga traditions but, much to the chagrin of the establishment, she transmits them in her vernacular Kashmiri to anyone and everyone. The teachings

---

30 Kwok Pui-lan, *Postcolonial Imagination and Feminist Theology* (Louisville, KY: Westminster John Knox Press, 2005), 30.

and practices of these women mark them as belonging within the borders of Christianity and Kashmir Saivism, but their mode of address marks them as outsiders to the authoritative structures of each tradition. They remain 'outsiders within', then as well as now, when religiously authoritative discourse is narrowly defined by language or genre.[31]

Doctrines of revelation in which women's contributions fail to qualify as scripture and theology would seem to prohibit us from reading the women in the world's religious traditions as theologians. The 2006 Statement states that although theology is not limited to textual and writing traditions, 'in the beginning at least, less attention will be paid to oral traditions and to the oral and popular dimensions of writing traditions – dimensions which, while highly important, are not normally seen as theological' (III.3). The phrase 'not normally seen as theological' would seem to invite a new definition of theology capacious enough to include women's wisdom in various genres. Women as well as men have always asked questions about the nature of ultimate reality and humanity's relationship to it, and they have answered these questions in various ways conditioned by their religious traditions. Texts and practices that address such questions should be recognized as theology.[32]

When the comparativist treats women's theological texts as theology, she or he must consider whether and how diverse genres (poetry, proverbs, narratives, scholastic treatises, etc.) may be compared with one another. Attention to theological metaphor is one way to bridge gaps between genres. There are certainly other possible approaches to cross-generic comparison; but comparison of metaphor has the potential to illuminate patterns of thought across diverse genres. It also corresponds with the heart of the theological endeavor.

Theological language is basically metaphorical. Theologians recognize that their words fall short of the ultimate mystery that surpasses human thought and language. Christian apophatic theology, Buddhist doctrines of emptiness, and some Hindu assertions of ultimate (*paramarthika*) nonduality serve this negative purpose. Although Lalleswari's *vaakh*s are replete with vivid images from everyday life, the images dissolve in meditation upon the void, the highest nondual source of everything that exists.

> Through constant practice objective reality is withdrawn
> The world of forms and colors suddenly merges with void
> When the void disappears nameless consciousness remains
> That is my teaching, O Pandit! (Odin #85)

---

31 Even though their texts have not been counted as theologically authoritative, they do enjoy the distinct advantage of being preserved in written record. The effort to uncover such records is an important theological task, but this task need not be restricted to the written word. The journal *Practical Matters*, for example, endeavors to 'read' non-literary sources such as quilting, mandalas, photography, ritual, and dance for theological content. The first issue of the journal is available online at http://www.practicalmattersjournal.org/issue/1.

32 Tracy Sayuki Tiemeier's work with the Indian poetess Antal is one of the few examples that treats women's poetry in a comparative theological context. See her essay in this volume.

Mechthild elaborates upon the nine choirs of heaven (III.1), but her speech falters in her ascent to God: '[The soul] soars further to a blissful place of which I neither can nor will speak. It is too difficult; I do not dare' (FL I.2). Both theologians resort to a scheme of cosmic hierarchy in which language drops away at its apex – for Lalleswari, the 'void' at the beginning and end of Kashmir Saiva scheme of creation,[33] and for Mechthild the mystery of the Trinity. In both, the meditating subject's transcendence of human thought and language relativizes theological speech; its metaphors remain (only) metaphors.

Most theologians, however, do not stop with apophatic deferral but proceed to kataphatic explication: they spin out metaphors, tell stories, and outline systems of thought and practice. The kataphatic images of Mechthild and Lalleswari provide a striking metaphor for comparison: each employs a metaphor of fluidity that subverts the hierarchizing impulse to leave material reality behind. Although Lalleswari has been criticized from a feminist angle for her emphasis on transcendence and the void,[34] she employs fluidity to bring reflection back to material reality.

> In the midst of being lost, I lost the sense of being lost
> After being lost I found myself in this worldly ocean
> Laughing and playing, I attained the all-pervading Self
> This philosophy became a part of me. (Odin #29)

For Lalleswari, the world is the embodiment of the consciousness of Siva. This in no way sullies or diminishes him – persons for whom false distinctions have melted away perceive him as both omnipresent (*sarvagath*) and stainless (*amol*) (Odin #128). Seeing the world in this light enables her to embrace the world and her embodied state. Mechthild praises the 'eternal spring of the Godhead, out of which I and all things flowed' (IV.21). The ebb and flow of mutual desire washes away the hierarchy between God and creation, as the 'playful flood of love . . . flows mysteriously from God into the soul/And through his power flows back again according to her ability' (VII.45). This fluid ontology is the basis for Mechthild's teachings on relations in the Church and society: we are to flow out to others as God flows out to us (VI.32).

The metaphor of fluidity bridges the differences between the two women's genres and serves as a basis for a comparison of their theological structures. Comparisons involving images from non-dominant subjects also destabilize dominant constructions of their traditions. Both Mechthild and Lalleswari

---

33 For an explication of this system, see Gavin D. Flood, *Body and Cosmology in Kashmir Saivism* (San Francisco: Mellen Research University Press, 1993). Excellent overviews of Lalleswari's religious tradition can be found in Flood, 'The Saiva Traditions', and Alexis Sanderson, 'Saivism and the Tantric Traditions', *The World's Religions: The Religions of Asia*, ed. Friedhelm Hardy (London: Routledge, 1988).

34 See chapter 4 of Odin, *To the Other Shore*.

employ traditional theological resources; but by exploring fluidity as a metaphor for divinity, they restore value to the material, social, embodied reality to which women historically and symbolically are relegated. Thus, they provide constructive alternatives to other more dualistic, hierarchical models of thought – models that, in George Lakoff and Mark Johnson's phrase, can become the very 'metaphors we live by'.[35]

Androcentric Hagiography

A second lesson for comparative theology derives from one of the genres that surface when we look to non-dominant theologians: their hagiographies. Feminist theology employs a hermeneutic of suspicion to evaluate what religious traditions do with these teachers' memories once they are gone. For example, Pamela Sue Anderson demonstrates how female dissent is gradually distorted in interpretations of the Greek myth of Antigone and the life of the Rajasthani poet-saint Mirabai. In Hegel's reading, Antigone's defiance of civil law is, ironically, removed from public life and interpreted as adherence to private, familial and religious duty. Similarly, Gandhi styles Mirabai, who rejects her class privilege for solidarity with a marginalized community, as the paragon of wifely devotion in her submission to the Lord Krsna. Women's acts of dissent are muted, made safe, when their actions can be explained in terms of patriarchal ideals of femininity.[36]

As a beguine, Mechthild treads a risky path. In the late twelfth and thirteenth centuries, an upsurge in laywomen's devotion led, briefly, to a third option to being a wife or a nun. Relatively unattached to the patriarchal institutions of the family and the Church, beguines lived alone or formed voluntary communities where they owned property and practiced contemplation and service in the world. They often appealed to the mendicant orders rather than parish priests for the institutional staples of their devotional practice, confession and the Eucharist. Mounting opposition to this movement near the end of Mechthild's life – as in 1261, when the Magdeburg Synod decreed that beguines must obey their parish priests – may be one reason Mechthild eventually left the beguinage to join the Cistercian convent at Helfta.[37]

Mechthild's early rejection of the traditional paths set out for women was smoothed over through the support of her Dominican confessor and the editorial comments of the Dominican editors of her writings. The Latin translators

---

35 George Lakoff and Mark Johnson, *Metaphors We Live By* (Chicago: University of Chicago Press, 2003 [1980]).

36 Pamela Sue Anderson, *A Feminist Philosophy of Religion* (Oxford: Blackwell, 1998), chapter 5. The issue of male mediation has been especially well explored with relation to the medieval Christian women mystics; see, for example, Catherine Mooney (ed.), *Gendered Voices: Medieval Saints and Their Interpreters* (Philadelphia: University of Pennsylvania Press, 1999).

37 Elizabeth A. Andersen, *The Voices of Mechthild of Magdeburg* (Oxford: Peter Lang, 2000), 80.

of her book added a hagiographical preface emphasizing Mechthild's assimilation of the values of the Dominican order. It describes her life of 'humble simplicity, in the poverty of exile, weighed down by scorn, and in heavenly contemplation' as 'following perfectly the footsteps of the brothers of the Order of Preachers'.[38] Although the male translators claimed her contemplation and poverty as their own, not everything in the book met their standards, for they 'toned down Mechthild's criticism of the clergy and some of her erotic imagery'.[39] Despite contemporary devotional trends surrounding the Song of Songs, the female desire articulated in her poetry disturbed her editors; and because she abstained from the official paths of religious life, her severe critiques of the clergy would have been doubly pointed. These thorns were further neutralized in the work's transmission. Portions of Mechthild's book were anthologized, often without her name attached, and her memory was largely lost until the complete text was rediscovered in the nineteenth century.[40]

Lalleswari's hagiographies also muffle challenges to her religious tradition. Her emphasis on transcendence functions as a tactic to circumvent patriarchal structures to a greater degree than Mechthild. Unlike Vedic schools of Hindu thought which profess the system of four *asrama*s or stages of life (celibate student, married householder, forest dweller, renouncer), Kashmir Saivism, a householder tradition, eschews renunciation. Lalleswari is an anomaly: she renounces her marital home to roam naked like an ascetic and convey her *vaakh*s to others.

> My guru gave me only one [piece of] advice –
> From outside transfer the attention within
> That became my initiation
> That is why I began to wander naked. (Odin #15)

Neither Kashmir Saivism nor the Vedic *asrama* system was designed with women in mind. When Lalleswari sets out to pursue liberation, institutional structures cannot hold her.

The hagiographers deal with Lalleswari's dissent on several fronts. First, the problem of the female body is neatly covered over with various translations and pictorial representations of her. J. L. Kaul interprets the last line of the above verse creatively: he reads *nangay* ('naked') as a corruption of the word for 'mountain flower'.[41] In twentieth-century pictures of Lalleswari, her body is covered

---

38 Mechthild of Magdeburg, *The Flowing Light of the Godhead*, 35.

39 Frank J. Tobin, 'Introduction', in *The Flowing Light of the Godhead* (New York: Paulist Press, 1998), 7.

40 Sara Poor meticulously traces the transmission of the German and Latin texts in *Mechthild of Magdeburg and Her Book: Gender and the Making of Textual Authority* (Philadelphia: University of Pennsylvania Press, 2004).

41 Jai Lal Kaul, *Lal Ded* (New Delhi: Sahitya Akademi, 1973), 12–13.

by long hair and a sagging stomach, or simply by text plastered over her midsection.[42] Second, the circumstances leading up to her renunciation, which include starvation by her mother-in-law and physical intimidation by her husband, are attributed not to the patriarchy of the tradition but to the impiety of one particular family. Nil Kanth Kotru suggests that she 'could not become an integral part of her husband's family because [it] was at variance with that in which she had been brought up in her early life . . . an atmosphere of piety and scholarship'.[43] Thus, despite her unorthodox renunciation of the household, Lalleswari's piety can be subsumed into a patriarchal framework by attributing it to her father's home.

In sum, a hermeneutic of suspicion makes comparative theologians vigilant for patriarchal values in the transmission of the lives and work of their subjects. Historical figures do not meet us unmediated. Anderson doubts whether the past dissent of non-privileged subjects can truly reach the center 'when, due to certain concrete differences, [their] gender, sexuality, or status is from the outset conditioned as marginal'.[44] If theologians notice places of discomfort in the hagiographical tradition, however, elements such as female desire and the female body that have been covered up might be recovered. If we attend closely to Mechthild and Lalleswari, the dissent that troubled institutions of their day might do so again today.

The hermeneutic of suspicion can be turned upon ourselves as well. Extant hagiographies and traditions of textual transmission challenge contemporary exclusions of these texts. Despite patriarchal packaging, these women *have* enjoyed a place in their religious traditions. *Yoginis*, beguines, female ascetics, nuns, wives, mothers, and laywomen may become our theological preceptors because they have already done so for others. Sara Poor reminds us that

> Mechthild's medieval reception shows not that she was excluded from canons of religious literature because she was a woman but rather that there were men who universalized her book because they believed it came through her from God. Mechthild's obscurity derives paradoxically from the success of the new mysticism and literary culture that her book helped to inaugurate.[45]

Even if Mechthild's name has not been prominent in Christian theology, her ideas were deemed important enough to circulate. Contemporary scruples about the authenticity of Lalleswari's oral verses are also misplaced because, as Lance Nelson explains, orality is inherent to the transmission of Kashmir Saiva teaching. The tradition

---

42 These concessions to the viewer's modesty may be viewed at P. N. Razdan, 'Gems of Kashmiri Literature and Kashmiriyat', http://www.koausa.org/KashmiriGems/LalDed.html. (Last accessed 5 March 2010.)

43 Nil Kanth Kotru, *Lal Ded, Her Life and Sayings* (Srinigar: Utpal Publications, 1989), vii.

44 Anderson, *A Feminist Philosophy of Religion*, 192.

45 Poor, *Mechthild of Magdeburg and Her Book*, 203.

has never intended that the texts that elaborate its various branches of knowledge (*sastras*) should function independently of an oral teaching tradition . . . The notion of mastering a field of knowledge without relying on a preceptorial tradition is unthinkable in a culture still oral in its most genuine expression . . . In such a setting, the written manuscript functions more as an outline or point of departure than final authority. The latter rested with the *guru*.[46]

Even without access to the language and lineage of scholarly commentary, women receive and pass on theological wisdom. The hang-ups with women as theologians may sometimes stem more from *our* androcentric concerns with acknowledged authorship as much as any historical exclusions due to gender.

Inclusion of genres 'not normally seen as theological' (Statement III.3) and the application of a hermeneutic of suspicion to women's received lives will necessarily alter our representations of religious traditions. Yet engagement with feminist theology must mean more than to 'add women and stir'. When we stir in women's voices, we do more than supplement androcentric theological discourse with projects that focus on women. In truth, we may no longer be baking the same cake when perspectives once muffled by hegemonies of gender, race, class, and sexuality begin to challenge hegemonic definitions of orthodoxy and orthopraxy.[47]

Liberative Ends

In light of the history of Christian hegemony, Francis Clooney has recommended dwelling in the space of creative tension between two traditions as long as possible before drawing normative conclusions. The difficulties of competency lead him to insist on 'patient deferral of issues of truth',[48] for the truth of comparative theology comes through the prolonged practice of reading texts of different traditions together. This restraint encapsulates many scholarly virtues; yet feminist commitment impels constructive work even while we keep our eyes on the horizon of greater understanding. J. Z. Smith comments that the '"end" of comparison cannot be the act of comparison itself'.[49] For him, redescription of exempla and rectification of scholarly categories must go hand in hand with careful comparison; and for feminists these assessments are particularly urgent given the formative power of theological metaphor for the lived experience of religion.

---

46 Lance E. Nelson, 'Foreword', in John Hughes (ed.), *Self Realization in Kashmir Shaivism: The Oral Teachings of Swami Lakshmanjoo* (Albany, NY: SUNY Press, 1994), xxxvi.

47 Cf. Johnson, *She Who Is*, 32.

48 Francis Xavier Clooney, *Theology after Vedanta: An Experiment in Comparative Theology* (Albany: State University of New York Press, 1993), 187.

49 Jonathan Z. Smith, 'The "End" of Comparison', in Kimberley C. Patton and Benjamin C. Ray (eds), *A Magic Still Dwells: Comparative Religion in the Postmodern Age* (Berkeley: University of California Press, 2000), 239.

Feminist theologians refuse a permanent deferral of issues of truth and look for ways to employ the comparative enterprise toward liberative ends. As in other liberation theologies, in feminist theology the preferential option goes to those on the underside of hierarchies: women under patriarchy, the poor, racial minorities, the ravaged environment, the very young and the very old. This norm operates across religious contexts. Kartikeya Patel articulates the end of our reflection as a 'beneficial direction' for religion that 'suggests that respect for . . . the female body lead[s] to the collective happiness of people'.[50] Because of the inherent diversity of religions and their margins, standards for liberation will depend heavily upon actual struggles and involve a broad set of contextual factors. Norms must arise from and positively affect the daily lives of the marginalized.

Feminist comparative theology aims for a level of efficacy that exceeds the Comparative Theology group's stated goals of 2006, yet the liberative orientation accords with the standard of speaking 'from a specific religious starting point' (Statement I.1). Theology is normative:

> Like other forms of theology, [comparative theology] is about and for the sake of knowledge of God or, more broadly, the ultimate mystery toward which life points. In a theology that is comparative, faith and practice are explored and transformed by attention to the parallel theological dimensions of one or more other religious and theological traditions. (Statement II.1)

Theologians have norms, and the religious norm of feminist theology is the flourishing of the marginalized. As Tracy Sayuki Tiemeier argues in her contribution to this volume, 'Comparative Theology as a Theology of Liberation', comparative theologians with feminist norms and perspectives may mobilize their work toward liberative ends.

As Tiemeier notes, the constructive task has some precedent for comparativists, especially in 'Asian and Asian American theologians [who] contribute to global conversations on liberation in their outstanding commitment to the oppressed in their multireligious and cultural realities.'[51] Aloysius Pieris, for example, considers Latin American Roman Catholic iterations of Christianity alongside the lived realities of Asia to argue that Christianity on that continent must be focused on alleviating Asia's poverty. Unlike some of the Christian ashram movements in Asia, he insists that voluntary poverty must serve the needs of those *forced* into poverty.

---

50 Kartikeya C. Patel, 'Women, Earth, and the Goddess: A Shakta–Hindu Interpretation of Embodied Religion', in *Hypatia* (9:4, 1994), 70.
51 See this volume, p. 137.

The positive role of Asian religiousness has to synchronize with the positive role of poverty. It is the hallmark of an Asian religion to evoke in its adherents a desire to renounce the ego and abandon the worship of mammon – indeed a fine complement to Jesus' messianic mission to the poor, which the church claims to continue in Asia.[52]

Pieris maintains that the Asian union of philosophy and religion includes both a program of action (*pratipada*) and a salvific path (*marga*), and he does not hesitate to elaborate a programmatic path with social, political, and economic implications.[53] This integral vision can be used to modulate his abstract 'feminine' principle of *agape*, for feminist comparative theology will be especially interested in applying these liberative interests to the lived realities of women in the world's religions.

The texts and lives of Mechthild and Lalleswari offer particular visions for liberation in relation to worldly power structures. For example, Lalleswari's striking image of all as 'one body' enlivened by the consciousness of Siva offers one particularly helpful way to envision our interconnectedness amidst difference.[54] The fluid imagery of both thinkers also shares a common interest in crossing boundaries and overturning hierarchies, but their ruptures with the religious institutions of their day indicate a breakdown of the fluid economy at the societal level. In their experience, the fluid interchange of being, love, and consciousness with divinity is often obstructed from flowing into interpersonal relations. The failure of past religious communities encourages contemporary theologians to imagine modes of relation that unblock the divine flow at the point where it would permeate worldly hierarchies.

Our comparative case study has uncovered two particular obstructions: the silencing of women's desire and the fear of women's bodies. Theologian Wendy Farley describes desire as the essence of theology – 'theology is not primarily texts but a kind of desire that employs thought as a religious practice'.[55] A feminist hermeneutic of suspicion looks beneath the various mechanisms that incorporate women's desire into a patriarchal framework. The censorship of Mechthild's erotic language of desire dovetails with a history of Christian mysticism that has thematized the erotic mode of devotion as particularly 'feminine' and subordinated it to other more 'masculine' (rational, apophatic) modes of discourse. Hindu women's religious desire has been similarly pigeonholed, as when an erotic tone has been imputed to Lalleswari's relationship with Siva beyond the

---

52 Aloysius Pieris, *An Asian Theology of Liberation* (Maryknoll, NY: Orbis Books, 1988), 42.

53 Pieris, *An Asian Theology of Liberation*, 24.

54 'O Lord, I understood neither self nor others. / I always knew one body' (my translation of Odin #22).

55 Wendy Farley, *The Wounding and Healing of Desire: Weaving Heaven and Earth* (Louisville: Westminster John Knox Press, 2005), xii.

permission of her texts.[56] Desire comes in many modalities, and the stock thematization of women's desire as (hetero-)sexual has the potential to obscure their agency and message.

Feminist theologians do nevertheless reclaim sexuality and female life processes (birth, menstruation, nursing, menopause) as sites of wisdom and bodily practice as a locus of spirituality. Lalleswari's bodily performance of dissent is a bit of an embarrassment for a non-renunciant religious tradition. The discomfort caused by the holy woman's naked body taps into the negative association of the body with the feminine.[57] Given this association of women with the body, comparativists might attend to what women have to say about the body. Both Lalleswari and Mechthild struggle with material conditions, Mechthild to the point of styling her body as her enemy (FL I.2, IV.2). Yet both also learn that the bodily and material aspects of religious life can bring healing – Lalleswari through yogic practice, and Mechthild through practices such as the sacraments in which 'the body gain[s] its share' (FL V.4). Comparativists might, therefore, illuminate gendered constructions of the body and retrieve practices that affirm its value in religious life.[58]

A liberative approach opens up an array of new subjects for comparative inquiry. Beyond the particular concerns I have cited here – institutional power, desire, and embodiment – comparative theologians might further consider what forms oppression takes in different settings, whether terms such as 'oppression' and 'patriarchy' apply across contexts, and who is permitted to name oppression. We can inquire how marginal subjects accommodate, survive, and resist hegemonies; and we can bear witness to the theological implications of their practices. From these vantage points we might further consider how the intersection of various identity markers (race, class, gender, sexuality) affects our ability to compare. We have only begun to experience the wealth of ways comparative theology can work toward liberative ends.

---

56 J. L. Kaul depicts Lalleswari's meditation as her 'daily tryst with God' (*Lal Ded*, 9), a phrase that is more appropriate to Mirabai and others. Among almost 150 *vaakh*s attributed to Lalleswari, only two contain even the possibility of an erotic theme (Odin #26, and possibly #17; see Kotru's interpolation, Kotru #99).

57 For an excellent discussion of the gender dynamics surrounding naked female saints, see chapter 8 in Vijaya Ramaswamy, *Divinity and Deviance: Women in Virasaivism* (Delhi: Oxford University Press, 1996).

58 I have explored this trajectory at greater length in Michelle Voss Roberts, 'Flowing and Crossing: The Somatic Theologies of Mechthild and Lalleswari', in *Journal of the American Academy of Religion* (76:3, 2008).

Conclusion

An alliance between feminist and comparative perspectives on theology awakens both to the types of power operative within them. Colonial and Christian hegemonies are not the only dangers to comparative theology: insofar as comparative theology focuses exclusively on texts and traditions by, for, and about men (and in which the view of women is slanted from a male perspective), it reifies androcentric hegemonies. The exclusion of women in the sources of comparative theology is rarely deliberate. Earlier generations did not have the benefit of the feminist theory that is now mainstream. There were also substantial obstacles to studying women's theology when the voices of 'outsiders within' were rarely deemed worthy of translation, let alone canonization. Today women's texts and practices are available as never before. Although much historical and textual work on 'oral and popular dimensions of traditions' (Statement III.3) remains to be done, this work *is* being done by scholars across diverse fields in religious studies. My hope is that comparative theologians will take up these materials with enthusiasm.

In making the case that attention to 'outsiders within' can avert unwitting essentialisms and oppressions, I am not arguing that comparativists must abandon their studies of the male theologians, texts, and traditions usually taken as authorities in their religious traditions. Even if such a sea change were desirable, a complete shift to local and non-dominant religious expressions (the 'little traditions') is about as likely as the elimination of the study of the world's major religions. It is crucial that we understand the 'big traditions' well, in light of their enormous influence for insiders and 'outsiders within' alike. I do, however, want to argue against the unnecessary narrowing of subjects for comparison to authoritative male theologians. With the addition of marginalized voices, the field is wide open for unexplored, creative pairings.

Comparativists will not be the only beneficiaries of an alliance with feminist theology. Feminist theology can learn from comparativists' increasing methodological sensitivity, exemplified in this volume, to the colonial legacy. Comparative habits of reading religious others – carefully, empathetically, and without taking individual theologians as representative of entire traditions – can prevent feminist scholars as well as comparative theologians from subsuming the voices of our exemplars to our constructive projects. Feminist theologians will do well to emulate comparativists' careful attention to the particularities within traditions and the long, difficult work of attaining competency in multiple religious traditions. Such practices inculcate a certain sensitivity to cultural essentializations that was absent in some earlier feminist work and can help feminists to welcome genuine religious differences even while searching for sites of convergence.

The intersection of feminist and comparative theologies promises a mutually beneficial exchange. If feminist thought takes its place alongside the postcolonial theory that comparative theologians have begun to embrace, it can act as a further prophylactic to the hegemonies and essentialisms of earlier comparative projects. In the conjunction of the two disciplines, each becomes more aware of the power operative within its respective field of discourse; and in overcoming these hegemonies, each can do liberative work.

7

Comparative Theology as a Theology of Liberation

TRACY SAYUKI TIEMEIER

Comparative theology is in its infancy. Although theologians such as David Burrell, Francis X. Clooney, James L. Fredericks, Robert Neville, and Keith Ward have profoundly shaped comparative theology, it is still developing its identity and emerging as a distinct discipline in theology. There is a variety of methods in comparative theology (and there is by no means agreement on what exactly defines it); but these different approaches do expose comparative theology as overwhelmingly Christian, white, middle-class, and male. My concern in this essay is to highlight the significance of different perspectives, opening up the method and practice of comparative theology. I ultimately argue that if comparative theology is to be relevant and avoid the domination of one perspective, it must become more like an Asian or Asian American liberation theology: responsive to the cultural, multireligious, and social contexts within which religions inhabit and responsible to the religious communities that the theologian studies.

I first look at Asian and Asian American theologies of liberation. Because of their contexts, they often consider cultural and multireligious issues in their theologies. I highlight how two major Catholic Asian and Asian American liberation theologians, Aloysius Pieris and Peter Phan, utilize the 'triple dialogue' of religions, culture, and liberation in their work. I also look at an Anglican theologian, Sathianathan Clarke, in order to show how the choices a theologian makes in setting up that dialogue significantly impact the resulting theology of liberation. Next, I move to method in comparative theology. One of the more troubling issues occupying the theory of comparative theology today is whether or not comparative theology avoids a new imperialism that 'plunders the riches' of other religious traditions in service to Christian theological interests. I propose that moving towards a comparative theology of liberation that takes into account the triple dialogue of Asian and Asian American liberation theology is an important step toward addressing the charge of imperialism. Finally, a comparative theology of liberation must recognize that it is not just concepts such as 'comparative theology' that can be problematic, if not carefully interrogated and

129

(re)constructed in interreligious conversation; 'liberation' itself must be constructed comparatively. Toward that end, I rethink 'liberation' through a comparative example.

As this essay argues for the personal engagement of the comparative theologian and careful attention to her presuppositions and goals, I want to situate myself at the outset. I am a biracial Japanese-German American Roman Catholic woman. Like much of comparative theology today, my own theology is Christian, middle-class, heterosexual, and even white (while being also Asian American and yellow). Yet, I speak as a feminist who privileges the flourishing of women, and also as an Asian American woman who privileges Asian and Asian American voices. My own Roman Catholic faith also means that I am bound by Catholic belief and practice. Thus, although I draw from a variety of sources, I also focus my comparative theology through Catholic, Asian American, and feminist concerns. These subjective elements limit my perspective, but they also offer important resources more widely significant for constructing a liberation method in comparative theology. Finally, my work as a theologian cannot be understood apart from my commitment to interreligious dialogue and my participation in the local Los Angeles Hindu–Catholic dialogue. This grounds my theology and offers fertile soil for reflecting on comparative and interreligious theology. I shall return to the Los Angeles Hindu–Catholic dialogue in my conclusion as a way of moving my methodological and theological considerations into wider communities of dialogue.

Asian and Asian American Theologies: Culture, Religions, and Liberation

In their joint 1991 statement, 'Dialogue and Proclamation', the Pontifical Council for Interreligious Dialogue and the Congregation for Evangelization of Peoples outline four kinds of interreligious dialogue: the dialogue of life, the dialogue of action, the dialogue of theological exchange, and the dialogue of religious experience.[1] Based on an earlier statement in 1984 by the then-called Secretariat for Non-Christians,[2] the joint statement warns, 'One should not lose sight of this variety of forms of dialogue. Were it to be reduced to theological exchange, dialogue might easily be taken as a sort of luxury item in the Church's mission, a domain reserved for specialists.'[3] As the statement makes clear, all of these dialogues are interrelated: theological interreligious dialogue will be

---

1 Pontifical Council for Interreligious Dialogue and the Congregation for Evangelization of Peoples, 'Dialogue and Proclamation' (Rome: 19 May 1991), 3.42, http://www.vatican.va/roman_curia/pontifical_councils/interelg/documents/rc_pc_interelg_doc_19051991_dialogue-and-proclamatio_en.html (accessed 9 July 2009).
2 Secretariat for Non-Christians, 'The Attitude Toward Followers of Other Religions: Reflections and Orientations on Dialogue and Mission' (Rome: 10 May 1984), http://www.melbourne.catholic.org.au/eic/pdf/art-Interfaith-attitudenonchristian.pdf (accessed 9 July 2009).
3 'Dialogue and Proclamation', 3.43.

enriched by other forms of dialogue, and will in turn enrich them. This emphasis on the interrelated nature of these forms of dialogue is an essential backdrop to understanding Catholic Asian and Asian American theologies, theologies which emphasize contextually grounded theological reflection and the engagement of the theologian in the life of the communities to which she belongs.

The Federation of Asian Bishops' Conferences had been thinking about dialogue even before the 1984 Secretariat document. The 1974 Statement of the First Plenary Assembly of the Federation of Asian Bishops' Conferences (FABC) in Taipei emphasized the need for Christians in Asia to build a truly local church. It states,

> The local church is a church incarnate in a people, a church indigenous and inculturated. And this means concretely a church in continuous, humble and loving dialogue with the living traditions, the cultures, the religions – in brief, with all the life-realities of the people in whose midst it has sunk its roots deeply and whose history and life it gladly makes its own.[4]

The bishops then go on to explain that this dialogue in Asia especially entails dialogue with Asian religions and the poor.[5] In a 2000 statement, the FABC emphasizes that

> As we face the needs of the 21st century, we do so with Asian hearts, in solidarity with the poor and the marginalized, in union with all our Christian brothers and sisters, and by joining hands with all men and women of Asia of many different faiths. Inculturation, dialogue, justice and the option for the poor are aspects of whatever we do.[6]

This 'triple dialogue' with culture, the religions, and the poor means that Asian theologies must also reflect on and interrelate these realities.

The triple dialogue can be seen beyond Asian and Catholic worlds. In fact, many Asian and Asian American theologians engage in a kind of liberation theology, emphasizing the flourishing of Asians and Asian Americans through their own life-stories and practices of personal and communal justice. While Asian theologians often do their work in the contexts of poverty, health crises, the history of missions, and European colonialism, Asian American theologians are in a distinct (though by no means exclusive or singular) context that contends with – among other issues – racism in America, the history of immigration,

---

4 Gaudencio B. Rosales, DD and G. C. Arévalo, SJ (eds), *For All the Peoples of Asia: Federation of Asian Bishops' Conferences Documents from 1970 to 1991* (Maryknoll, NY: Orbis Books, 1992), 14.
5 Rosales and Arévalo, *For All the Peoples of Asia*, 14–15.
6 Seventh Plenary Assembly of the Federation of Asian Bishops' Conferences, 'A Renewed Church In Asia: A Mission of Love and Service' (Samphran, Thailand: 3–12 January 2000), http://www.ucanews.com/html/fabc-papers/fabc–93.htm (accessed 9 July 2009).

inter-Asian and Asian American conflicts, and questions of assimilation and acculturation.[7] There is no essential 'Asian' or 'Asian American', and there can be no one 'Asian theology' or 'Asian American theology'. Despite these differences, however, a deep concern for justice can be seen in many Asian and Asian American theologies. In such theologies, the contextualization into a Korean theology, a Vietnamese American theology, or (like mine) a multiracial Japanese American theology, means a stance of solidarity and advocacy. It also often means a commitment of solidarity with other Asian and Asian American communities, even if a pan-Asian or pan-Asian American identity is socially constructed. Dialogue and justice are essential for those who suffer, are marginalized, or are oppressed.

Moreover, the entangled nature of Asian and Asian American religious and cultural practices highlights how complicated it is to separate 'religion' and 'culture'.[8] Both Asian and Asian American communities are highly ethno-religious, blending ethnic identity and practice with religious identity and practice – in ancestor devotion, rites of passage, or New Year celebrations, for example. Such festivals and rituals can seem syncretistic or even dangerous to 'outsiders'. Yet the religious plurality of many Asian and Asian American contexts often leads to multiple practices as a basic fact of life. Christian Asian and Asian American theologians have therefore typically shown interest in that religious diversity, recognizing that Asian Christianities have been profoundly impacted by the religions of their soil. While this reflection has, in some cases, been done in an uncritical way, there has been increasing attention to the complexities and power dynamics involved in the appropriation of religious symbols, rituals, and narratives from outside of 'Christianity', but which are nevertheless a part of wider cultural networks. In dialogue with culture, religions, and 'the poor', Asian and Asian American Christian theologians have developed ways of negotiating their multireligious contexts, attentive to the complicated power dynamics between religions.

I now briefly consider three different Asian and Asian American liberation theologians, in order to show how the triple dialogue of religions, culture, and liberation interact. Aloysius Pieris, SJ, is a Sri Lankan Catholic theologian who has developed an Asian theology of liberation that emphasizes dialogue with

---

7 There is much crossover, however. See Rita Nakashima Brock, 'Interstitial Integrity: Reflections toward an Asian American Woman's Theology', in Roger A. Badham (ed.), *Introduction to Christian Theology: Contemporary North American Perspectives* (Louisville: Westminster John Knox Press, 1998), 183–96, 184–5.

8 I loosely understand 'culture' to be a way of life that expresses the shared values and beliefs of a community in its many practices and institutions. 'Religion' is a part of this way of life, though it often crosses cultural boundaries. Religion is therefore both a cultural product and cultural carrier. Asian and Asian American theologians tend to emphasize ethnic and racial practices in their understanding of culture, though many other cultural practices are also considered, such as music, art, common narratives, community rituals, etc. See Kathryn Tanner, *Theories of Culture: A New Agenda for Theology* (Minneapolis: Augsburg Fortress Press, 1997), 25–9.

Buddhism, social justice, and an active resistance against western consumerist culture. Peter Phan is a Vietnamese American Catholic theologian who explicitly utilizes the triple dialogue in his work. Finally, Sathianathan Clarke (Church of South India) develops an Indian Dalit (low-caste, non-caste, or out-caste) liberation theology through an in-depth narrative, ethnographic, and theological encounter with Dalit religion. Clarke does not have an equivalent body of work to Pieris or Phan, but he does offer a comparative approach to Indian Christian liberation theology that can be an instructive bridge for our conversation on comparative theology.

Aloysius Pieris

Aloysius Pieris has developed a theology of liberation through his encounters with Buddhism in major works, such as *An Asian Theology of Liberation*,[9] *Love Meets Wisdom*,[10] and *Fire & Water*.[11] In the context of this interreligious commitment to liberation, Pieris offers theological insight in light of Buddhist teachings and practices, rethinking everything from the Eve–Mary polarity,[12] to the Spiritual Exercises,[13] to monasticism,[14] to marriage,[15] to Christ.[16] Aloysius Pieris brings together liberation in Asia with the religions through the model of symbiosis. Playing off of Christian base communities in Latin American liberation theology, Pieris develops the notion of basic *human* communities. These communities are intentional interreligious communities working for justice; and it is in their 'ongoing liberative praxis' that adherents find the uniqueness of their own religious traditions.[17] Here, there is no room for the traditionally understood categories of inclusivism, exclusivism, and pluralism. Instead, Pieris uses the categories of syncretism, synthesis, and symbiosis. Syncretism is a 'haphazard mixing of religions', where the interaction actually changes the meanings and values of narratives, rituals, and symbols. Synthesis is the creation of a third way from the integration of two or more religions, which destroys the uniqueness and identity of those original religions. However, in basic human communities, symbiosis occurs and, 'each religion, challenged by the other religion's unique approach to the liberationist aspiration of the poor . . . discovers and renames itself in its specificity in response to the other approaches'.[18] Pieris says further,

9 Aloysius Pieris, SJ, *An Asian Theology of Liberation* (Maryknoll: Orbis Books, 1988).

10 Aloysius Pieris, SJ, *Love Meets Wisdom: A Christian Experience of Buddhism* (Maryknoll, NY: Orbis Books, 1988).

11 Aloysius Pieris, SJ, *Fire & Water: Basic Issues in Asian Buddhism and Christianity* (Maryknoll, NY: Orbis Books, 1996).

12 Pieris, *Fire & Water*, 29–37.

13 Pieris, *Fire & Water*, 183–94.

14 Pieris, *Love Meets Wisdom*, 89–96.

15 Pieris, *Love Meets Wisdom*, 97–109.

16 Pieris, *Love Meets Wisdom*, 124–135.

17 Pieris, *Fire & Water*, 158.

18 Pieris, *Fire & Water*, 161.

The Basic Human Community is not a group that has come together for interreligious dialogue. Dialogue is not an end in itself. Nor is there any preoccupation about one's religious identity or uniqueness. The origin, the development, and the culmination of the activities of a BHC is, ideally, the total liberation of nonpersons and nonpeoples. It is within the process of this ongoing liberative praxis that each member of the BHC discovers the uniqueness of his or her religion.[19]

The symbiotic liberationist approach is essential, and Pieris vigorously critiques academic interreligious dialogue. Dialogue for dialogue's sake is pointless, even dangerous. Certainly, dialogue has its place, as it can bring certain clarity to differing viewpoints; but it must not become mere intellectual exercise.

Pieris is concerned with the history of Christianity and colonialism. In response to a Buddhist monk who decried the 'Christian west', which has originated 'the evils of capitalism and colonialist exploitation', Pieris argues that,

Beneath this indignant verdict lies a deeply ingrained Asian conviction that colonialism, Christianity, and the West form an inseparable trio. This is because Asia is not being given a chance to taste the monastic flavor of Western Christianity. For capitalism, which turned money into a god, and colonial Christianity, which made God depend on money, appear as a Western attempt to reconcile what Jesus had declared irreconcilable: God and mammon. Therefore, only a monastic Christianity that, in word and deed, through life and death, proclaims God's pact with the poor, will be the seed of an authentically Asian church.[20]

Christianity is inevitably implicated in the project of colonization; yet, there must not be a simple conflation of 'the west', capitalism, colonialism, and Christianity. An Asian theology of liberation stands against poverty and the importation of western consumerism. Thus, although Asian religiosity and poverty are the primary concerns of Pieris's work, purging Christianity of its western consumerist culture in favor of a more authentic monastic culture (shared between Christianity, Buddhism, and other Asian religious traditions) is also essential. Christianity becomes truly Christian in becoming truly Asian: religiously (and interreligiously), culturally, and liberationally.

---

19 Pieris, *Love Meets Wisdom*, 3.
20 Pieris, *Love Meets Wisdom*, 95–96.

Peter Phan

Peter Phan has developed one of the most comprehensive Catholic Asian American interreligious theologies, seen most fully in his controversial trilogy. The volumes reflect the triple dialogue in Asia: *Christianity with an Asian Face*[21] focuses on liberation; *In Our Own Tongues*[22] focuses on culture; and *Being Religious Interreligiously*[23] focuses on the religions. Although each volume is dedicated to a different mode of dialogue, each does so interreligiously. *Christianity with an Asian Face* rethinks Catholic Christology through the lens of Confucianism and popular Vietnamese religion, offering a model of Jesus as Eldest Son and Ancestor. *In Our Own Tongues* puts forward Mary and the Buddhist Bodhisattva Kwan-Yin as an important theological comparison for interreligious dialogue in Vietnam, and rethinks the relationship between liturgy and culture through ancestor veneration. Finally, *Being Religious Interreligiously* dialogues with Buddhism and Judaism, proposing Jesus as the Enlightened Enlightener (or Buddha) and rethinking Asian liberation theology after the Holocaust. In these volumes, Phan shows the interrelated nature of culture, the religions, and liberation.

One of his more surprising interreligious reflections is on Asian theology in its relationship with Judaism. Phan grounds the dialogue in the history of Jewish and Christian interaction in Asia, the reality of unwitting anti-Judaism in some Asian theology, and how post-Holocaust theology and Asian liberation theology can benefit from continuing dialogue. [24] For Phan, cultural retrieval in Asian and Asian American theology cannot occur without careful interreligious and sociopolitical consideration. Such consideration is aided by careful attention to history.

> In 1995, fifty years after atomic bombs were dropped on Hiroshima and Nagasaki, Japan remembered not only Japanese victims of the war but Jewish victims as well. A Holocaust museum dedicated to the memory of 1.5 million Jewish children murdered by the Nazis was opened in June of the same year in Fukuyama, a city near Hiroshima. Anne Frank's diary, translated into Japanese, was also exhibited in Hiroshima's Peace Park.
>
> Less known is what has been called the Fugu Plan, Japan's top-secret plan to create an 'Israel in Asia'. Conceived by Japanese diplomats, industrialists, and military leaders, this scheme involved offering displaced European Jews a safe haven in Japanese-controlled Manchuria. Its purpose was twofold:

21 Peter C. Phan, *Christianity with an Asian Face: Asian American Theology in the Making* (Maryknoll, NY: Orbis Books, 2003).

22 Peter C. Phan, *In Our Own Tongues: Perspectives from Asia on Mission and Inculturation* (Maryknoll, NY: Orbis Books, 2003).

23 Peter C. Phan, *Being Religious Interreligiously: Asian Perspectives on Interfaith Dialogue* (Maryknoll, NY: Orbis Books, 2004).

24 Phan, *Being Religious Interreligiously*, 147–85.

obtaining Jewish financial and technical resources in exchange for physical safety, and improving Japan's image with the United States and gaining the sympathy of America's influential Jewish population . . . Though this plan foundered with Japan's entry into the Tripartite Pact with Nazi Germany and Italy in 1940, it saved from the Holocaust thousands of Jews who were issued Japanese transit visas and given wartime refuge in Asia.[25]

In this shared historical space, interreligious theological dialogue between Asian liberation theology and Holocaust theology is an 'unexpected reunion'.[26] Here, they can unite in their commitment to justice and their struggle for liberation.

Sathianathan Clarke

Sathianathan Clarke brings together and interrelates Dalit religion, culture, and liberation in his Indian theology of liberation.

> First, Indian–Christian theology tends to be exclusionary and non-dialogical by turning a deaf ear to the collective religious resources of the Dalits. Second . . . , Indian–Christian theology fosters the hegemonic objectives of the caste communities. Thus, in order to capture the dialogical, inclusive and liberative dimensions of theology, it is determined that the religious world of the Dalits must be re-collected and re-membered.[27]

Clarke closely examines the Paraiyar Dalit community in South India and retrieves the sacred symbol of the drum for a renewed vision of Christ as drum. This move to the drum draws on the ritual function of the drum in Paraiyar religion, the cultural power of sound (what Clarke calls 'subaltern-based orality'),[28] and the drum as an instrument of resistance to caste colonialism and violence.

Clarke makes a critical choice in his theology that shows what is at stake in relating religions, culture, and liberation. There are two important religio-cultural Dalit symbols that Clarke argues could serve as an important interreligious symbol for an Indian Christian theology of liberation: the drum and the goddess Ellaiyamman. His choice to privilege the drum over Ellaiyamman is based on three reasons: first, Clarke believes that the drum is 'safer and more neutral' than the goddess; second, Clarke is ambivalent about the appropriateness of using a goddess symbol in Christian theology; and finally, Clarke argues that any use of the goddess would require a careful study of her relation to Dalit women and feminist theology – which he is admittedly neither ethnographically

---

25 Phan, *Being Religious Interreligiously*, 184.
26 Phan, *Being Religious Interreligiously*, 185.
27 Sathianathan Clarke, *Dalits and Christianity: Subaltern Religion and Liberation Theology in India* (New Delhi: Oxford University Press, 1999), 2.
28 Clarke, *Dalits and Christianity*, 162.

nor theologically prepared to take up.[29] The awareness of his own bias is both admirable and realistic (for we cannot address all things in our theology), but his failure to examine this bias more carefully is problematic for his own stated framework. Clarke points out in his study that the relationship between the goddess and the drum is inextricable, but assumes he can sidestep his discomfort with the goddess by using the drum. In the process, the liberative/oppressive power of the goddess for men (to say nothing of her power for women) and the liberative/oppressive power of the drum for women (to say nothing of its power for men) go unexplored. This limits his consideration of the drum, and therefore his appropriation of it for an Indian Christian liberation theology. Clarke illustrates the reality that the theologian (not just the Asian liberation theologian, but *any* theologian) must make choices – and that these choices matter.

The Contribution of Asian and Asian American Theologies to the Theology of Liberation

Asian and Asian American theologians show how entangled cultural and inter-religious concerns are with social justice. Indeed, although Asian and Asian American liberation theologians negotiate quite different national, economic, and cultural locations, significantly shifting how they understand flourishing and liberation, their attention to the triple dialogue is quite instructive. The choices that theologians make arise out of their own cultural contexts and the lenses that they utilize impact not only their theological conclusions, but also the political ramifications of those conclusions.

As Tissa Balasuriya argues, 'The Asian contribution [to the liberation of theology] can include a certain understanding of the human person which the Asian religions and philosophical traditions can contribute, as well as a sharpening of the strategies due to the demands of the Asian revolutionary processes.'[30] Aloysius Pieris adds that, 'It follows, then, that the reclaiming of our original charisma – that is, our Christian uniqueness – is the task of the poor and the powerless, who have God as their covenant partner in the mission of redemption.'[31] Asian and Asian American liberation theologians contribute to global conversations on liberation in their outstanding commitment to the oppressed in their multireligious and cultural realities.

---

29 Clarke, *Dalits and Christianity*, 141.

30 Tissa Balasuriya, 'Toward the Liberation of Theology in Asia', in Curt Cadorette, Marie Giblin, Marilyn J. Legge and Mary Hembrow Snyder (eds), *Liberation Theology: An Introductory Reader* (Maryknoll, NY: Orbis Books, 1992), 41.

31 Aloysius Pieris, 'The Option for the Poor and the Recovery of Christian Identity: Toward an Asian Theology of Religions Dictated by the Poor', in Daniel G. Groody (ed.), *The Option for the Poor in Christian Theology* (Notre Dame: University of Notre Dame Press, 2007), 275.

Developing a Comparative Theology of Liberation

The interest in multireligious perspectives has not yet led large numbers of Asian or Asian American theologians to the field of comparative theology (though the numbers are growing); and comparative theology has largely stayed away from such debates on liberation and social justice. Instead, comparative theology's search for a stable identity has often led theologians to root comparative theology in Christian historical or systematic theology. This has been important in setting the initial boundaries for an emerging discipline, but it also has led to comparative theology's remaining dominated by (white) (male) Christian theological interests. Such interests are not problematic in and of themselves, but become so when not complicated by other perspectives and questions.

John Renard brings together a wide array of 'comparative theologies', grouping different approaches into historical and systematic models.[32]

> As a historical discipline, Comparative Theology investigates the mechanisms and assumptions behind both the implied and expressed comparisons that have resulted in theological change in a variety of historical and cultural contexts. As a systematic discipline, Comparative Theology builds on the historical data as it seeks to elaborate not only the relationships between Christianity and other theological systems, but the very shape of Christian theology itself.[33]

Renard helpfully brings together and interrelates quite different approaches to 'comparative theology' (though a number of the scholars profiled would not call themselves 'theologians', much less 'comparative theologians'). These differing approaches nevertheless have a symbiotic relationship.[34]

Renard argues that comparative theology does not require (Christian) religious belonging. '[O]ne can use any of the models from either explicitly confessional or non-confessional standpoints, depending on one's ultimate theological purpose. The important proviso is that one be as clear about one's evaluative criteria as possible from the outset.'[35] Renard goes out of the way to find examples by scholars using non-confessional approaches or confessional approaches from outside of the Christian tradition. However, Renard often presumes a Christian theological context. He also depends on western Christian categories, such as systematic theology, to construct and explain his models. While this clearly does not exclude religious questioning from outside of Christianity, it still depends on a framework that would favor western Christian scholarly methods.

---

32 John Renard, 'Comparative Theology: Definition and Method', in *Religious Studies and Theology* (17:1, June 1998), 3–18.
33 Renard, 'Comparative Theology', 5.
34 Renard, 'Comparative Theology', 15.
35 Renard, 'Comparative Theology', 15.

Another strategy in the definition of comparative theology is to articulate a general definition that can accommodate a wide variety of approaches. This strategy can be seen in the Group Statement of the American Academy of Religion's (AAR) Comparative Theology Group, which frames comparative theology through Anselm's (eleventh-century Archbishop of Canterbury) formulation of theology as 'faith seeking understanding'.

> Comparative (Interreligious) Theology is, like other forms of theology as familiarly understood, primarily a matter of faith seeking understanding (or, in some traditions, perhaps 'meditative perception' or 'insight'), and this faith as enacted in meditation, visualization practice, ritual, and ethical behavior. Like other forms of theology, it is about and for the sake of knowledge of God or, more broadly, the ultimate mystery toward which life points. In a theology that is comparative, faith and practice are explored and transformed by attention to the parallel theological dimensions of one or more other religious and theological traditions. As theology that occurs within the academy, this communal and inter-communal faith and practice are open to the analysis, comment, and questions of both insiders to the involved traditions, and to other scholars, not necessarily defined by such commitments, who are nonetheless able and willing to explore the full range of dynamics of faith seeking understanding in a comparative perspective.[36]

Similar to Renard's approach, the AAR Statement tries to hold together confessional and non-confessional approaches and balance a constructive definition with openness to change.

A Christian definition of theology by the Statement again raises the specter of Christian imperialism and the hegemony of privileged perspectives. If comparative theology is largely defined in Christian terms and practiced by Christian theologians from privileged communities, comparative theology can be seen as yet another attempt by Christian theologians to define (and thereby dominate) the religious 'other' (whether that 'other' is from religious traditions other than Christianity or from underrepresented Christian perspectives). In light of the history of Christian imperialism, therefore, a Christian theology that is 'explored and transformed by attention to the parallel theological dimensions of one or more other religious and theological traditions' is suspect. If the goal of comparative theology is to be enriched by the religious 'other', it can easily serve a covert (even if unintended) agenda of conversion, apologetics, or 'plundering the riches' of other religious traditions.

The typological approach of Renard and the flexibility built into the AAR Group Statement (of suggesting loose analogues for theology, such as 'meditative perception' or 'insight') are helpful for addressing the problem of imperialism.

---

36 'Statement for the Comparative Theology Group for the AAR', revised May 2006, II.1, http://myweb.lmu.edu/ttiemeier/GroupStatement.html (accessed 5 November 2008).

Typologies inherently resist reduction to one perspective and leave open the possibility for adding or revising models in light of new evidence. The Group Statement begins realistically from the framework of the major author (Francis X. Clooney, SJ) and the majority of signatories, but it recognizes that 'theology' may not be able to translate exactly in differing religious contexts. More importantly it recognizes that, 'in establishing a Comparative Theology Group, one of our goals will be to test the limits and prospects of the term "theology" in a comparative perspective. In any case, we expect the very definition of "comparative theology" to be a topic for fruitful disagreement and argument in the first years of the Group'.[37] The AAR Comparative Theology Group expects comparative theology to be redefined in Group discussions.

Also important is the AAR Statement's recognition of the cultural complexes within which and through which religions exist, whether they have to do with race/ethnicity, gender, or class:

> [The] Comparative Theology Group will also be a forum in which attention to cultural and religious differences makes us notice and problematize standard historical priorities, and to bring to the fore concerns regarding gender, race/ethnicity, and socio-economic status. We will examine questions such as the kinds of theology produced by women and the institutional structures that have facilitated and/or hindered such production in a variety of world religious traditions. Other issues will concern ethnic identity and difference as they bear upon theological thinking and institutional recognition, and how various religious [traditions] have welcomed or excluded participants from a variety of socio-economic classes.[38]

Such recognized complexities allow Christian comparative theologians to rethink their own concepts of theology and rework them in order to address any charges of Christian hegemony. Inherent to the method of comparative theology is the principle that one is fundamentally changed in encounter with the 'other'. Even the definition of 'theology' shifts in a conversation not wholly governed by one partner, but a dialogue shared among partners who both have something significant to say about Reality. However, until the imbalance in comparative theology is resolved, and more comparative theologians emerge from religious traditions other than Christianity and from other underrepresented perspectives, comparative theology is inevitably going to be defined and articulated by Christian theologians from privileged backgrounds, and the possible charge of imperialism is bound to remain.

Integrating some of the insights from Asian and Asian American liberation theologies can also help comparative theology to counter the charge of imperialism. Asian and Asian American Christian theologians practice their theologies

---

37 'Statement for the Comparative Theology Group for the AAR', II.2.a.
38 'Statement for the Comparative Theology Group for the AAR', III.2.a.

with the historical realities of Christian conquest and colonization in Asia. They moreover must contend with contemporary neo-colonialism and the imposition of western cultural-political-sociological modes of discourse in Christian theology. The question of Christian imperialism is therefore often an implicit or explicit theme in their work. Additionally, Asian and Asian American theological approaches to religious plurality are helpful for developing a method in comparative theology that is hermeneutically sensitive to its wider socio-political horizon.

Asian and Asian American liberation theologies (along with other interreligious theologies) show the extent to which religions other than Christianity are historically and practically entangled with Christianity. The comparative theologian may practice comparative theology in order to find a better understanding of her own tradition; but she cannot do so without herself becoming entangled in the religious tradition(s) she compares. The comparative theologian therefore has a certain responsibility to all the traditions considered in the theology. Just as she bears some responsibility to represent her own religion in faithfulness to its traditions (though with a critical faithfulness) she must represent the other religion in a way that is in continuity with its traditions. This does not mean that religions must be seen as rigidly bounded wholes with a clear center of authoritative belief and practice (the question of which traditions and voices 'count' make the representation of any religion an immeasurably complicated prospect); but there must be some accountability and recognition that religions function in communities of interpretation, belief, and practice. One cannot construct a comparative theology – even a historical comparative theology – without saying something (whether intentionally or not) about and to those wider communal traditions.

Asian and Asian American liberation theologies (along with other contextual theologies) also show that theology always occurs in a cultural context. If culture is a way of life that expresses shared beliefs and values, religion is inexorably bound with culture, expressing and constructing those shared cultural beliefs and values. The practices, beliefs, and narratives of religions – however divinely revealed they may be – are not immune to human cultural creation, and therefore shift fundamentally in meaning as they enter and take root in other cultural contexts. Theology and the theologian are no exception, being products of national, gendered, economic, and racial/ethnic complexes. Therefore, no comparative theology operates in a vacuum, and a theological dialogue must be contextualized, both within the traditions considered and in relationship to the theologian who makes the choices about the theological dialogue. Questions addressing how material is chosen and why certain questions are posed must be clarified in order to answer possible charges of imperialism.

Finally, Asian and Asian American liberation theologies (along with other theologies of liberation) show that theology is never value-free. Theology inevitably takes sides; as a result, there must be a specific stance in solidarity with the traditions it investigates and those within them who suffer, are marginalized, or are oppressed. There are complex power dynamics involved in appropriating and comparing religious traditions, and the liberative retrieval of traditions for some may mean the erasure of others. Indigenous traditions, in particular, are in a vulnerable position to be co-opted. The comparative theologian must therefore become more critical in how she relates to her theological 'objects' as 'subjects'. She cannot be out simply for her own theological insight or liberation. Liberation and justice must be important commitments of the comparative theologian, but they must be commitments for all traditions involved in the comparison.

All three of the elements made explicit in many Asian and Asian American theologies of liberation – culture, religions, and justice – are fundamentally interrelated. The distinction between religion and culture is not easily made in contexts that are ethnoreligious like Asia and Asian America. Religious and cultural investigations inevitably involve values and commitments. It is therefore essential to understand the contexts out of which and about which comparative theology and the comparative theologian speak, and the values/ideology inevitably communicated and supported. Comparative theologians must be responsible to (all of) their subjects: intellectually, ethically, socio-politically, and spiritually. If comparative theologies of the future can become much more akin to Asian and Asian American liberation theologies in their interrelation of religions, culture, and justice, they will be better equipped to address charges of imperialism (Christian or otherwise).

The danger of imperialism in comparative theology is actually a productive problem, for it pushes comparative theologians to be critical of their interests, aims, and practices. The tendency to turn the religious 'other' into a tool for self-enhancement must be resisted, even as comparative theology (re)articulates itself in light of another religious tradition. The responsibility that the comparative theologian has to all the parties in the comparison must not be forgotten. Contextualizing comparative theology culturally, multireligiously, and liberationally will enhance the possibilities of comparative theology and avoid the pitfalls. Balancing these commitments, however, is no easy task. There must be a constant process of contextualization, revision, self-critique, and openness to change in light of new challenges and encounters. Such a process may raise more questions than it solves; but the failure to engage other religious traditions seriously in today's globalizing world is an even more perilous prospect.

Rethinking Liberation, Comparatively

I have used a number of terms, such as 'religion', 'culture', 'liberation', etc., that are clearly coming from my own western Christian context. Just as the AAR Comparative Theology Group statement recommends a flexible use of 'comparative theology' that will inevitable change in comparative dialogue, all theological and other specialized terms will need revision in light of interreligious encounter. As a result, a comparative theology of liberation not only has to be aware that the definition of 'theology' must be revised through interreligious encounter, it must also be willing to change its own understanding of liberation. Christian concepts of 'poverty', 'liberation', 'solidarity' and 'human flourishing' are all subject to revision.[39] Toward that end, I now provide one example of how the consideration of another religious tradition can enrich the conversation. The songs of the ninth-century Hindu saint, Antal, can provide a resource for interreligious feminist conversations on liberation and illustrate the ways in which a comparative approach to liberation is mutually illuminative. Although I utilize a feminist hermeneutic that privileges the flourishing of women, I still seek to articulate themes within Antal's poetry that are in continuity with the dynamic of her thought and tradition.

Antal was one of twelve saints, called Alvars, who lived between the sixth and ninth centuries CE in Tamil South India and wrote devotional poetry to Visnu and his many forms (one of his most well-known human incarnations is Krsna). The poetry of the Alvars is authoritative for the Srivaisnava tradition, which is a South Indian Tamil Vaisnava tradition (devotees of Visnu as the One God) that worships the One Divine Reality as God-with-Goddess, Visnu-with-Sri, ontologically united and One. In this tradition, the Alvars are themselves worthy of devotion and are believed to be secondary incarnations of Visnu's companions and attributes.

Antal is believed to be a secondary incarnation of Bhudevi, the goddess Earth and the consort of Visnu. Although little is known about her life, her poems reveal that she is the daughter of Periyalvar (another Alvar). Two incidents from her hagiography have made Antal particularly famous. Dedicated to Visnu from a young age, Antal would secretly wear garlands dedicated to Visnu: a disturbing ritual pollution that Visnu nevertheless found pleasing. Antal also refused to marry a human male and resolved only to marry her divine lover, Visnu. Visnu ultimately accepted her desire; and when during her wedding ritual Antal embraced the temple image of Visnu, she vanished, physically and spiritually merging with her lover.[40] Over the course of her life, she composed two poem-songs, the *Tiruppavai* and *Nacciyar Tirumoli*. I will focus on the *Tiruppavai*.

The *Tiruppavai* centers on the ritual of the *pavai*, a Tamil ritual that takes place in the Indian month of Markali (mid-December through mid-January).[41] The month-long vow is undertaken by unmarried girls, who bathe every morning in the cold waters of a river or pond in the hopes of securing a blessing for a happy married life.[42] Antal has taken the ritual, exclusive to unmarried girls, and used it

---

39 See Dan Cohn-Sherbok (ed.), *World Religions and Human Liberation* (Maryknoll, NY: Orbis Books, 1992).

40 See Vidya Dehejia, *Antal and Her Path of Love: Poems of a Woman Saint from South India* (Albany: SUNY Press, 1990).

41 Dehejia, *Antal and her Path of Love*, 16–17.

42 Dehejia, *Antal and her Path of Love*, 17.

as a focal point for devotion to Krsna and the human being's unification with him. At the end of the song, the girls sing,

> The holy moon-faced, ornamented ladies worshipped Kesava [Krsna],
> Madhava, who churned the ship-ocean, and obtained the drum there;
> Kotai [Antal], of the chief of brahmins, with refreshing green lotus garland,
> And from beautiful Putavai, wrote thirty literary Tamil garlands;
> Those who declare without fault this gift here will obtain wherever
> The grace of Tirumal [Visnu],
> Prosperous, with red eyes, a holy face, and four great hill-shoulders;
> They will attain bliss; Oh, our *pavai*! (Verse 30)[43]

The fulfillment of the vow is not only for those select few to find husbands. Through the song, the *pavai* becomes a universal unitive goal, to find one's divine husband, Visnu/Krsna.

The song follows the girls in their *pavai* vow. Verses 1 through 5 form the introduction of the song. The *pavai* ritual is explained and clearly set within the legendary stories of a young Krsna in his cowherd village, Ayarpati. The girls in the song who are called to perform the *pavai* are identified with the *gopis,* the cowherd lovers of Krsna. Visnu is described in his beauty, and praised as the one who bestows the ritual drum (symbol of his grace). In verses 6 through 15, the *gopis* chastise a girl or series of girls who failed to awaken for the *pavai*. The slumbering maiden(s) finally respond and join the other girls. In verses 16 through 20, the *gopis*, rather than going to the *pavai* grounds, go to the house of Krsna. The girls call to the gate guard and Nappinnai, cowherd wife of Krsna, asking her to open the door and wake up her husband. In the final section of the song, verses 21 through 30, there is an extended direct appeal to Krsna himself. The *gopis* praise Krsna, proclaiming that they have come to serve him and receive the drum. They sing of their desire for the lord. Then they make a startling claim: they say they do not want the drum that they have been previously seeking. Instead, the girls bind themselves in servitude to the lord and ask for no other desires. This twist points to an essential moment in the song. The sounding of the drum indicates the fulfillment of the vow; however, it also symbolizes the bestowal of the lord's blessings. Thus, the giving of the drum to the *gopis* by the lord, confirmed in verse 30, indicates that their vow is complete and fulfilled. Indeed, the *gopis* fulfill their *pavai* vow, not by bathing in water, but by bathing in their lord: they are married to their lord, and all the results of the *pavai* will be bestowed.

Antal's song about union with Krsna illustrates human responsibility in devotion and discipline, as well as what precisely constitutes this liberative union.

---

43 Translations are my own.

You who live on the earth,
Listen to what we do for our *pavai*;
We praise the Supreme One [Visnu] who sleeps gently on the milk ocean;
We do not eat ghee; we do not drink milk; we bathe at dawn;
We do not paint our eyes; we do not put flowers in our hair;
We do not do bad deeds; we do not speak evil;
We offer charity, alms, as much as possible;
Gladly hoping for heavenly bliss; Oh, our *pavai*! (Verse 2)

If we sing the name of the Perfect One [Visnu] who rose up and
    measured the earth,
And bathe in the water for our *pavai*,
All the country will be free from blemish; it will rain three times a month;
Red rice will flourish; carp will leap;
Bees will sleep in water lily buds;
With overflowing udders,
Abundant cows will fill their pots;
Unceasing prosperity will abound; Oh, our *pavai*! (Verse 3)

Dazzling One [Krsna], Son of everlasting Matura in the north,
Chief of Yamuna's pure waters,
Ornamented Lamp of the cowherd tribe,
Damodara, who made his mother's womb illustrious,
To him we come pure, worshipping him and scattering flowers;
Singing with our mouths; contemplating with our mind;
Our past crimes, as well as the ones to come, which we have not yet
    conceived,
Will become like cloth in a fire; Oh, our *pavai*! (Verse 5)

Verse 2 explains the *pavai* vow, and in doing so, explains significant aspects of the ritual (both for the *gopis* in the song and for the devotee singing the *Tiruppavai*). Bathing, singing the lord's praises, and ascetic and moral practices are all important aspects of the *pavai* vow. Through this, the devotee lives a joyful and graced life. Because the song is the verbalization of the vow, and not a simple replacement for it, these practices also indicate the requisites for proper chanting of the *Tiruppavai*. Verse 3 situates unification and liberation in the context of earthly goodness and abundance. Verse 5 refers to disciplines (meditation and recitation) undertaken as a part of the ritual vow, pointing to the personal results of this devotion.

In the *Tiruppavai*, female desire is transposed onto erotic union with Krsna. This liberation, this unification, is not a spiritualized or disembodied activity pursued in private, but is physically in relation to a human and cosmic community. The *gopis* devote themselves together and hold each other accountable. This necessary ritual community operates for the *Tiruppavai* on two levels: the level of the song's narrative in the practice of the *pavai* and the level of the song's ritual purpose. The song itself is a ritual text, meant for chanting in a community. Antal's song is a process of visualization and sound, as the singers become incorporated into the narrative and become cowherd maidens. It is important not to see the declaration in verse 30 as an internalization of the *pavai* that forgoes the rigors of the vow. Although the song universalizes a bridal ritual and highlights its significance for devotion, it is still meant for ritual chanting and bodily practice. Liberation does not require the abandonment of the body or of the world; rather, liberation occurs as bodily devotee, in a ritual community, and has real ramifications for the wider world. As devotees are united to Krsna, the lord's grace also fulfills all material reality. Through the devotee's practice and the grace of Krsna, there is earthly, creaturely, and human prosperity. Even though these material goods are not the *ultimate* end, they are nevertheless fulfilled as the grace of Krsna bathes the devotees in their ecstatic union and overflows onto all things.

So, then, what is liberation? Antal's *Tiruppavai* suggests that liberation involves body, community, and environment. Liberation occurs in and through the body, as certain forms of desire and physical living become channeled, refocused, and purified into the desire for serving the lord and relating with him. Ritual, visualization, sound, and physical and ethical observances are a part of this process of purification and preparation. Liberation also requires a ritual community. The *gopis* awaken themselves and perform their vow together. Liberation is therefore a community process, utilizing both individual and community-oriented practices of devotion. Finally, because self-realization (or the lack thereof) has ramifications for earthly prosperity and goodness, liberation also involves the environment and wider world. The devotees' actions have direct effect on their environment. Ritual performances and devotional activities influence not only the liberation of the self, but also the liberation of the earth. The *Tiruppavai* therefore envisions an entangled process of liberation between individual, community, and the earth, where devotees have deep responsibilities in their lives and practice. Individual and communal bodies become loci for Krsna's grace, a grace that unites the self and the ritual community to him, bathes these bodies in prosperity, and spills over onto the entire earth.

Antal's *Tiruppavai* presents a view of liberation that is profoundly holistic and unitive. It balances human discipline and divine grace, human prosperity and earthly goodness, sensual desire and ascetical practice. The grace that overflows from the human person and her community is not a celebration of consumerism and consumption. It is an abundance that depends on and cannot be separated from ascetical practice, self-discipline, and charitable action. Antal's attention to body and bodily practices can therefore bridge feminist theologies of liberation that reclaim desire and bodily abundance and other theologies of liberation that stress the need for asceticism and voluntary poverty. Bodily desire is valued as a primary strategy of liberation, but it is also in need of discipline. Thus, in rethinking 'liberation' through Antal's *Tiruppavai*, individual, communal, and environmental flourishing must arise together, 'materially' and 'spiritually'. This integrated and holistic approach to liberation is framed through female desire, a woman's ritual, and women's narrative voices. Women are agents of liberation: socially, environmentally, and spiritually.

The notion of liberation found in Antal's *Tiruppavai* offers one way to hold together, interrelate, and enrich the dynamic of culture, the religions, and liberation that is so prominent in Asian and Asian American theologies of liberation. This Hindu Srivaisnava approach illustrates cultural negotiations of gender and gender roles (Antal's poetry manifests the very practical and not uncommon strategy of refusing to marry a human male by insisting on divine marriage), thereby subverting traditional social expectations of women. The girls are active, insistent, and downright stubborn in obtaining their desires from their divine lord. This leads to a revelation on what liberation truly consists of, and provides Hindu and Christian women with images and language to rethink liberation together.

Nevertheless, it must be noted that a Srivaisnava or Christian feminist retrieval of Antal cannot be without critique. Antal's songs are sung today for *human* (not divine) marriage, and so the songs in these contexts often function to reinforce the religio-social function of marriage, rather than providing authoritative sanction for women to subvert such obligations. Antal becomes an ideal spiritual devotee, but is not seen as offering a legitimate social path for women: her story becomes a miraculous exception, rather than the rule. Moreover, Antal's song-poems themselves cannot be said to be unproblematic from a feminist perspective. First, there is an androcentric devotional focus on Visnu (not to mention his male incarnations like Krsna). Second, the female voice as representative of human dependent on male independent divine maintains an overarching power structure of male over female, divine over human. Thus, although the language of female bodily desire may be promising, the hierarchical gender binary serves to support patriarchal and heterosexist interests.

Such problematic issues can, however, become productive points for dialogue. For example, there are structurally similar problems in Christian theologies of a male Father/Son and the Christian mystical portrayal of the female human soul in relation to the male divine. Although Antal cannot be appropriated uncritically to address these issues, she also can be an important part of religious and interreligious liberationist reconstructions. The Srivaisnava theo(a)logy of Visnu-with-Sri frustrates easy gender binaries. The ontological unity of God-with-Goddess that is seen in Antal's poetry challenges the exclusivity of a divine independent male. The thealogical interpretation of Antal as incarnation of Bhudevi and goddess for devotion is also significant. The female divine, though not as prominent as in Hindu Goddess traditions, is nevertheless an important part of Srivaisnava tradition that can undermine some of its androcentric elements. Finally, the female anthropology constructed by Antal is a decidedly bodily one, and one that requires male devotees to take on female desiring bodies in their love for Krsna. This transgendering element of devotion to Krsna – even if still the result of imagining erotic union through a male–female binary – can also serve to problematize that binary. Therefore, even if Antal is not entirely unproblematic, she can nevertheless offer some concrete possibilities for thinking beyond Srivaisnava and Christian patriarchal theologies.

Some Concluding Reflections

The Los Angeles Hindu–Catholic dialogue is a small, but dedicated group of people. Every six weeks or so we gather together, share a meal, and chat about our lives. This 'dialogue of life' provides an important foundation of friendship for our year-long 'dialogue of theological exchange'. During our regular meetings we will discuss an article or book, or listen to a participant present some current work. Over the course of that year, the group also plans a public dialogue event (including such topics as human rights, celibacy, and consciousness). The group will also attend other public events together (for example, an icons exhibit, temple or church dedications, or local lectures). This 'dialogue of action' attempts to promote mutual understanding and respect among the wider Los Angeles population. Finally, we participate in the 'dialogue of religious experience', sharing in each other's religious communities and spiritual practices. Thus, the 'dialogue of theological exchange' that is essential to comparative theology is importantly a part of a wider dialogical process. Indeed, comparative theology is most beneficial when consciously a part of that wider process.

The dialogue group is currently reading a series of Christian commentaries on the *Bhagavad Gita*. In one of the most interesting conversations I have been a part of with the group, several Hindu dialogue partners had a debate among themselves on whether choosing to read a commentary on the *Gita* presumed a false understanding of the role of the *Gita* among vastly diverse Hindu traditions. We ultimately chose to proceed with the book, but were all the wiser about 'insider' debates on the status of the *Gita* and how some Christians and Hindus, in looking for shared Hindu scripture, may over-emphasize the place of the *Gita* in Hindu thought and practice. In a subsequent meeting, several Christian members pointed out how one of the Christian commentaries provided deep insights into Christian theology that we otherwise would not have considered. But we remained silent about the author's mistakes on the *Gita* and on how two of the *Gita's* well-known Hindu commentators were presented (though we had noted the errors in the margins of our reading). When one of the Hindu participants rightfully criticized the reading for those inaccuracies, she pointed out that there must be a prior responsibility to the Hindu text and Hindu traditions of interpretation before there can be a responsible retrieval for Christian theology. And yet – another Hindu participant interjected – Hindus have not seemed to have any trouble appropriating Christian texts without any consideration for their integrity; so why should Christians worry about 'responsible' interpretation?

Both participants, of course, were correct. Hindus and Christians have a long history of cross-appropriation without concern for responsible re-presentation.

Theological insights can be made without any consideration of texts' and traditions' wider networks of meanings, values, symbols, and practice. But the social and political dynamics of the twenty-first century make necessary the development of a more attentive process of appropriation (within all religious traditions). There is a long history of Christian imperialism, militarism, and dominance. But Christianity is not the only religion responsible for contributing to the realities of violence and injustice in the contemporary world. Fundamentalism and oppression are on the rise in many traditions. Interreligious dialogue and co-operation will be necessary to remedy these problems, and so it is essential that we not contribute to those problems further by uncritical appropriation or superficial interreligious interaction. A comparative theology that is also a theology of liberation can participate in the wider process of dialogue, functioning to promote interreligious theological knowledge, cultural understanding, and social justice.

In the end, perhaps not every comparative theology needs to be an explicit theology of liberation. Theologians are limited by their method, training, and perspective. They cannot be expected to be adept in all areas of constructive theology (much less all areas of theology and religious studies). But if comparative theologians do not more carefully interrelate culture, religions, and liberation, they run the (even if unintended) risk of being at best irrelevant and at worst a tool of the new imperialism. Grounding comparative theology in cultural and socio-political considerations will not 'dilute' the intellectual rigor of the discipline; rather, it will deepen it. In this way, comparative theology will be able to find a more grounded identity that is still flexible enough to accommodate the varying approaches and backgrounds of the comparative 'theologian'. It will also enjoy a broadened appeal that will bring more students, scholars, theologians, activists, clergy, and lay persons to the comparative theology table.

8

(Tentatively) Putting the Pieces Together: Comparative Theology in the Tradition of Sri Ramakrishna

JEFFERY D. LONG

Introduction

The world's spiritual traditions are like different pieces in a giant jigsaw puzzle: each piece is different and each piece is essential to complete the whole picture. Each piece is to be honored and respected while holding firm to our own particular piece of the puzzle. We can deepen our own spirituality and learn about our own tradition by studying other faiths. Just as importantly, by studying our own tradition well, we are better able to appreciate the truth in other traditions. (Pravrajika Vrajaprana)[1]

The pluralistic view expressed here by Pravrajika Vrajaprana is not uncommon in Hindu traditions, and it is absolutely foundational to the tradition of Sri Ramakrishna, in which both Vrajaprana and I are located. It is a view that is widely misunderstood, both by its supporters and by its critics. But it is also a view that many of us hold to be vital to the survival of humanity, particularly in a time that is characterized not only by intense interreligious conflict, but also by the proliferation of weapons of mass destruction.

Because of all these factors – the importance of this pluralistic outlook, the fact that it is poorly understood, and its centrality to my religious tradition – I see my chief task as a theologian to be its reconstruction and re-articulation. One could argue that the body of work I have done in this regard might be more properly termed a *theology of religions* than a *comparative theology* in the strict sense; for one of the primary concerns of this work is the articulation of a tradition-specific perspective on religious diversity.

---

1 Pravrajika Vrajaprana, *Vedanta: A Simple Introduction* (Hollywood, CA: Vedanta Press, 1999), 56–7.

On the other hand, the pursuit of this task has involved me in engagement with other traditions at every step. I do not know if I would be justified in asserting that the theology of religions and comparative theology must, by necessity, occur in concert or feed into one another in a symbiotic fashion. But this has certainly been the case for my work. My articulation of a Neo-Vedantic pluralistic theology has involved extensive engagement with Jain and process thought, as well as Buddhism, Christianity, and other Hindu traditions under the rubric of Vedanta, such as classical Advaita and Dvaita.[2]

In this essay, I intend to illustrate a Neo-Vedantic understanding of comparative theology by unpacking Vrajaprana's image of the world's religions as 'pieces in a giant jigsaw puzzle', using my own practice of comparative theology as an example of how this approach might be applied. My thesis will be that, at least for a Neo-Vedantist in the tradition of Sri Ramakrishna, the theology of religions and comparative theology are not, in practice, separable.

Following definitions outlined by Francis X. Clooney, SJ, the *theology of religions* 'is a theological discipline that discerns and evaluates the religious significance of other religious traditions in accord with the truths and goals defining one's own religion', whereas *comparative theology* is theological reflection that is 'rooted in a particular faith tradition but which, from that foundation, venture[s] into learning from one or more other faith traditions'.[3] The centrality of an irreducible pluralism to the Neo-Vedanta tradition, to the spiritual experiences of its principal founding figure, and to the life experiences of many of its adherents, is such that any attempt to articulate its theology of religions must involve one in extensive engagement – positive engagement – with other religions. To the degree that such engagement does not occur, a Neo-Vedantist theology of religions risks becoming, in the words of one of its harshest critics – my old teacher, Paul J. Griffiths – 'pallid, platitudinous, and degutted'.[4]

But to the degree that such engagement with other religions *does* occur, a real deepening of both spirituality and knowledge – knowledge of one's own tradition and of others – is enabled. This is the deepening to which Vrajaprana alludes in saying, 'We can deepen our own spirituality and learn about our own tradition by studying other faiths.'[5]

---

2 The locus of the bulk of my theological work is my first book, entitled *A Vision for Hinduism: Beyond Hindu Nationalism* (London: I. B. Tauris, 2007). This book covers Neo-Vedanta, Jain philosophy, and process thought in some depth, and gestures, in its autobiographical introduction, to my engagements with Christianity and Buddhism. My engagement with Advaita and Dvaita is covered chiefly in my recent article, 'Advaita and Dvaita: Bridging the Gap – The Ramakrishna Tradition's both/and Approach to the Dvaita/Advaita Debate', in *The Journal of Vaishnava Studies* (Spring 2008). I hope to do an in-depth comparative theological project on Christianity and Hinduism in a future book, the working title of which is *A Hindu Jesus? Hindu Reflections on Christ and Christianity*.
3 Francis X. Clooney, SJ, *Comparative Theology: Deep Learning Across Religious Borders* (Wiley-Blackwell, 2010), 10.
4 Paul J. Griffiths, *An Apology for Apologetics: A Study in the Logic of Interreligious Dialogue* (Maryknoll, NY: Orbis Books, 1991), xii.
5 Vrajaprana, *Vedanta*, 56–7.

My Practice of Comparative Theology

As I have mentioned, my work of articulating a Neo-Vedantic, pluralistic theology of religions has involved me in engagement with other traditions at every step. In order to get to the depths of my Neo-Vedantic perspective and articulate it properly, I have, in my earlier work, drawn heavily upon two other traditions: Jainism and process thought.

In both cases, I adhered, broadly speaking, to the principles that are illustrated by Vrajaprana's metaphor: seeing my own tradition as essentially true, but also incomplete, and looking to other traditions for complementary truths – additional pieces of the puzzle – that might be used to broaden and deepen my understanding of truth. In both cases, this process has led to an expansion and a transformation of my own perspective. I shall begin with my engagement with process thought.

When I first began my project in earnest of developing a Neo-Vedantic theology of religions – initially and tentatively in college at Notre Dame, and then more seriously in graduate school, at the University of Chicago – I was in search of a way to express in a systematic fashion the ideas that I had found so appealing in the teachings of both Gandhi and Ramakrishna: the many paths up one mountain, the many rivers flowing into one sea, and so on. In the spirit of these aphorisms, I had pieced together an eclectic worldview that was a mix of a wide range of elements from various religions and philosophies.

What was lacking in this worldview at the time was a coherent system of ideas through which it could be expressed. Or rather, the system was *there*, but it was mute – in search of a vocabulary through which it could be articulated without simply sounding like a New Age grab bag.

It was at this point that the philosophy of Alfred North Whitehead came into my life. Through Franklin I. Gamwell's course on Whitehead at the University of Chicago, and subsequent further explorations of the work of other process thinkers, such as Charles Hartshorne, David Ray Griffin, John Cobb, and Gamwell himself, I felt that I had found the vocabulary for expressing the system of thought underlying my pluralistic worldview. Brilliant and inspired though they were, gleaning a system from the varied sayings and writings of Sri Ramakrishna, Swami Vivekananda, and Mahatma Gandhi is, to say the least, a challenge – at least as great a challenge as developing a single system of Vedanta from the *Upanishads*, the *Brahma Sutras*, and the *Bhagavad Gita*, a task that even today eludes the Vedanta traditions, divided as they are over the interpretation of these texts.

Whitehead saw his metaphysics as, 'the endeavour to frame a coherent, logical, necessary system of general ideas in terms of which every element in our experience can be interpreted'.[6] This seems, at first glance, like the ultimate

---

6 Alfred North Whitehead, *Process and Reality: An Essay in Cosmology* (corrected edn) (New York: The Free Press, [1929], 1978), 3.

hegemonic discourse. He also saw this system as a way to bring back together the fractured discourses of science and religion, which had, in the modern period, carved out for themselves separate realms of fact and value with little or no mutual relevance. Where these realms did overlap, there was considerable conflict, conflict which resonates even today in debates about creation and evolution, intelligent design, bioethics, the nature of consciousness, and so on.

But one page later, Whitehead also asserts that this ideal philosophical system can only be approached asymptotically.[7] This is epistemic modesty coupled with the sense of a metaphysical realist that there is a reality *there*, a truth to be approached – the relative truth and the absolute truth, the blind men and the elephant.

The beauty of Whitehead's system is that it is an *open* system. As such, it is an excellent model for interreligious dialogue and comparative theology. It is rooted in a rational analysis of common human experience – of things that we already know – but it is also aware of the limits of such analysis, and displays a profound sense of the limits of language and rational reflection. It is a 'middle path' between positivistic, reductionistic philosophies, which see all experience as ultimately reducible to 'bits of matter', and the negative, deconstructive philosophies, which undermine the idea of *any* true knowledge.

As such, it is a highly expansive system. Whitehead reintroduces the category of the divine to western philosophy – after God had been relegated by Kant to the status of a 'postulate of practical reason', a necessary but unprovable assumption of the science of ethics. Process thought contains three ultimate realities. There is the unchanging, timeless absolute – which Whitehead calls the principle of creativity. There is the cosmos of actual entities, which enact this creative principle. And there is the Supreme Being, or supreme embodiment of the creative principle, who makes it available to actual entities in such a way as to constitute a coherent reality.

As Whitehead explains,

[T]he Universe, as understood in accordance with the doctrine of Immanence [the principle that a rational explanation of the universe requires that the universal order be inherent, and not imposed by the fiat of an arbitrary deity] should exhibit itself as including a stable actuality whose mutual implication with the remainder of things secures an inevitable trend towards order.[8]

There is a close correspondence between Whitehead's three ultimate realities and the various aspects of Brahman as understood in Neo-Vedanta. The unembodied, pure principle of creativity correlates with both the *nirguna Brahman* and

---

7 Whitehead, *Process and Reality*, 4.
8 Alfred North Whitehead, *Adventures of Ideas* (New York: The Free Press, [1933], 1967), 115.

maya of Advaita. The cosmic process made up of actual entities correlates with the world or 'flow' (*jagat*) of souls (*jiva*-s) of theistic, realist forms of Vedanta. And God, of course, correlates with the personal divinity, or Lord (*Isvara*) of these systems.

As I have argued elsewhere, these mutual correlations or 'translations' of process and Vedantic categories are illuminating to both. Seeing *maya* as creativity, for example, recovers the positive sense of this term from the confusion and assumption of negativity toward the world perpetuated by its widespread translation as 'illusion'. And the sense of Brahman as a totality encompassing all three of these categories is an idea otherwise not found in process thought, and idea that addresses a common criticism addressed against process thought that it diminishes the role of the divine in ways unacceptable to more orthodox intuitions about the nature of God.[9] For if, by 'God', we are referring to the totality of being – to Brahman – as Hindus often do, then attributes like omnipotence, which process thought otherwise finds incompatible with the existence of a universe of free actual entities, become more coherent with the total system.[10]

The potential for process thought to form a template for a pluralistic theology of religions has been perceived by a number of Christian process theologians – most notably, John Cobb and David Ray Griffin, who have used it to develop what they call a 'deep religious pluralism' that does not reduce all religious ultimates to one.[11] I have similarly used it to develop a Hindu process theology of religious pluralism.[12]

The way this works, specifically, is that the concept of the three ultimate realities can be used to affirm the very distinct ultimate goals of the world's religions – realization of an impersonal ultimate principle, loving union with a supreme deity, and harmonious existence among the beings making up the cosmos – without doing away with the idea of a larger, coherent worldview in terms of which all of these realities and their accompanying goals can be affirmed simultaneously. To paraphrase John Cobb, process thought allows for a universe in which Christian salvation and Buddhist *nirvana* can both occur without either being reduced to the other. In terms of Neo-Vedanta, both can be seen as modes

---

9 These and other related ideas are explored in greater depth in the second chapter of *A Vision for Hinduism* and in my article, 'A Whiteheadian Vedanta: Outline of a Hindu Process Theology', in Donna Bowman and Jay McDaniel (eds), *Process Theology: A Handbook* (St Louis, Missouri: Chalice Press, 2006).

10 In terms of the universe of actual entities, then, divine omnipotence becomes an eschatological ideal – a state in which all beings co-operate perfectly with the promptings of the divine will, which is otherwise only ever imperfectly realized, and is sometimes even thwarted, due to the freedom exercised by the actual entities. But if one is referring to Brahman, the totality, as divine, then omnipotence is an already-realized fact, for there is nothing that is not Brahman, and so all power belongs to it – that of the *jiva*-s and of Isvara.

11 See David Ray Griffin (ed.), *Deep Religious Pluralism* (Louisville, KY: Westminster John Knox Press, 2005)

12 See my 'Anekanta Vedanta: Toward a Deep Hindu Religious Pluralism', in Griffin, *Deep Religious Pluralism*, and my *A Vision for Hinduism*.

of liberation either through loving union with, or realizing, respectively, different aspects of Brahman, the totality: the supreme being and the ultimate principle. Finally, the open-endedness of process thought, the understanding that process itself is always 'in process', the capacity of this system for 'self-relativization', minimizes any hegemonic tendencies to which such a totalizing perspective might otherwise be subject.[13]

My engagement with Jain philosophy occurred simultaneously and in symbiosis with my engagement with process thought. In exploring the pre-modern antecedents of Neo-Vedanta, I found that, contrary to the strong emphasis on religious pluralism found in the tradition of Ramakrishna, the classical systems of Vedanta, such as Advaita and Dvaita, were engaged in constant – and often bitter – polemical conflict, no less so than the religions of the west (albeit with much less actual bloodshed). Despite such pluralistic aphorisms in the Vedic literature as 'Truth is one, the wise speak of it in various ways', or Sri Krsna's, 'All paths lead to me', the predominant mode of much traditional Hindu philosophy was logical argumentation.[14] At best, traditions would rhetorically subsume one another in hierarchical inclusivisms – such as in Madhava's *Sarvadarshanasamgraha*, in which the various systems of Indian philosophy are presented as steps leading from the least adequate view (the materialism of the Lokayatas) to the perfected, *siddhanta* view of Madhava (in his case, Advaita Vedanta). But one would not typically see other views represented as authentic expressions of even partial truth.

Buddhism seemed more promising than the orthodox systems in this regard. The Mahayana doctrine of the Buddha's 'skillful means' (*upaya kaushalya*), according to which various Buddhas and Bodhisattvas teach a variety of doctrines to different types of spiritual aspirant, according to each one's needs and capacities. But this doctrine still tended to be affirmed by means of inclusivist hierarchies, much as in the Hindu systems.

In the Jain tradition's doctrines of relativity, however, I found a pre-modern Indic system of thought that seemed to comport well with the pluralism of Neo-Vedanta – and even to extend and deepen it. It also went further than process thought, whose threefold typology of ultimate realities corresponding to the three major types of religious path was good for addressing the issue of the different goals of these types of religion, but was too blunt an instrument for looking at intra-religious issues, or issues among religions within a single category. For much of the world's religious conflict has not been about whether the ultimate nature of reality is personal or impersonal – a relatively abstract issue – but over *which* form of personal deity one should worship, or how a particular deity should be worshiped, or which community holds that deity's favor.

The Jain doctrines of relativity are a complex of three distinct doctrines that

---

13 John Cobb, 'Metaphysical Pluralism', in Joseph Prabhu (ed.), *The Intercultural Challenge of Raimon Panikkar* (Maryknoll, NY: Orbis Books, 1996).
14 *Rg Veda* 1.164:46c and *Bhagavad Gita* 4:11.

make up the traditional Jain approach to comparative theology. The Jains, having been a tiny minority community in India throughout their history, have had numerous occasions to engage theologically with religious others. Having to defend their views and practices and show the distinctiveness of these to their followers, Jain monks have made close studies of both Hindu and Buddhist philosophical positions over the centuries. Though a good deal of this work has been polemical in nature and intent, a distinctively Jain method of argumentation gradually emerged which presented the views of opponents as expressing partial truths, with the Jain view expressing the 'big picture'. This approach was distinct from the hierarchical inclusivisms of Hindu and Buddhist thinkers. It viewed other perspectives not as rungs on a ladder leading up to Jainism, but as parts of a larger truth expressed most fully in Jainism: pieces of a puzzle, as in Vrajaprana's metaphor.

Halbfass distinguishes Jain inclusivism from Hindu and Buddhist inclusivisms by describing it as 'a horizontally [rather than vertically] co-ordinating inclusivism which recognizes other views as parts and aspects of its own totality'. He notes, though, that like the Hindus and the Buddhists, '[T]he Jainas, too, claim a superior vantage point, and a higher level of reflection.'[15] In other words, the main difference between the Neo-Vedantic view and the Jain view was that the Jains tended to identify the 'big picture' of which other traditions were 'pieces' with their own perspective.

An important exception to this, however, was the third century CE Digambara Jain mystic and philosopher, Kundakunda, who affirmed a 'two truths' doctrine similar to that of Nagarjuna – and later of Sankara, and much later of Neo-Vedanta. According to the view of Kundakunda, which has been tremendously influential upon the Digambara Jain tradition right up to the present day, even Jain doctrine yields only a 'relative view' (*vyavaharanaya*). The absolute view (*nishcayanaya*) can only be known through a direct realization of the true nature of the soul (*jiva*).[16] This is closer to the Neo-Vedantic view that one's own perspective is true, but always incomplete, this side of enlightenment. It anticipates the Neo-Vedantic emphasis on direct experience over received doctrine.

According to the Jain doctrines of relativity, the universe is irreducibly complex, having a great variety of forms and aspects. This is *anekantavada*, the doctrine of 'many-ness'. Corresponding to each aspect of reality is a perspective, or *naya*, which reveals that aspect. This is *nayavada*, the 'doctrine of perspectives'. In regard to any particular aspect of reality, there are seven possible truth claims that can be made about it. Each of these claims is true, but partial. If any of them is affirmed absolutely, then one has fallen into the error of *ekantata*, or 'one-sidedness'. This is the error that leads to the rise of the only partially true, absolutist systems of belief. But if one qualifies one's claims with the word *syat*,

---

15 Wilhelm Halbfass, *India and Europe: An Essay in Understanding* (Albany, NY: State University of New York Press, 1988), 414.
16 See my *Jainism: An Introduction* (London: I. B. Tauris, 2009), 125–31.

which, in Jain technical usage, means 'in some sense' or 'from a certain point of view it is the case that x', then one has captured the truth. This is called *syadvada*, the doctrine of conditional predication.

The seven logically possible truth claims that can be made about a given topic are:

1. In one sense, or from one perspective, x is true.
2. In another sense, or from another perspective, x is not true.
3. In another sense, x both is and is not true.
4. In another sense, the truth of x is inexpressible.
5. In another sense, x is true and inexpressible.
6. In another sense, x is not true and is inexpressible.
7. In another sense, x is true, not true, and inexpressible.

Further non-redundant combinations of the first four truth claims are not possible.

One can readily see that, in combination with process thought, and in its 'two truths' version as advocated by Kundakunda, the Jain system of hermeneutics can readily lend itself to the analysis of a wide range of religious claims: from the nature of reality as permanent or impermanent (a topic endlessly debated by Hindu and Buddhist thinkers, with the Jains holding the view that both views are true of different aspects of reality), to the survival of the person after death (with materialism and the affirmation of a soul both being true of different aspects of the complex person), or even to the divinity of Christ.[17]

The deep compatibility of the Jain doctrines of relativity with process thought are the key to synthesizing both into a Neo-Vedantic pluralistic theology of religions. The Jain doctrines of relativity are traditionally interpreted by Jain philosophers in terms very similar to the process concept of positive and negative *prehensions* – the ways in which an actual entity both does and does not embody particular possibilities, or 'eternal objects', made available to it in a given moment through its relations to the mind of God, one role of whom is to be a repository for possibilities for actualization, not unlike the Yogacara Buddhist concept of the *alayavijnana*, or 'storehouse consciousness'. A particular entity can be said both to exist and not to exist, for example – a seemingly contradictory pair of predications – inasmuch as it does exist *vis-à-vis* certain qualities, and does not exist *vis-à-vis* others.

---

17 In terms of process thought, the divinity of Christ, or of any *avatara*, can be analyzed as a function of the degree to which that entity prehends and responds positively to the reality of God. Divinity, therefore, can admit of degrees, with a being whose will is perfectly in accord with the will of God being seen as fully divine (though not *numerically* identical with God), a being whose will is largely in accord with the will of God being seen as a highly inspired person – a prophet or saint – and so forth. The concept of degrees of avatar-hood is found in Vaishnava Hindu traditions, and can be used as a matrix by which one can assess the relative divinity of such persons as Jesus, the prophet Muhammad, the various Buddhas and Bodhisattvas of Buddhism, the Jinas of the Jain tradition, the saints and sages of various world religions and philosophical systems, and so on.

A pen, for example, embodies those qualities (*guna*-s) that are distinctive to a pen, but does not embody those qualities that are distinctive to a jar. It exists *vis-à-vis* pen qualities, does not exist *vis-à-vis* jar qualities, both exists and does not exist *vis-à-vis* both sets of qualities jointly, is inexpressible inasmuch as its actual existence is beyond the ability of language to communicate, and so on. Such positive and negative relations to particular possibilities are what constitute an actual entity at a given point, according to both Jain and process thought. It is in terms of this fundamentally relational worldview that the truth claims of any given religion or philosophy can be assessed as, in a certain sense true, in another sense false, etc.

On the basis of a synthesis of Jain and process thought – or, more specifically, the addition of the Jain doctrines of relativity to process thought, an augmentation that is justified by the fundamental relational worldview that both share – one can approach any worldview, religious or non-religious, and see it as partially true and partially false. If a new claim is logically compatible with the existing system, it is a good truth candidate, even if it is not already present in one's own system. This is an 'open inclusivism'. And if a new claim is not so compatible, as currently understood, the possibility of a return to the issue is not foreclosed, as the system continues to expand and transform itself.

This open, perpetually synthesizing, expanding, and self-correcting system is a formalized, systematic version of the approach to truth already at work in Neo-Vedanta. It is a systematization of the direct, experiential method followed by such giants of Neo-Vedanta as Sri Ramakrishna and Mahatma Gandhi. And, not to place myself on the same level as these figures – or even anywhere near it – it also reflects the approach to truth that I followed intuitively prior to my formal engagement in systematic theological work – the approach that led to my adoption of a Neo-Vedantic Hindu worldview and practice in the first place. In other words, my religious identity is itself the product of comparative theological reflection and the application of a theology of religions (albeit largely implicit and unsystematic for much of my life) with the basic structure that has been described.

I was neither born nor raised in the tradition of Ramakrishna, but in the Roman Catholic tradition of Christianity. My eventual self-identification as a Hindu in the Neo-Vedantic tradition was the result of a lengthy internal Hindu–Christian dialogue that arose out of a process of questioning and a spiritual search accelerated by personal tragedy – the death of my father when I was twelve years old.[18]

I refer to an 'eventual self-identification as a Hindu' rather than a 'conversion to Hinduism' because my experience has not been one of rejecting a Christian identity in favor of a Hindu one, but of having an originally Roman Catholic Christian worldview and practice that was gradually transformed, through a

---

18 My transition from Roman Catholic Christianity to Ramakrishna Vedanta is traced in greater detail in the autobiographical introduction to *A Vision for Hinduism*.

process of reflection and dialogue, to the point where it became a Vedantic Hindu worldview and practice in the tradition of Ramakrishna.

I see this process as being not unlike the biological evolution of one species from another. If one were to place my Catholic beliefs and practices at the time I was twelve alongside the Hindu beliefs and practices of my adulthood, the differences might appear quite striking. But there were also intermediate phases – other 'selves' between my twelve-year-old self and my current 40-year-old self – that would appear much more mixed and ambiguous. There are also very consistent themes and ideas that connect all these selves, revealing them to be far more alike than a superficial analysis would suggest. I have always sensed, for example, the benevolent, sustaining, and guiding presence of God in my life.[19] I do not *feel* like a different person, but I clearly must be.

Outline of a Neo-Vedantic Theology of Religions

In terms of Alan Race's threefold typology,[20] which has become standard in the theology and philosophy of religions, a Neo-Vedantist theology of religions is, in one sense, pluralist, and in another sense, inclusivist. It is pluralist in the sense that it takes as axiomatic the basic claim that has united most of the pluralist theologies developed over the course of the last few decades: that there are many true religions, the practice of which can be salvifically efficacious.

But it is also inclusivist (as, indeed, are all pluralistic theologies, try as their authors may to avoid this) inasmuch as it proceeds from a specific worldview that is held to be true and in terms of which the truth claims and the salvific efficacy of other religions may be evaluated. The fact that such giants of Neo-Vedanta as Vivekananda and Gandhi[21] affirm religious pluralism, while at the same time do

---

19 Except for a period of about a year, which I call – following St John of the Cross – my 'dark night of the soul', in which prayer and meditation were very difficult, and a void seemed to fill the place normally occupied by the divine presence. But this period was followed by one of an intensified sense of the divine presence, and a feeling that the period of darkness was not one of absence, but of dormant potential preparing to manifest itself. This resurgence came just in time for my doctoral qualifying examinations and the writing of my dissertation.

20 This is the well-known typology of religious exclusivism, inclusivism, and pluralism. See Alan Race, *Christians and Religious Pluralism: Patterns in the Christian Theology of Religions* (Maryknoll, NY: Orbis Books, 1982).

21 Though Gandhi was not formally a member of Ramakrishna's tradition, in the sense of having a guru or taking *diksha*, his thought bears all of the hallmarks of Neo-Vedanta, as a broad movement of modern Hindu thought, as I describe it in this essay. A more systematic argument for the appropriateness of characterizing Gandhi as a Neo-Vedantist is developed in a forthcoming article by Nicholas F. Gier (Gier, personal communication). I would make a distinction between Neo-Vedanta as a broad movement, starting with Ram Mohan Roy in the early nineteenth century, and the Ramakrishna tradition, which is a prominent sub-set of this larger movement. This distinction is somewhat elided in this essay, but is not of great significance for my thesis here.

so using unabashedly Hindu categories and extolling the distinctive inclusiveness of Hindu Dharma, is a case in point.[22]

The inclusivist character of a Neo-Vedantic theology of religions is a necessary logical result of the fact that it is a set of truth claims rooted in a specific worldview. As Wilhelm Halbfass observes, '[A]ny kind of tolerance which is allied with, and committed to, religious absolutism, and which keeps itself free from relativism, skepticism or indifferentism, is by definition inclusivistic.'[23] Or, to return to Vrajaprana's image of the giant jigsaw puzzle, 'Each piece is to be honored and respected while holding firm to our own particular piece of the puzzle.' We shall see that Neo-Vedantists make strong, and sometimes quite radical, claims about the truth and efficacy of multiple religious paths. But we do so from a particular religious perspective that we do take to be essentially true.

It is very important to acknowledge and emphasize this point quite frankly at the outset. A widespread misconception, among adherents and critics alike, is that Neo-Vedantic religious pluralism – and pluralistic theologies of religion more generally – must necessarily involve what Race calls a 'debilitating relativism' – or the view that all religions are equally true and equally false.[24] This view is widely taken to have the debilitating implication that holding any perspective which might involve one in apologetic debate with an adherent of another tradition is an unacceptably hegemonic move.

As Kristin Beise Kiblinger points out in her essay in this volume, the valid concern about avoiding hegemonic claims has led many theologians to eschew the project of the theology of religions, favoring instead a direct engagement in comparative theology.

However, as Kiblinger also points out, an at least implicit theology of religions must underlie any effort at interreligious dialogue. And it is possible to develop a theology of religions that is not – or is at least minimally – hegemonic, affirming as a central value that one must honor and respect – while not necessarily

---

22 Vivekananda says famously that, 'I go forth, to preach a religion of which Buddhism is nothing but a rebel child, and Christianity, with all her pretensions, only a distant echo' (Swami Vivekananda, *Complete Works* (Kolkata: Advaita Ashrama, 1989), 1:161). And Gandhi says that, 'What of substance is contained in any other religion is always to be found in Hinduism. And what is not contained in it is insubstantial or unnecessary' (Mohandas K. Gandhi, *Collected Works* (1958–99), 28:194). In the thought of both Vivekananda and Gandhi, while Hinduism, *in practice*, might be as flawed as any other religion, the *ideal* of Hindu Dharma is an absolute, in terms of which all religions can be measured, sometimes being found praiseworthy, and at other times found wanting. This particular quotation of Gandhi, a relatively early one, does not seem to reflect his mature view – a view that comports better with the view outlined in this paper, according to which a Hindu *can* learn something new from another tradition. (Nicholas F. Gier, personal communication.) To try to reconcile this quotation with my position would involve interpreting Gandhi as referring not to the actual practice of Hinduism, but to the ideal of Hindu, or Sanatana, Dharma. I explain this distinction in greater depth in 'Anekanta Vedanta: Toward a Deep Hindu Religious Pluralism', in Griffin, *Deep Religious Pluralism*.

23 Halbfass, *India and Europe*, 416.

24 Race, *Christians and Religious Pluralism*, 78.

agreeing in every way with – the point of view of the other. It is also important to note that engagement with the other is always a *process*. The fact that one does not, at this moment, assent to some particular doctrine held by one's interlocutor does not mean that, in light of further dialogue and reflection, that same doctrine may not later reveal itself to carry profound, and even salvific, truth.[25]

From whence does the impetus come, in Neo-Vedanta, for its pluralistic theology of religions, and beyond that, for its engagement with other religious traditions through comparative theology? I presume most readers are familiar with the many statements of Sri Ramakrishna, Swami Vivekananda, and Mahatma Gandhi on the truth and the salvific efficacy of many religions, and the many beautiful and enduring images that they have utilized to convey this concept: the many words in different languages for one and the same substance – water – or the many streams flowing into the one ocean, or the many paths leading to the summit of the same mountain. To these I have added, in this essay, Vrajaprana's image of the giant jigsaw puzzle. And I am personally fond of the Buddhist and Jain image, also cited by Gandhi, of the blind men and the elephant.[26] (I will show, though, that these last two images put an important pluralistic twist on the more widely known metaphors that emphasize the unity of the ultimate goal.)

If one were simply to stop there, as many do, with the *a priori* affirmation that all religions are ultimately one, then one would end up with the heavily critiqued and widely rejected pluralism which is often attributed to the Neo-Vedanta tradition: a superficial and platitudinous, if goodhearted, sentiment divorced from any actual engagement with the world's religions, in all of their complex, rich, messy variety. Such an approach gives pluralistic theologies a bad name, leading to their widespread rejection by those who see the adherents of this view as lacking in seriousness and depth.

But if Neo-Vedantic religious pluralism is actually *true*, if it discloses something important about the nature of reality, then those who reject it as false end up throwing the proverbial baby out with the bathwater. As I mentioned at the outset of this essay, my conviction that Neo-Vedantic religious pluralism is not only true, but also *important* for the survival of humanity, has been my impetus

---

25 On a personal note, I recently experienced such a revelation with regard to the Christian view, also held by Mahayana Buddhists and within my own tradition of Ramakrishna Vedanta, that an enlightened being – in the Christian case, Christ – can take on the negative karmic effects of others' actions. I found this idea incoherent, seeing karma as a matter of learning life lessons, until I saw that one can create a great deal of negative energy in the universe through one's actions – energy that needs to be processed – and that the fact that one has 'learned one's lesson' does not obviate this fact. An enlightened being, like Christ, can process this negative energy on one's behalf, in order that one may continue one's path of spiritual progress unhindered, so long as one has truly learned the relevant lessons – or, as a Christian would say, as long as one is truly repentant. This is done as a free gift, purely out of compassion, to facilitate the progress of the individual soul on the way to God-realization and liberation. This understanding has caused a pronounced positive shift in my attitude toward Christianity.

26 Mahatma Gandhi, *Young India: 1919–1931* (Vol. VIII, 1926) (Ahmedabad: Navajivan Publishing House, 1981), 30.

for reconstructing and rearticulating it in my work as a Neo-Vedantic theologian. And this work has led – inevitably, I would say – to an extensive engagement with traditions other than my own; in particular, to engagement with Jain and process thought, Christianity, Buddhism, and other forms of Vedanta.

Broadly speaking, one could say that a metaphysical justification for engagement comparative theology arises, in Neo-Vedanta, from the doctrine of the 'two truths' – a concept this tradition inherits from its ancient forebear, the Advaita of Sankara, and before that, from the Madhyamika Buddhist philosophy of Nagarjuna and the Jain mystical thought of the Digambara master, Kundakunda.

At its most basic, the doctrine of the two truths is the idea that there is a relative truth that is expressible in words, gestures, symbols, and concepts, and an absolute truth beyond the relative that is not so expressible, but which can be experienced and which is the foundation upon which relative truth rests and to which it points beyond itself.

Neo-Vedanta is distinguished from traditional forms of Vedanta, such as Advaita, by its attitude toward the text of the *Veda*, the sacred revelation, or primordial wisdom (*veda*) of which Vedanta is the end or ultimate goal (*anta*). Traditional forms of Vedanta, like Advaita, Vishishtadvaita, Dvaita, Bhedabheda, and so on, regard the *Veda* much as the Abrahamic religions traditionally regard their respective scriptures: as absolute and fixed repositories of truth in terms of which other truth claims and the validity of all spiritual experiences are to be evaluated.

According to Neo-Vedanta, however, it is the spiritual experience that is primary. In the state of *samadhi*, or absorption in ultimate reality, one experiences the absolute. It is only in this state that the absolute or ultimate truth is really and fully known.

On this understanding, scriptures are the records of the experiences of enlightened sages. They can act as road maps – as guides – to the truth revealed in the experience of enlightenment. As the words of highly spiritually advanced beings, they are, for most of us mere mortals, *virtually* absolute. But because they are linguistic artifacts that are in need of interpretation, they belong to the realm of relative truth. They are neither infallible nor beyond criticism, and some of their claims, even if appropriate at the time and place of their composition, may no longer be acceptable. On this basis, many Neo-Vedantists, such as Ram Mohan Roy,[27] have taken on the task of reforming Hinduism in practice, advocating for the abolition of caste prejudice, for example, and such abusive patriarchal practices as dowry, child marriage, and the forbidding of widow remarriage.

From a Neo-Vedantic perspective, all of the traditional forms of Vedanta, and

---

27 Roy, a predecessor of both Ramakrishna and Vivekananda, and the founder of the reformist Brahmo Samaj, is widely regarded as the first Neo-Vedantist. Often called the 'father of modern Hinduism', he famously campaigned for the abolition of the fairly rare, but justifiably notorious, practice of *sati*.

indeed all religions, embody genuine insights and paths appropriate to different kinds of spiritual aspirant. This is a form of relativism, but not the kind of debilitating relativism that does not enable one to make distinctions with regard to the relative truth of competing claims. It is not, in other words, identical to the skeptical relativism prevalent in popular western thought, according to which it is impossible to say what may or may not be true because the absolute truth is held to be unknowable. Rather, it is the affirmation that religious doctrines, symbols, and so forth partake of the realm of *relative* truth.

According to Neo-Vedantic thought, the absolute truth can be known – and indeed must be known, in order for *moksha*, or spiritual liberation, to occur – *directly*, being immediately apprehended through the experience of *samadhi*. But whenever this truth is communicated through the medium of language, it is always filtered through the relative realm of words and concepts. So it is possible to make valid distinctions between competing sets of truth claims. For example, a religious tradition that affirms the reality of the process of rebirth is more adequate, at least in this respect, than one which explicitly denies it. But it must also be affirmed that even the *Veda* is only relatively true, being merely the record, in words, of the direct experiences of the absolute truth of the sages who wrote them. If contemplating the *Veda* does not lead to an experience of direct God-realization – of *samadhi* or *brahmanirvana* – it is of no value. In the words of Swami Vivekananda, 'All scriptures, all truths are Vedas in all times, in all countries, and these truths are to be *seen*, and any one may discover them.'[28] Nor, for the one who has achieved such realization, is scripture necessary.[29]

This, again, is a reversal of the attitude of all the traditional systems of Vedanta, and, one could say, of most of the world's religions, towards scripture. Neo-Vedanta sees itself as, in a broad sense, 'scientific', because it tests the words of scripture against the experience of the spiritual aspirant, rather than yielding that experience to the test of the words of scripture.

In practice, this distinction is not as dramatic as it might seem; for it is widely understood that the authors of scripture were far more advanced than the average devotee, who is well advised to heed what the sages say, just as a traditional practitioner would by viewing the scripture as an infallible guide – again, as *virtually* absolute. But in terms of how teaching authority is conceived – as flowing from scripture or from direct experience – Neo-Vedanta represents a paradigm shift in Hindu thought.[30]

---

28 Swami Vivekananda, *Complete Works* (Kolkata: Advaita Ashrama, 1989), 7:9.

29 Though associated with modern, or 'Neo' Vedanta, such an attitude toward the *Veda* is strongly evident in the *Bhagavad Gita*. 'As useful as a water tank in a flood is the *Veda* for one who has insight' (*Bhagavad Gita* 2:46) There is, I think, a stronger continuity between traditional forms of Vedanta and modern Vedanta than some scholars have been willing to credit.

30 Though, again, not one without precedent in pre-modern Hindu thought, and with considerable precedent in Jain and Buddhist thought – which, in this sense, have 'won' the classical debate over the authority of the *Veda*.

If scriptures and spiritual lineages are relative *paths to* the absolute truth, and are not the absolute truth itself, and if the absolute truth is universal, with no particular text or tradition having a privileged access to it, then Swami Vivekananda's claim follows that, 'All scriptures, all truths are Vedas in all times, in all countries.'[31]

According to the Neo-Vedanta of Sri Ramakrishna – of whom Swami Vivekananda was a pre-eminent disciple – this teaching of the relative, and therefore plural, nature of truth as manifested in scriptures and religious traditions is not only a logical deduction from the two truths doctrine, but was embodied in the spiritual path of Sri Ramakrishna. During the middle period of his life – the period of his *sadhana*, or spiritual discipline – Ramakrishna, according to the tradition, experienced *samadhi* by means of a variety of religious paths: Vaishnava, Shaiva, and Shakta or Tantric Hindu practices, meditation on the impersonal absolute in the mode of Advaita Vedanta, devotion to Jesus Christ, and the practice of Islam. Critics have pointed out that these practices occurred within what could broadly be called a Vedantic Hindu rubric. One might therefore doubt whether Ramakrishna *really* attained *samadhi* through the practice of either Christianity or Islam, for example, because one could argue that he never really 'converted' to one or the other of these traditions, rejecting fundamental Hindu assumptions such as the idea of rebirth, but practiced them as a Hindu, from within a Hindu view of reality. But this is actually consistent with the inclusivist nature of Ramakrishna's Neo-Vedanta. In Ramakrishna's 'experiments with truth',[32] he held firm to his piece of the puzzle, while yet respecting and honoring, and even exploring, the others.

But this does raise a question that is not so easily dissolved: namely, what is the relationship between Hinduism, or Vedanta philosophy, and the absolute truth? Are the world's religions equidistant from the absolute truth? Or did Ramakrishna's Hinduism give him some special advantage? Has the two-truths doctrine, in the end, not simply deferred the issue of relativism? For if the absolute truth is, for all intents and purposes, an empty set, conceptually speaking, then this is no different from John Hick's widely critiqued – and Vedanta-inspired – view of ultimate reality as a Kantian *noumenon*, beyond description and categorization. On the other hand, if the absolute truth is simply identical with a Vedantic Hindu worldview, then we have not a true pluralism, but an inclusivism of the hegemonic variety that many pluralistic theologians have rightly rejected: a closed system with nothing, really, to learn from engagement with other traditions.[33]

It is to just such a situation that the theologian in the tradition of Sri Ramakrishna comes, in urgent need of articulating a 'middle path' between

---

31 Vivekananda, 7:9.
32 This phrase is associated with Gandhi, but is, I think, a fair characterization of Ramakrishna's even more radical approach to truth.
33 As the earlier Gandhi quotation about all substantial truth being located in Hinduism suggests.

the debilitating relativism to which one reading of this tradition lends itself, and the absolutist, Hindu supremacist view to which another reading points. (And the many and varied statements made by the adherents of this tradition – Sri Ramakrishna, Vivekananda, Gandhi, Radhakrishnan, and others – can point in both directions at different times and in different contexts.)

It is here that Vrajaprana's image of the giant jigsaw puzzle becomes instructive. The absolutist or inclusivist 'pole', one could say, of Neo-Vedanta rests with the specific beliefs and practices that define this tradition and invest it with identity: the doctrines of karma, rebirth, and liberation; the idea of the four yogas, or forms of spiritual discipline, as articulated by Swami Vivekananda; the institution of guru and disciple; the practices of meditation and *puja*, and so forth. This is the piece of the puzzle to which we 'hold firm' while respecting the others and honoring them. It is not identical, though, to the big picture: the puzzle in its entirety, which, on this analogy, would be the absolute truth. We know, in other words, as Neo-Vedantists, that certain doctrines are true and that certain practices are efficacious. But we also know that there are pieces we do not possess.

The relativist or comparative 'pole' of Neo-Vedanta, then, would consist of our being open to the teachings and practices of others: teachings and practices which might enrich and deepen our knowledge and experience of the larger truth of which our path is only one part.

In the writings of Vivekananda and Gandhi, this understanding is suggested by a distinction that both make between Hindu Dharma as a lived practice, and a kind of ideal, eternal dharma, *Sanatana Dharma*, beyond all religions. Gandhi speaks, for example, of the 'Religion beyond religions'. 'The one Religion is beyond all speech. It is not less real because it is unseen. This religion transcends Hinduism, Islam, Christianity, etc. It harmonizes them and gives them reality.'[34] And Vivekananda holds as his ideal not that all people would become Hindu, but that they would learn from one another and together evolve toward a higher understanding. 'The Christian is not to become a Hindu or a Buddhist, nor a Hindu or a Buddhist to become a Christian. But each must assimilate the spirit of the others and yet preserve his individuality and grow according to his own law of growth.'[35] This, one could say, is holding firm to one's own piece of the puzzle, while at the same time incorporating as much of the big picture as possible into one's own view by being open to the others and seeing how they might fit into it. And it avoids becoming hegemonic by acknowledging that others are doing the same thing, from their particular perspectives, and that this is as valid for them as one's own project is. One author, in critiquing my work, has called this approach a 'Hindu Pan-Inclusivism' – that is, a form of inclusivism that acknowledges and accepts that everyone else is also an inclusivist; yet he does not

---

34 Gandhi, cited in Glyn Richards (ed.), *Source-Book of Modern Hinduism* (Richmond, England: Curzon Press, 1985), 156.
35 Richards, *Source-Book of Modern Hinduism*, 89.

see this as a problem, but rather an inevitability of being in the realm of relative truth.[36]

Another famous Indic image for this concept of pluralism, and to which I alluded earlier, is the parable of the blind men and the elephant, according to which a group of blind men, when asked to describe an elephant, proceed to feel its various parts – the legs, the trunk, the tail, the tusks, and so forth – and then fight amongst themselves over what an elephant is like: a tree-trunk, a snake, a broom, a spear, and so on.[37]

This image is particularly appropriate because, rather like the puzzle image, it is able to convey both the 'absolutist' and 'relativist' poles of the Neo-Vedantic position. It is absolutist in the sense that there really is an elephant *there*, with particular attributes that are ordered in a particular way. It is an objective reality. But it is relativist inasmuch as the various perceptions of the blind men, though capturing these attributes in specific ways appropriate to the perceivers' modes of perception, are each incomplete, and none is, in isolation, adequate for describing the whole elephant. It would only be through a calm and careful sharing one another's perceptions, and a concerted attempt to co-ordinate these – on the assumption that each captured a *piece* of the truth, rather than simply being mistaken – that the contours of the whole elephant would begin to emerge for each of the participants in the conversation. This, I would argue, is the task of comparative theology, from a Neo-Vedantic perspective: the sharing and attempted co-ordination of our various pieces of the puzzle – or perceptions of the elephant, depending on which of these two metaphors one prefers – in order to expand and deepen our own understanding. As an activity that occurs in the realm of relative truth – the realm of discourse – theology of this kind involves acquiring and engaging with specific knowledge of the other pieces of the puzzle – the other religions. It does not presume that one has already reached the realm of absolute truth – that one is an enlightened being – but only that one has a *piece* of the truth in the form of the particular spiritual tradition that one inhabits.

I call this, in the title of this essay, a *tentative* putting together of the pieces of the puzzle on the understanding that it is a process without a foreordained end. Who knows what new perceptions of reality, and consequent transformations of one's existing point of view, will result from embarking upon such an enterprise? In the realm of relative truth, our conclusions must be, on the whole, provisional. I say 'on the whole' because even to affirm provisionality in an absolute way is a form of absolutism inappropriate to the realm of relative truth. One's moral revulsion at cruelty, for example, seems like a good candidate for a sentiment that one would hesitate to 'adjust', no matter what additional truth one

---

36 Matt Lopresti, 'Sanatana Dharma as a Whiteheadian Religious Pluralism?', in *The Journal of Process Studies* (36:1, August 2007).
37 The first extant textual reference to this story attributes it to the Buddha, and is found in the Theravada Buddhist canon (*Udana* 6.4:66–9). It has also been widely used in the Jain tradition, though, as well as by Mahatma Gandhi.

came to realize. And the love of truth itself, as well as the longing for spiritual liberation (*mumukshutva*), seems to be a necessary condition for the pursuit of the project. It may also be the case that particular doctrines simply express quite well certain relative truths about the universe where others fall short, and so need to be kept. (Hindu claims about the age of the universe, relative to literalist biblical claims about it, come to mind.)

The model for both comparative theology and interreligious dialogue that I am suggesting, on the basis of Neo-Vedanta and its claims about a relative and an absolute truth, is one in which each of us begins with a piece of the puzzle – a piece of the truth to which we must hold fast so long as we remain persuaded of its truth and efficacy. But this *satyagraha*, or 'holding fast to truth', to borrow a term from Gandhi, involves a complementary realization that our piece of the truth, while being true, is also only one piece of the larger puzzle. In order to advance in our understanding of that larger truth, a twofold process is involved – engaging in dialogue with the other, with an openness to any new insights that may 'fit' with our piece of the puzzle, that may be consistent with it and complementary to it, while at the same time engaging with our own piece of the truth in ever greater depth. Again, as Vrajaprana says, 'We can deepen our own spirituality and learn about our own tradition by studying other faiths. Just as importantly, by studying our own tradition well, we are better able to appreciate the truth in other traditions.'[38]

Conclusion

In relating religion to philosophy, Whitehead writes that:

> Religion should connect the rational generality of philosophy with the emotions and purposes springing out of existence in a particular society, in a particular epoch, and conditioned by particular antecedents. Religion is the translation of general ideas into particular thoughts, particular emotions, and particular purposes; it is directed to the end of stretching individual interest beyond its self-defeating particularity.[39]

Perhaps it could be said that theology represents the next phase in this process. If philosophy, like science (which is, after all, a type of philosophy), is concerned primarily with general truths – principles widely, if not universally, applicable – and religion with the translation of these truths into particular symbols, narratives, practices, and so forth, then perhaps theology, with its attentiveness to the unique particulars of specific communities of belief and practice, is the drawing out of those general truths in a new way, with new insight that is made possible only by their prior translation into the particular in the form of religion.

---

38 Vrajaprana, 56–7.
39 Whitehead, *Process and Reality*, 15.

Comparative theology, then, could be seen as taking this process to yet another level, by drawing general truths not only from the particulars of a specific tradition, in a new and unique way not otherwise possible, but by drawing these general truths from the interaction of two or more such traditions – again, in ways not possible through philosophy alone, nor even through theological reflection occurring within one tradition in isolation. The applicability of the relational ontology at the basis of process thought to the analysis of the relative truth of religious claims might not be possible without the comparison and engagement of process thought with the Jain doctrines of relativity. And the implications for Jainism of the compatibility of its doctrines of relativity with process thought open up new avenues of inquiry for Jain thinkers. Might Jainism, for example, which traditionally affirms a non-theistic worldview, be compatible with a process version of theism, free of the logical defects to which Jain thinkers have historically objected? Might this open up a space for Jain practices and views now regarded as heterodox?[40]

The task of the comparative theologian is to engage responsibly, with the fullest self-awareness and self-disclosure possible, with the particulars of her own tradition and the traditions of others in a way that draws out general truths potentially applicable to all traditions, and to all persons. This work will occur pre-eminently in the service of the theologian's tradition, which is natural. But it is ultimately undertaken in the service of all of humanity.

The hope underlying my development of a Neo-Vedantic theology of religions – a development that has involved comparative theological engagements with process and Jain thought, with the occasional nod towards Buddhism, and has arisen out of my early reflections on Hinduism and Christianity – is that this highly particular, and in some ways idiosyncratic, approach might resonate with the views and the experiences of others, who might thereby be inspired to develop their own pluralistic theologies, based on their own traditions and interactions with others. As John Cobb writes:

> Global theology in a pluralistic age need not cut its ties to the particularities of religious traditions . . . [T]here is no global strategy for developing global theology in a pluralistic age. The strategy [itself] is pluralistic. It will be quite different for Muslims, for Hindus, for Sikhs, for Jains, for Buddhists, for Jews, and for Christians.[41]

---

40 Many Jain laypersons in the modern period, for example, interact increasingly in Hindu ritual contexts that are avowedly theistic, and also increasingly interpret the Jinas – traditionally seen not as deities but as enlightened human beings – in theistic ways. Might such tendencies, traditionally seen as heterodox, be justified, on Jain grounds, if the Jain doctrines of relativity are seen as being rooted in a relational ontology that implies Whitehead's modified theism? I explore this idea in a tentative way in both *A Vision for Hinduism* and in *Jainism: An Introduction*.

41 Cobb, 'Metaphysical Pluralism', 56.

We all start on our pilgrimage toward pluralism and interreligious dialogue, if we do so at all, from our own unique starting points. Just like religions, there can potentially be as many theologies of religious pluralism as there are people. Yet, as we each hold firm to our particular 'piece of the puzzle', we move, through comparative theology and through engagement with the worldviews of others, towards a more universal view. This is an ongoing process of engagement and mutual enrichment, moving asymptotically toward the absolute truth. The impetus for engaging in this process varies with each tradition and situation. For the Neo-Vedantist, this impetus arises from a need to articulate the pluralistic insight at the heart of Ramakrishna's tradition in a way that moves beyond platitudes, toward substantive engagement with others and a deepening of insight and appreciation for the pieces of the puzzle – the pieces of *truth* – at the heart of all traditions.

9

Solidarity through Polyphony

JOHN N. SHEVELAND

In this chapter I propose the musical aural experience of 'polyphony' as an inter-disciplinary model by which to envision the reconciling work of comparative theology. A theological appropriation of musical polyphony as I understand it can reorient the theological task as conceived in the theologian's imagination away from judgement of others – typified in many theologies of religions however well intentioned – to an appreciation of them, away from comparison predicated on latent competition to comparison predicated on aesthetic appreci-ation and moral identification.[1] In short, polyphony prizes theological aesthetics over antagonism, and concrete human persons over abstract or reified religious ideas.

This chapter offers three proposals concerning a theological appropriation of musical polyphony, and then offers a concrete example of it involving the voices of Paul the Apostle, the Buddhist teacher Santideva, and the Hindu teacher Vedanta Desika. The intended outcome of both the methodological proposal and the theological comparison I present, is solidarity, first as an intel-lectual virtue[2] conditioning theological thinking and speech, and second as a

---

1 Peter Phan's clarification is instructive. Theologies of religions like Inclusivism and Pluralism are best understood not as ill-fated attempts at interreligious dialogue upon which a moratorium should be imposed, but as examples of a more preliminary *intra*-religious dialogue in which the Christian community discerns the scope and limits of Christian doctrine in light of religious pluralism. Phan's observation is useful for two reasons. It preserves a limited appropriateness of theologies of religions by clarifying their function as doctrinal discourses internal to the Christian community not meant for use in interreligious encounter. It also preserves the basic critique registered against these theolo-gies by Comparative theologians like Clooney and Fredericks who rightly worry about the ineluctable inhospitality of abstract, *a priori* conceptualizations of the other, however well intended. Cf. Peter Phan, 'Praying to the Buddha: Living amid Religious Pluralism', in *Commonweal* (26 January 2007), 14.
2 'By *intellectual solidarity* I mean a willingness to take other persons seriously enough to engage them in conversation and debate about what makes life worth living, including what will make for the good of our deeply interdependent public life. . . . [intellectual solidarity] differs radically from

moral virtue[3] capable of healing our fractured experience and ideological tendencies.

Musical Polyphony: Impressions on the Theological Imagination

Proposal #1: Polyphony preserves distinction-in-unity

The musical genre of polyphony – also called counterpoint – flourished in the Renaissance and Baroque periods in the Latin west and grew out of the more simplistic Gregorian Chant, specifically, the style of harmonized chant called *Organum*, the sung prayer of Christian monks. A composer in this genre brings together multiple voices sounding their own individual melody lines.[4] It is important to note that each voice, rather than being a mere harmonic part in relationship to a dominant melody, represents a distinct melody with its own integrity and musical logic that could feasibly refrain from interaction with other melodies. But in this genre, three, four, five and rarely even six melody lines are combined deliberately to produce an emergent structure of greater depth than any single melody line could produce on its own.[5] John Rain remarks that '[i]t is hard to write a beautiful song. It is even harder to write several individually beautiful songs that, when sung simultaneously, sound as a more beautiful polyphonic whole.'[6]

Here, Rain suggests that the difficult compositional task of combining multiple melodies, beautiful individually in their own right, can give rise to more beauty than could be perceived in temporally isolated soundings of those melodies. Multiple melody lines superimposed on each other collaborate to

---

pure tolerance by seeking positive engagement with the other through both listening and speaking.' David Hollenbach, 'Is Tolerance Enough? The Catholic University and the Common Good', in *Conversations* (Spring 1998), 13.

3 'The fact that men and women in various parts of the world feel personally affected by the injustices and violations of human rights committed in distant countries, countries which perhaps they will never visit, is a further sign of a reality transformed into awareness, thus acquiring a moral connotation. It is above all a question of interdependence, sensed as a system determining relationships in the contemporary world, in its economic, cultural, political and religious elements, and accepted as a moral category. When interdependence becomes recognized in this way, the correlative response as a moral and social attitude, as a "virtue", is solidarity. This then is not a feeling of vague compassion or shallow distress at the misfortunes of so many people, both near and far. On the contrary, it is a firm and persevering determination to commit oneself to the common good; that is to say to the good of all and of each individual, because we are all really responsible for all.' John Paul II, *Sollicitudino rei socialis*, 38: http://www.vatican.va/holy_father/john_paul_ii/encyclicals/documents/hf_jp-ii_enc_30121987_sollicitudo-rei-socialis_en.html. Last accessed 9 August 2009.

4 Leading composers included Jacob Obrecht (*d.* 1505), Josquin des Prez (*d.* 1521), Giovanni Pierluigi da Palestrina (*d.* 1594), and William Byrd (*d.* 1623), and later, Johann Sebastian Bach (*d.* 1750).

5 Aaron Copland, *What to Listen for in Music* (New York: Penguin Classics, 2002), 86.

6 John Rain, *Music Inside and Out: Going Too Far in Musical Essays* (Singapore: G+B Arts International, 2001) 177.

create a polyphonic whole more beautiful than the sum of its parts. Rain continues with a remark very much at home in a comparative theological framework:

> The internal structures that create each of the voices, separately must
> contribute to the emergent structure of the polyphony, which in turn must
> reinforce and comment on the structures of the individual voices. The way
> that is accomplished in detail is . . . 'counterpoint'.[7]

Not only do individual voices, when combined, give rise to a more beautiful
emergent structure; that emergent structure also bends back, reflexively, as a
movement that now sheds further light on the individual voices comprising it.
An individual voice changes *while it sounds* as a consequence of the movement's
other voices.[8] As Zuckerkandl explains, 'the musical meaning of a tune is
affected and may be changed by the other tonal motions that go on at the same
time'.[9] The emergent structure or polyphonic chord offers the hearer a new
vantage point, a new aural context or set of resources with which to appreciate
individual voices. That new vantage point affords unexpected insight into the
previously isolated voices. Rather than assaulting the ear with dissonance,
polyphony reveals the character and depth of individual voices in a way only it
can, as consonance.[10] Parallel motifs, tensions, and disagreements among the
voices are sharpened in the chord. A previously unobserved quality in a given
melody line breaks through more clearly on account of a separate melody line
contrapuntally drawing out its quality by way of contrasting with it. Contrast
functions as a pedagogical tool training the ear to appreciate both the emergent
structure and the irreducible particularity of the voices constituting that structure. Indeed, contrast and even tension between voices represents the condition
for the possibility of consonance. To articulate the point in negative terms, one
hears a comparatively impoverished version of a given voice when it remains
isolated within its own logic.

Transposing all of this to a comparative theological discussion involves recognizing that an audience understands an individual religious speaker with greater
nuance and sophistication when her speech is heard communally in a shared
context with other speech. Polyphony resists the temptation to caricature other
voices or pass over their real differences; it thrives on texture and difference as

---

7 Rain, *Music Inside and Out*, 177.
8 Victor Zuckerkandl, *The Sense of Music* (Princeton: Princeton University Press, 1959), 149.
9 Zuckerkandl, *The Sense of Music*, 150.
10 'The theologically minded musicians of the Middle Ages saw in the two states of consonant and
dissonant sound the tonal counterpart of Good and Evil: That Which Should Be, and That Which
Should Not Be. One thing the two pairs certainly have in common: the distinction as such of consonance and dissonance has been questioned as little as the distinction of good and evil; but as to the
specific question as to what sounds should be called consonant, what dissonant, the opinion of the
ages differ just as much as they do about specific moral questions.' Zuckerkandl, *The Sense of Music*,
152.

the condition of its possibility. So too, comparative theology acknowledges difference as a *sine qua non* for engaging the other with hospitality and integrity.[11] The dynamics of counterpoint within polyphony assist us with the moral imperative of taking our companions in dialogue seriously precisely in their difference, but not isolation, from us. This aural image represents a nuanced and effective way to understand the dynamics of similarity and difference in analogical relationships.

These two features of polyphony – recognition of difference and attention to an emergent structure of intelligibility – are the same features prized by comparative theologians. On the one hand, comparative theologians wish to underscore the real differences, contrasts, and tensions between voices in order to resist domestication, caricature, and hegemony. On the other hand, they are keenly interested in the possible emergence of a unitive framework of intelligibility making comparison both possible and profitable. Polyphony encourages the comparativist to pursue both tasks, with the additional benefit of underscoring the aesthetic qualities imbedded in the emergent structure of intelligibility which impact the listener and drive her to continue and repeat the exposure. This task is demanding both in music and in the theological application. As Aaron Copland indicates,

> Music that is polyphonically written makes greater demands on the attention of the listener, because it moves by reason of separate and independent melodic strands, which together form harmonies . . . Polyphonic texture implies a listener who can hear separate strands of melody sung by separate voices, instead of hearing only the sound of all voices as they happen from moment to moment, vertical fashion [*sic*].[12]

Reading texts comparatively or engaging in concrete dialogues with persons requires this same degree of sophisticated discernment, which hears not simply the overall sound of the voices in play but patiently discerns their rich and independent individuality within the movement. The aesthetic experience depends on this 'greater intellectual participation', a patient and discerning listening.[13]

Proposal #2: Polyphony amplifies the aesthetic dimension of theological comparison

The transportation of polyphony into comparative theological method contributes a new, aesthetic understanding of interreligious dialogue and learning. That new understanding is grounded in the latent potential of the texts and

---

11 For more on the application of hospitality to the encounter with religious 'strangers', see Martin Marty, *When Faiths Collide* (Oxford: Blackwell, 2004), 124–48.
12 Copland, *What to Listen for in Music*, 84–85.
13 Copland, *What to Listen for in Music*, 89. Cf. 132.

traditions to induce in the comparativist an affective appreciation of the new vocal tone and its effects on the new communal tone. Not only are the texts, voices, and traditions viewed in terms of beauty, but the sound they create in the new listener is likewise apprehended as beautiful. The overworked speculations concerning the status of another religion's truth claims *vis-à-vis* those of one's own become less urgent in this model and replaced by a readiness to be edified by the tonality of the dialogue and the learning it produces. Such tonality includes a principle of non-competition since musical polyphony depends on multiple melody lines combined in a non-competitive fashion for its own production of beauty. No one voice occupies the melody line to the exclusion or expense of other voices. To be sure, at various points in a score of music certain voices become more prominent than others. But no single voice in polyphony is continually dominant or even continually present; dynamics of augmentation, diminution, and rest apply to all voices.[14] Each voice represents a melody that cannot be reduced to a mere harmonic relationship to a dominant melody. Individual movements within the score might bring some voices to the fore and others to the background, but when viewed from the entire score of music, no one voice holds precedence over the other. Precedence and subsequence are replaced by musical dynamics such as augmentation and diminution, which focus the audience on contextual dynamics of interaction, on the (re)discovery of one's own familiar voice as a member of the community of voices, and on the emergent beauty of the whole.

The analogy with comparative theology is clear, as are the implications for hegemony resistance. Transportation of this motif into comparative theology suggests that no one speaker should be self-preoccupied in ways which exclude other voices or construe some voices in terms of fixed positions of precedence and subsequence relative to other voices. Rival truth claims may be of interest in the distant future, but only after the laborious work of comparison, i.e., repeated listening and reading, takes place. While the theologian learns from colleagues and texts in other traditions, she does well to consider the affective or aesthetic component of the sound produced in community and heard in an even wider community. This common sound (to use an aural image) or this public square (to use a spatial image) functions in the first instance as the condition for the possibility of comparison. She does well to let her ear become trained, sensitive to, and accountable to the larger whole of which her voice is a part. The dialogue of which she is a part is not a dialogue over which she exercises control but one of unpredictable development, of reciprocal illumination, and perhaps surprising edification. This dialogue can, just like polyphony, be marked by a great complexity of voices educating the careful listener, and it can also be marked by great tension begging for resolution. She will perceive this tension and valorize its place in the theological community as voices contributing to a complex score of

---

14 Copland, *What to Listen for in Music*, 134.

music, each of which speak to – in isolation and in community – the irreducible mystery grasping and shaping them. The polyphony model can shift the theologian's attention somewhat away from theological learning as information gathering and transfer, toward theological learning as the development and attunement of aesthetic appreciation.

Her task will be to arrange or intellectually organize polyphony from the voices present. She, as a composer-theologian, will be responsible for deducing moments of consonance as well as dissonance, in each case explaining how this is so and what the dynamics between voices reveal about them. If the analogy with music holds even further, the theologian will perceive that in the very fact that voices can sound dissonant anticipates their possible resolution into consonance. Not a theology of religions as such, this anticipation preconditions hearing without structuring it.

Proposal #3: Polyphony contributes a new metaphor by which to imagine the corporate membership of all (individual melodies) in a global community (a polyphonic score of music) of theological reflection

This third proposal suggests that theological speakers are bound together in a common enterprise or symphony *because of* their diversity, which has now become not a problem to be solved or overcome but a richness to be pondered and preserved. Theological investigation now can be seen as the aesthetic and possibly edifying endeavor it is, as an endeavor in which all voices actively contribute to the beauty of the whole. My neighbor contributes to my own self-understanding and helps me to locate myself in solidarity with the global community of theological reflection. Our differences and distinctions no longer relegate us to a competitive zero-sum game but instead find shelter together under a larger rubric of unity, though not identification.

This change in the perception of religious difference is immense. If this sort of corporate endeavor seizes the theological imagination, the prospects for inter-religious learning and conflict resolution are encouraging. The change in perception would spell humility in the best sense of the word: an awareness of our individual limits and gifts coupled with a willingness to learn from others who have now become resources ignored at our own peril, voices whose diminishment signals a lost opportunity to deepen wisdom and understanding. In short, the polyphony model renders 'enclave theology' a peculiar contradiction in a world that is better described as an interactive commons wherein no voice sounds or is heard alone.[15]

---

15 'By enclave theology I mean a theology based narrowly in a single tradition that seeks not to learn from other traditions and enrich them, but instead to topple and defeat them . . . Whether openly or secretly it is not really interested in dialogue but in rectitude and hegemony . . . It is in danger of what Paul rejected as "party spirit" or "works of the flesh", namely, enmity, strife, and factionalism (Galatians 5.20).' George Hunsinger, *The Eucharist and Ecumenism: Let us Keep the Feast* (Cambridge: Cambridge University Press, 2008), 1.

A principal virtue and vocation from Catholic Social Teaching, which may help to describe this interdependence, is solidarity. It represents a thick species of empathy and action predicated on the experience of interdependence that characterizes modern persons in the world today. While solidarity (and its inter-religious cognates or approximate values) is a virtue which all persons can under-stand and enact, the depth of its meaning in the Christian community is to be found in qualities of Christian faith and life which regard one's neighbor 'as the living image of God the Father, redeemed by Jesus Christ, and placed under the action of the Holy Spirit'.[16] To date, the elaboration of solidarity in Catholic Social Teaching, especially by John Paul II, has privileged the political and economic interdependence of human persons and societies, linking it to social, economic, and political justice. Yet the principle of solidarity can also obtain meaningfully in the arena of interreligious dialogue. Such solidarity must be retrieved in today's troubled religious and global climate.[17]

The polyphony model cultivates a shared sense of solidarity in the context of interreligious encounters, illuminating perhaps another dimension of social justice. The term 'solidarity' is used here tentatively as a formal term or place-holder for what will be given specific content by the three theologians; it is used as what Robert Neville and Wesley Wildman have called a 'deliberately vague category' to allow comparison to commence.[18] We now turn to three discrete textures of that vague category.

Theological Polyphony: Soundings of Solidarity

The vocal contributions of St Paul, Santideva, and Sri Vedanta Desika are but brief excerpts from these authors focusing on their analogous concepts of a common body to which all belong in solidarity. The following interpretation merely suggests the appropriateness of the polyphony model without exhaus-tively demonstrating it. Others might tease out additional nuance or contribute separate examples of theological polyphony.

---

16 Charles E. Curran, Kenneth R. Himes and Thomas A. Shannon, '*Sollicitudo rei socialis* (*On Social Concern*)', in Kenneth R. Himes (ed.), *Modern Catholic Social Teaching* (Washington, DC: George-town University Press, 2005), 429.

17 John Paul II, Sollicitudino rei socialis, no. 38. Cf. Charles E. Curran, et al., '*Sollicitudo rei socialis* (On Social Concern)', *op. cit.*, 427; and James L. Fredericks, *Buddhists and Christians: Through Com-parative Theology to Solidarity* (Maryknoll, NY: Orbis Books, 2004), 112–15.

18 'Vagueness in a category allows all the potential specifications to be brought under one head with the proviso that specific relations among them remain to be determined.' Robert Cummings Neville and Wesley J. Wildman, 'On Comparing Religious Ideas', in Robert Cummings (ed.), *Ultimate Realities* (Albany: SUNY, 2001), 198.

St Paul

In his letters, Paul privileges a theological motif of participation relevant to moral solidarity and ideology critique. Of the many passages we might consult to learn of the mystical incorporation of Christians into the body of Christ, one can start simply with Galatians 3:28, a signature text of Paul's, which reads, 'There is no longer Jew or Greek, there is no longer slave or free, there is no longer male or female, for all of you are one in Christ Jesus' (NRSV). This passage and others like it (1 Corinthians 10:14–17, 27–31; 1 Corinthians 12:12–26) have lengthy traditions of commentary about which much can and should be said. While it is difficult to make sweeping or uncontextualized statements about the Pauline corpus on this matter since his writings were more occasional than systematic, two interpretive comments are appropriate.

First, his declaration that 'all of you are one in Christ Jesus' should be noted for its use of the preposition 'in'. Paul is known for having invested prepositional phrases with considerable theological meaning. Prepositions like 'through', 'into', 'with', and 'in' all denote a theology of participation in which persons are incorporated into Christ, forming one body, united in that body even while comprising distinct members of it. As Joseph Fitzmyer notes, with the prepositional phrase 'into Christ' (*eis Christon*) Paul holds that one is:

> Torn from one's original condition ('in Adam', 1 Corinthians 15:22), from one's natural inclination ('in the flesh', Romans 7:5), and from one's ethnic background ('under the law', 1 Corinthians 9:20), one is solemnly introduced 'into Christ' in faith and baptism. *Eis Christon* denotes, then, the movement of incorporation.[19]

Fitzmyer also notes that the prepositional phrase 'in Christ', used some 165 times in the Pauline corpus, intends a mystical genitive of possession, suggesting that one literally is Christ's, or belongs to Christ, or is of Christ, on account of membership in his body.[20] This membership amounts to a new creation. The genitive of possession implies Christ's mystical influence over the one incorporated into his body, a domain of power in which the effects of Christ take hold in persons. That domain is at once objective in that it is caused by the work of Christ for all and has become a cosmic reality, and subjective in that it is apprehended in the response of

---

19 Joseph Fitzmyer, 'Pauline Theology', in Raymond E. Brown, Joseph A. Fitzmyer et al. (eds), *The New Jerome Biblical Commentary* (Upper Saddle River: Prentice Hall, 1990), 1409. Fitzmyer's verb in this paragraph – 'torn from . . . ethnic background' – along with Paul's statement that there is 'neither Jew or Greek', might be heard as subversion if not elimination of Jewish identity. It should be noted that the selection below from 1 Corinthians 12 valorizes difference as a necessary feature of a body, which cannot be merely one organ. Paul's motif eliminates any antagonisms wrought *on the basis of* distinctive identities, but not the identities themselves.
20 Fitzmyer, *The New Jerome Biblical Commentary*, 1409; Patrick T. McCormick, *A Banqueter's Guide to the All-Night Soup Kitchen of the Kingdom of God* (Collegeville: Liturgical Press, 2004), 73–5.

faith/trust (*pistis*) and baptism.[21] The turbulence of Paul's own ecclesial context helps to underscore his theological intentions with this language, enmeshed as he was in young and fractured Christian communities. He claims that Christ is one even while incorporating great diversity within the body, and that such unity in Christ grounds members' unity with each other (e.g. Romans 12:5). The body of Christ (*soma Christou*) remains a unity which not only invites but reconciles difference, distinctness, and otherness.[22] The community comprising this body, moreover, should be marked by a justice which brings the alienated back into the community, honors them, and enacts solidarity with them precisely because 'if one member of the body suffers, all suffer together; if one member is honored, all rejoice together' (1 Corinthians 12:26). Several verses from chapter 12 speak well:

> For just as the body is one and has many members, and all members of the body, though many, are one body, so it is with Christ. For by one Spirit we were all baptized into one body – Jews or Greeks, slaves or free – and all were made to drink of one Spirit. For the body does not consist of one member but of many. If the foot should say, 'Because I am not a hand, I do not belong to the body', that would not make it any less part of the body. And if the ear should say, 'Because I am not an eye, I do not belong to the body', that would not make it any less part of the body. If the whole body were an eye, where would be the hearing? If the whole body were an ear, where would be the sense of smell? But as it is, God arranged the organs in the body, each one of them, as he chose. If all were a single organ, where would the body be? As it is, there are many parts, yet one body. The eye cannot say to the hand, 'I have no need of you.' On the contrary, the parts of the body which seem to be weaker are indispensable, and those parts of the body which we think less honorable we invest with the greater honor, and our unpresentable parts are treated with greater modesty, which our more presentable parts do not require. But God has so adjusted the body, giving the greater honor to the inferior part, that there may be no discord in the body, but that all members may have the same care for one another. (1 Corinthians 12:12–25)[23]

---

21 For analyses of the tension between objective and subjective redemption in Paul's theology, which is never systematized or resolved by Paul, see Leander Keck, *Paul and His Letters*, 2nd edn (Philadelphia: Fortress, 1988), 55; Luke Timothy Johnson, 'Romans 3.21–26 and the Faith of Jesus', in *Catholic Biblical Quarterly* (44, 1982), 77–90; John N. Sheveland, 'The Gita's Equal Eye: Resourcing a Christian Concept of Neighbor without Limit', in *Louvain Studies* (32, 2007), 408–21.

22 Victor Paul Furnish, *The Moral Teaching of Paul: Selected Issues* (Nashville: Abingdon Press, 1979), 93.

23 Consider a parallel Islamic use of the Body metaphor from the *Hadith* or Sayings of the Prophet Muhammad which could become a fourth voice in this polyphonic experiment: 'Numan said, the Messenger of Allah (peace and blessings be upon him) said: Thou wilt see the faithful in their having mercy for one another and in their love for one another and in their kindness towards one another like the body; when one member of it ails, the entire body (ails), one part calling out the other with sleeplessness and fever.' Maulana Muhammad Ali, *A Manual of Hadith* (Lahore: The Ahmadiyya Anjuman Ishaat Islam, 1990), 379.

Paul's experience of the mystical body of Christ offers prophetic witness to our contemporary experience of division, antagonism, and violence between and within our religious traditions by incorporating and reconciling distinct members within the one body, 'that all members may have the same care for one another'. The egalitarian – or simply Christological – character of these passages urges one to see all persons as members of one's own body, to act in ways that confirm this objective reality, and to be cognizant that degradation of one part of the body – including the parts conventionally least valued – throws the entire body into a solidarity of degradation and suffering.[24]

Second, despite the objective truth of solidarity that Paul's theological claim signifies, common human experience tells us that the body of Christ is a broken body wherever some-bodies are treated as no-bodies, as ones who either fail to count or count less according to the in-group's aberrant determinations of worth.[25] Against such distortions stands an objective reality, namely, that all bodies are some-bodies because all bodies, by virtue of the gracious work of God in Christ, are members of this redeemed, justified body, because of which they are also members of each other. Membership in the body of Christ and solidarity with one another obtains independent of the extent to which one's own or group's narrative supports it. Narratives that compete with that objective reality amount to views and opinions held fast under the sign of sin and self-contradiction. They are clung to as objective and true when in reality they are not merely subjective, but false and sinful in a subjectivity habitually dissociated from the objective truth determined by God in Christ. For Paul, the objective reality of God's redeeming, justifying, and transforming work in Christ exists alongside of and within a world in which sin remains pervasive, unannounced, and threatening to the human person and her interpersonal encounters. Yet the victory of the cross, which concretizes God's redeeming activity on behalf of humanity, means that the narratives of grace and sin are not pitted against each other as equals in a Manichean struggle groping for an elusive resolution. Those narratives instead mean that within the human community which is both redeemed and sinful (*simul justus et peccator*), our subjective self-understandings can either affirm or flout the object reality circumscribing them. In other words, the objective reality of the gracious work of God in Christ transferring a sinful humanity from membership in Adam's family into the body of Christ constitutes the higher narrative which envelops, conditions, and relativizes the lower narrative.

---

24 For a comparison of the corporate membership of all in the body of Christ with the unity of reality suggested in the Zen notion of *Satori*, see Ruben L. F. Habito, *Living Zen, Loving God* (Boston: Wisdom, 2004), 98–9.
25 McCormick, *A Banqueter's Guide*, 80.

Vedanta Desika (Venkatanatha) with Paul

Add to Paul's voice that of a South Indian *acharya* (teacher) and famous exponent of the Qualified Non-dualist position known as Vishishtadvaita, Vedanta Desika (thirteenth century, South India) who in his large systematic text *Srimad Rahasy-atrayasara* proposes an ontology of participation that is at once ontological, linguistic, and moral.

With respect to ontology, Desika's understanding of God as 'Narayana' ('ayana' means resting place, abode, or refuge of 'naras' or living beings) involves a view of the divine as both radically immanent in creation and not exhausted by it.[26] By immanent (*antarvyapti*) Desika means 'being . . . inseparably connected with other things and beings in such a way that it cannot be said He is not present where they are', whereas, '[t]ranscendent (*bahirvyapti*) means being present also in places where they are not present'.[27] By virtue of the divine nature (*svarupa*) and will (*sankalpa*), the Lord indwells all conscious and unconscious things as their inner controller. The anthropological corollary of the Lord indwelling conscious and unconscious beings is that they exist as the Lord's inseparable modes or attributes (*prakaras*):

> [Isvara] is called the inner self or soul (*Saririi*), because as long as they exist, He is, in regard to sentient and non-sentient substances (*dravya*), their support (*adhara*), their controller, or ruler (*niyanta*) and their Lord or Master (*Seshi*) for whose purpose they exist. Sentient beings and non-sentient things form His body, since, with regard to Him, they stand as substances supported by Him, controlled by Him, and existing solely for the fulfillment of His purposes, throughout their existence.[28]

This ontological conceptualization represents, in our polyphonic experiment, an 'augmentation' on Paul's body motif in that Desika's is ontological and therefore conceptually prior to Paul's, whose conceptualization denotes reconciliation and eschatology. That is, Desika's voice is consonant with Paul's in that both speak to a common body but under different conceptual categories. In this sense the contrast draws out more clearly both the similarity and difference between them.

Desika's ontological conceptualization also gives rise to the linguistic claim of 'co-ordinate predication', which states that because living beings are understood as modes (*prakaras*) of the divine body, speech about the Lord and his essential nature necessarily entails speech about the attributes or *naras* which participate in Narayana, and vice versa. Co-ordinate predication is a direct consequence of the ontological reality of participation.

---

26 Vedanta Deshika (Venkatanatha), *Srimad Rahasyatrayasara*, trans. M. R. Rajagopala (Kumbakonam: Agnihothram Ramanuja Thathachariar, 1956), ch. 3, 26–9; ch. 27, 378–9. Henceforth cited as *RTS*.
27 Deshika, *RTS*, ch. 27, 381.
28 Deshika, *RTS*, ch. 3, 22–3.

The relationships between Isvara [the Lord] and the world of sentient things is that between soul and body, because of which every word, whatever its ordinary denotation may be, such as 'cow', 'man' and the like, refers ultimately to Isvara who is within them as their innermost soul.[29]

In a more poetic text, Desika perceives in co-ordinate predication the implications for praise and worship:

'Brahman, Samkara, Indra, Self-ruler, Self, Universe', O Self of all beings animate and inanimate, by these words, O Lord of the Hill of Elephants, the unfailing utterances aim at you, who are the place where all words end, who are the cause of everything.[30]

Because all words denote the inner-controller, a pious, doxological acknowledgement of the indwelling Lord is appropriate. Words move within – and therefore beyond – their obvious referent to denote, more fundamentally, the decisive referent – Narayana – whose internal immanence and support to all beings must be acknowledged for things to be designated properly by words.

Such service or glorification (*kainkarya*) of God has moral implication: it drives devotees to serve their fellows in community. This (moral) service is the highest form of glorifying the Lord, because the Lord counts such ones most dearly as his inner self.

[S]ince the jiva [person] is absolutely subject to the will of the Lord and since the service of the sesha [the Lord's servant] is due also to those who are favorites of the Lord, our being a sesha to the Lord extends even to Bhagavatas [devotees] and should last as long as the self lasts. Our being seshas to bhagavatas arises from their being devotees of the Lord and pertains to our essential nature. It arises also from their qualities and knowledge, which cause a desire in us to serve them.[31]

One can serve God indirectly or through the mediation of his devotees whom he regards intimately as his inner self. Those who wish to glorify God comprehensively will place themselves at the disposal of both their ultimate *Sesin* or Master and their proximate *sesins* in community. This dual service of God and neighbor hinges on Desika's ontology of all persons resting in the body of God.

Consonance between Paul and Desika is clearly struck in the body motif's momentum from ontological (Desika) or redemptive (Paul) statements to statements concerning moral solidarity. For Desika, ontology and worship give rise to ethics, whereas for Paul redemptive participation in Christ gives rise to ethics.

---

29 Deshika, *RTS*, ch. 3, 22.

30 Vedanta Deshika, *Varadarajapancasat*, trans. Pierre-Sylvain Filliosat (Bombay: Ananthacharya Indological Research Institute, 1990), v. 12, 15.

31 Deshika, *RTS*, ch. 16, 164.

For both, the body motif is crucial to that shared conclusion. They clearly do not state the same thing ('imitation' or 'canon') but their analogical consonance is beyond doubt.

Santideva with Desika and Paul

To Paul and Desika we add the aural texture of Santideva's eighth-century north Indian voice and gain another contrapuntal effect. The Mahayana monk builds on – or, to use a verb associated with polyphony, 'imitates' – the common body motif with which Desika and especially Paul were concerned in analogous ways, but with critical differences as well.

The body motif in Santideva's *Bodhicaryavatara* [*Guide to the Bodhisattva Way of Life*] functions as a thought experiment to help recondition the mind of the reader to appreciate more fully the emptiness of our habitual in-group out-group mapping, our chronic dualism of self and other.[32] He instructs his reader on the basic equality of self and other in that both equally desire to be free from suffering and to be happy. He recognizes that honoring this insight into equality requires habituated patterns of thought be exposed, arrested, and replaced by other habitual patterns of thought in sync with the objective reality of persons.

Just as a body, with its many parts from division into hands and other limbs, should be protected as a single entity, so too should this entire world which is divided, but undivided in its nature to suffer and be happy.[33]

Because we had heard Paul and Desika before, different light is thrown on the Santideva's heuristic use of the body image. In the verses to follow, attention falls on the performative outcomes of *lovingkindness* and compassion, for which the body motif serves as a thought experiment to help cultivate those mental states. Whereas for Paul, the Body of Christ is an objective reality of cosmic, redemptive, and moral significance, and for Desika the body motif signals an ontological participation of all persons in the Lord and each other, for Santideva it functions as a pedagogical tool to prompt in readers the recognition of non-duality and sameness between self and other. While enormously provocative and indicative of a profound truth, the image holds no ontological significance. But where 'ontological' significance might yet be found is in the outcome, namely, lovingkindness and compassion, mental states corresponding with the objective reality of persons.[34] In any case, the contrast in voices allows us to separate the strands of sound more clearly, because together.

---

32 Santideva, *Bodhicaryavatara* [*Guide to the Bodhisattva Way of Life*], trans. Kate Crosby and Andrew Skilton (Oxford: Oxford University Press, 1998), 8:91.

33 Cf. John Makransky, 'No Real Protection without Authentic Love and Compassion', in *Journal of Buddhist Ethics* (12, 2005), 25–36, and *idem, Awakening Through Love: Unveiling Your Deepest Goodness* (Boston: Wisdom Publications, 2007).

34 Santideva, *Bodhicaryavatara*, 8:92–3.

The next two verses utilize the reader's own familiar experience of suffering to generate compassion for the sufferings of others.

> Even though suffering in me does not cause distress in the bodies of others, I should nevertheless find their suffering intolerable because of the affection I have for myself,
>
> In the same way that, though I cannot experience another's suffering in myself, his suffering is hard for him to bear because of his affection for himself.[35]

Next, verses 94 and 95 explore the equality of self and other more fully, because of which there should arise a moral resolve to help others, a determination associated with what Mahayana Buddhist traditions know as *bodhicitta* – the mind of Awakening – which resolves to attain Buddhahood as the unconditioned state from which one can be of the greatest benefit to all living beings.

> I should dispel the suffering of others because it is suffering like my own suffering. I should help others too because of their nature as beings, which is like my own being.
>
> When happiness is liked by me and others equally, what is so special about me that I strive after happiness only for myself?[36]

Then follow two arguments on behalf of the appropriateness of boundless compassion (*karuna*) toward other beings.

> If I give them no protection because their suffering does not afflict me, why do I protect my body against future suffering when it does not afflict me?
>
> If you think that is for the person who has the pain to guard against it, a pain of the foot is not of the hand, so why is the one protected by the other?[37]

The first argument unravels ego-conditioning by imagining one's future body and taking steps in the present to prevent it from suffering, despite the fact it does not presently suffer and one does not stand to benefit presently from such prevention. By this logic, indifference at the suffering of an 'other' is a misapprehension, for suffering is suffering no matter whom it belongs to or when it occurs.

If one asks why suffering should be prevented, no one disputes that! If it must be prevented, then all of it must be. Why is any limitation put on this?[38]

---

35 Santideva, *Bodhicaryavatara*, 8:94–5.
36 Santideva, *Bodhicaryavatara*, 8:97, 99.
37 Santideva, *Bodhicaryavatara*, 8:103.
38 Kate Crosby and Andrew Skilton, 'The Perfection of Forbearance', in *op. cit.*, 47.

Santideva, like Paul and Desika, proposes the image of a single body with many members. He does not propose a complete identity of persons erasing difference and distinction, but poses instead the equalizing of self and other so that love and compassion can be radiated toward all beings without restriction. Resembling Paul's use of body imagery, Santideva communicates a profound non-difference between persons – in their state of suffering and desire for happiness – that should give rise to compassion, a moral solidarity that acts on their behalf to remove suffering and its causes. More akin to Paul than Desika, Santideva's body insists on particularity and individuality, albeit under the rubric of unity: the hand and foot are indeed different, yet they belong together in the one body which suffers holistically without isolating and delimiting suffering on account of its location in the body. Difference holds but also belongs conceptually under the umbrella of unity. Just as a hand moves spontaneously to protect other parts of the body, so should persons recognize their equality with others and act spontaneously on their behalf, as a hand moves pre-reflectively to protect members of its own body. It is a misapprehension to view members of the body separately or reciprocally unaccountable.

To be sure, the body imagery Santideva uses in chapter eight must be placed in a wider context within the *Bodhicaryavatara*, most notably the discussion of patience in chapter six. Patience (*kshanti*), one of the six perfections or virtues in Mahayana, is perhaps the most important in preventing mental states which destroy the bodhicitta resolve to assist all beings. Chief among these is anger, for it alienates the Dharma practitioner from the very persons she has undertaken to save. In place of anger, which projects misapprehensions onto others, she substitutes a boundless compassion, which cuts through those projections to sense beings fundamentally as they are.[39]

Additional tensions can be teased out with further reading and by other readers: for instance, to what extent do our authors intend the body to include all persons whatsoever? In Paul, there is a definite tension between objective and subjective redemption, between what Christ has done for all and what Christians must do, in faith (*pistis*) and baptism, to apprehend those effects and be Christ's body. Desika bears out a tension strongly analogous to Paul's. On the one hand, all of reality exists as modes (*prakaras*) of the Lord, and on the other the Lord holds *bhagavatas* (devotees) in a uniquely intimate way such that *bhagavatas*

---

39 Dan Joslyn-Siemiatkoski brought to my attention the Sufi genre of Qawwali music, dating back to the thirteenth-century Punjab region of North India, as a possible analogy with western polyphony. A 'Qaul' is an utterance of the Prophet Muhammad, and a 'Qawwal' is one who sings or repeats those utterances. The analogy is loose because the sung portions of this genre consist of the Qawwal singing an utterance of the prophet which the accompanying singers then repeat, sometimes with mild improvization but audibly the same melody as the original Qawwal, whereas polyphony relies on multiple separate but interrelated melodies. In that respect Qawwali might be more analogous to the western canon. Yet the analogy with polyphony should be pursued in that both Qawwali and polyphony have their origins in worship and are meant to induce a unitive state or consciousness precisely through vocal complexity. Cf. Zuckerkandl, 146.

should serve other *bhagavatas* in a uniquely intimate way. Who counts, finally, as members of these bodies? Is the scope expansive or restrictive? How that question is answered will impact the degree to which these authors enact the (deliberately vague) category of solidarity. Santideva's use of the image does not pose the same question; for him the body is a thought project meant to drive the Dharma practitioner to an indiscriminate solidaristic identification with all beings.

This experiment in polyphony has been but suggestive; much more reading, listening, and space are required to tease out further nuance and complexity. Yet these three discrete attestations of a corporate body bear the potential to increase readers' domain of affectivity, to recondition their imagination toward a solidaristic affiliation and love of neighbor. All the more so when sounded together.

Conclusion (By Way of Caution)

An interdisciplinary offering of this sort can complicate matters and place significant demands on those who would apply it to theological reflection. While this essay's use of polyphony is meant to reinvest theological discourse with aesthetics, affect, and solidarity, it also brings with it some potential stumbling blocks, as do all highly particular methodological constructs. I list three of these now as a caution and indicator of nuances yet to be teased out before this model can be considered satisfactory.

Superficiality

It will not do to enlist the model without adequate compliance to the demands of music as an independent field of original application. The theologian-composer will need to acquire a working knowledge of polyphony, including its historical antecedents, development, ecclesial context, and possible non–western and non–Christian parallels.[40] She might also *experience* musical polyphony by listening to actual examples of this type of music in order to train the ear better to hear the complexity of vocal polyphony, voices' similarity-in-difference, tensions, consonance, dissonance, resolutions, and other meaningful dynamics of a musical score. With that aesthetic grounding one can then imagine if and how theological voices might similarly be arranged. Like classic texts, musical polyphony solicits repeated exposures which can give rise to a progressively deeper understanding of the individual voices heard separately and heard together. Like reading and reflecting on theological texts, musical polyphony can exercise a self-transcending and edifying effect on listeners and participants, and should not therefore be perceived as an interdisciplinary metaphor bearing a pale, or even no, relation to theology. The significant relation between vocal

---

40 Francis X. Clooney, SJ, 'Comparative Theology', in John Webster et al., *The Oxford Handbook of Systematic Theology* (New York: Oxford University Press, 2007), 662.

polyphony and interreligious theology should not, however, induce sloth in theologian-composers with respect to compliance to the demands of music as an independent and highly nuanced discipline. Once musical polyphony edifies theologians, their challenge will be to understand better not only the dynamics of music itself, but the way in which the hearing of polyphonic voices can rearrange the theologian's intellectual vocabulary, sensitivities, and imaginative frames of reference. All of this must be done responsibly.

Incommensurability

Neither in music nor in comparative theology is polyphony designed to tolerate an unlimited degree of difference. Where even marked differences can be organized and understood as polyphony, we need theologian-composers sensitive to harmonic depth in the voices and texts being compared and who are able to anticipate possible resolutions to movements marked by tension or even dissonance. Where harmonic depth and resolution of dissonance into consonance elude the listener, we need patient and attentive theologian-composers who can rest in and navigate through that tension through a deeper listening that resists finality of interpretation. A deeper listening may not, in all cases, render unnecessary the application of theological norms to determine the line of demarcation between, on the one hand, differences that together create polyphonic consonance and, on the other, differences which together lack resolution and are dissonant. Just as not all tension can or should find resolution, nor should companions in dialogue be expected to reduce their confessional stance or delimit their understanding of what counts as true and real.[41] To be sure, theological polyphony optimistically privileges a hope for harmonic consonance or solidarity; the very model preconditions in this way.[42] For, with musical polyphony, the arrangement of voices contrapuntally anticipates, in its tensions, a resolution yet to be had, and the listener hears dissonance as a deviation capable of resolving itself in consonance. But when this expectation is applied theologically, the model must not *a priori* presume or require such consonance, nor can the model tolerate a self-abusing bending to the point of non-recognition. Thus, one must ask how comparative theologians should navigate the important demands of communal norms while not sacrificing the hospitable and solidaristic outcomes polyphony offers. Here a (new) theology of religions may be appropriate if comparative theologians are to honor and respect the normative dimensions both of their home traditions and the irreducible particularity of their

41 Zuckerkandl, *The Sense of Music*, 158. In theological comparisons, the expectation for consonance is grounded in the recognition that theological 'thinking occurs in ways that are broadly and commonly human, cultural and linguistic differences notwithstanding'. Francis X. Clooney, SJ, 'Comparative Theology', 660.

42 See the essay in this volume by Kristin Beise Kiblinger on the relationship between Theologies of Religion and Comparative Theologies.

companions in dialogue.[43] With respect to music, the 'canon' is a form of polyphony in which all parts sing exactly the same thing but at different intervals and time signatures. That form of polyphony, when transported to theological comparison, becomes problematic in its supposition that all traditions, texts and voices speak essentially what I speak but in different linguistic or cultural contexts. Theologians may need to await patiently the resolution of dissonance. They may also need to prepare themselves for the possibility that such resolution might take a long time, or even may not come at all.[44]

Reception

How will my companions in dialogue and all people of goodwill receive my construal of their voices according to this model? Is this interdisciplinary musing, like so much theology to date, plagued by a western cultural hegemony, however aesthetic and well-intentioned?[45] Theologian-composers must tend to concerns that this method prioritizes a norm alien to the traditions to which it is being applied and that it is just one more cloaked version of a western or Christian imperialism indifferent to the perception of those to whom the metaphor is meant peaceably to apply. Otherwise, a metaphor proposed for its irenic qualities may alienate the other and ironically give rise to the antagonism it seeks to redress. Because musical polyphony is imbedded in highly particular historical, cultural, and ecclesial contexts, comparativists employing it will need to be fully self-conscious of their methodological particularity, and be willing to change suppositions – methodological or otherwise – which fail to listen responsibly to the voices of their companions in dialogue. But *that* it comes from a particular western, Christian, context is not in itself sufficient grounds for dismissal. It includes voices precisely in their deep specificity; when this fails to occur, polyphony fails to occur, and one must change or abandon the model, not the voices. While no discussant should have to apologize for her particularity, it is also wise to wield one's particularity prudently, sensitively, and dialogically. In such cases of methodological failure, the comparativist bears the responsibility of clearly stating the model's irenic intentions with respect to intellectual and moral solidarity and accepting the possibility that in these cases the model may serve those intentions inadequately.

As was true above in the concern with incommensurability, here too it will be critically important to sidestep domestication: the error of listening to others because they represent 'in their own words and concepts' what 'we' already

---

43 Zuckerkandl, *The Sense of Music*, 146, 155. '[T]he inevitably and permanently dialogical character of an interreligious and comparative theology does not mean that such a theology always eventuates in mutual agreement and understanding. Such a theology can remain confessional, even apologetic.' Clooney, 'Comparative Theology', 662.

44 See the chapter by Tracy Tiemeier for illustrations of the ways in which recent work in comparative theology has been vulnerable to this criticism.

45 'Statement for the Comparative Theology Group of the AAR' (revised May 2006), II.4; 4.

mean and say.[46] That move succumbs to what Anne Clifford, borrowing from Emmanuel Levinas, calls an 'Egology', in which the 'I' in encounter 'becomes a "living from" that uses up the other in order to fulfill its own needs and desires.'[47] The comparativist will thus need to state clearly that the companions in dialogue are not included as participants whose contributions are deemed *a priori* to be univocal with our own, but rather as participants whose voices, texts, and questions are 'homologous' to our own – voices, texts, and questions bearing a relation to and perhaps at times corresponding with our own, but not identical to or explained without remainder by our own.[48]

While the model helps theologians to appreciate consonance, some experiments in comparison may reveal that it is only marginally helpful, or even not helpful at all. Such instances may demonstrate the limits of this limited – because contextual – model. Such judgements could be made only after a prolonged and thorough exposure, a good in and of itself. Any final, unresolved dissonance would in no way delimit the intellectual solidarity enacted in the careful, repeated listening the polyphony model recommends. That depth of attention will have enhanced accountability to the companion in dialogue and, in Christian terms, will become an act of neighbor love.

The merit of polyphony as an organizing principle for theological comparison will stand or fall on the basis of its capacity to characterize the dynamics of theological comparisons in ways illuminating, meaningful, and possibly edifying. Comparative theologians will need to test its fitness as a principle capable of organizing the independent voices of companions in dialogue. This essay offered but one brief example in very few pages. Other experiments are needed which deal in highly specific subject matter and which are largely unrelated to each other, in which case the model will gain credence if shown to pass the test of multiple attestation, that is, if it can organize multiple sets of discrete comparisons sharing minimal overlap in subject matter from an array of religious traditions and theological subject matter. Such attestations will speak to the fitness of the model and its promise for future efforts.

Use of this interdisciplinary metaphor should be suggestive, imaginative, and heuristic. It should not be absolute or rigid. One will meet with little success by rigidly transporting the many rules entailed in musical polyphony directly into theological comparison as though their relationship is one of univocity or one-

---

46 Anne M. Clifford, 'The Global Horizon of Religious Pluralism and Local Dialogue with the Religious Other', in Terrence Tilley (ed.), *New Horizons in Theology,* The College Theology Society Annual Volume 50 (Maryknoll, NY: Orbis Books, 2005), 171. Cf. Ronald Thiemann, 'Toward a Christian Theology of Religions: Some Philosophical and Theological Reflections', in *Union Seminary Quarterly Review* (56, 2003), 157–66, esp. 161–3; and Catherine Cornille, *The im-Possibility of Interreligious Dialogue* (New York: Crossroad, 2008), 189–96.

47 'Statement for the Comparative Theology Group of the AAR', II.4; 4.

48 Clooney, 'Comparative Theology', 661.

to-one correspondence, as though theological voices resemble fixed, static sounds rather than dynamic and developing tones subject ineluctably to change in history, community, and encounter with the other. Far from a pre-determined template fitted onto theological voices, polyphony should instead function heuristically to represent the promise of consonant voices, the promise of dissonant voices finding consonance in the one chord, and the promise associated with multiple voices sounding together complexly and richly in such a way as to change how all voices are heard. Polyphony should be imported into comparative theological reflection as an aesthetic and even moral paradigm but not as a system of fixed rules according to which voices are then promptly deemed to comply with or deviate from.

In these ways the model of polyphony, not yet adequately verified but replete with potential, may contribute an interdisciplinary model by which theologians can be comparative, that is, aware of theological differences contrapuntally and aesthetically rather than antagonistically, and in so doing help us to move toward the transformative experiences of intellectual and moral solidarity to which our traditions rightly call us.[49]

---

49 I am deeply grateful to the contributors to this volume for their helpful remarks on an earlier draft of this chapter.

10

Response

FRANCIS X. CLOONEY, SJ

Of course I am honored to respond to so interesting a set of essays. But since as editor, I bestowed this task upon myself, I do better simply to say I am very pleased to see how this project has come to fruition. It was very interesting to work with this varied and promising group of young scholars – who throughout were quite collaborative in reading and criticizing one another's work. It has been particularly pleasing to me precisely because the essays are by younger scholars, fresher to the field of comparative study, whose work gives us hope regarding the future of this field. They are full of new ideas, expected and sensible critiques of the previous generation (including James Fredericks and myself) – and also the burden of the questions that burden their particular generation. Jim has already narrated the genesis of the project in the AAR panel on hegemony, from which it grew into the present volume, a nuanced and rich set of essays that go well beyond the bounds of that original panel. In this brief response I need not restate where the field is today, nor need I summarize what the essays have already said with clarity. Rather, I will simply pick up on points that I find of particular interest with respect to my own work.

Responses rarely arise from purely neutral perspectives, so it will be helpful to locate this response in the context of the work I am now doing. Two of my recent books (both published in 2008) count as comparative theology – *The Truth, the Way, the Life* and *Beyond Compare*. Both draw on Vedanta Desika's *Srimad Rahasyatrayasara*; the first is a Christian commentary on the three holy mantras of Srivaisnava Hindus, and second a comparative reflection on loving surrender to God in Desika read along with Francis de Sales's *Treatise on the Love of God*. Both are instances of my accustomed approach, an intuitive sense that some particular Hindu text is theologically interesting for the Christian, and that when such a text is carefully read, it will generate good choices of Christian texts to read with it, for the sake of insights that are religiously and theologically rich. My view of my own work, in such cases, is that there are enough intellectual safeguards built into the reading process that major pitfalls of misunderstanding

and misuse will either be avoided or quickly made evident and liable to correction. Since my work is provisional and does not claim general truth, it is also
open to correction by further examples.

Finished projects are generally safe – until the reviewers show up – but I am
on less certain ground with respect to my new project, tentatively entitled *When
God is Absent*. This is a study of divine absence and departure/non-return in the
medieval sermons of St Bernard and his successors on the *Song of Songs,* and
the sermon-like commentary of Nampillai (thirteenth century) on the songs of
the young woman bereft of her beloved in Satakopan's Tamil religious classic,
Tiruvaymoli. As usual, I am settling down for the long haul with just a few potent
texts. In this new project, my initial intuition is that old wisdom can shed new
light on our contemporary scene, where God may seem to have gone missing.
This sense of absence is not primarily due to a general theoretical judgement on
God's existence or transcendence, but due to an insight into God's nature as a
vividly real and concrete being who, as particular, can come and go at will. This
unpredictability of God can frustrate the expectations of believers who expect to
find God present in just this way or that way. Such is the starting point of a
project that will take several years to complete. It is the kind of experiment – its
fruits uncertain but promising – that I like to think of as quintessential comparative theological learning, since not only is a comparable theme taken up in two
traditions, but the study of divine unpredictability through attention to two traditions aggravates our uncertainty, since neither religious narrative stands alone:
when we ask where God is, with respect to both traditions at once, it becomes
all the more difficult to decide that God is just here or just there. I undertake
such experiments without tidying up the theory, hoping that the beauty of the
texts and what is generated from the reading of them will carry the day; I see
myself as a kind of instrument by which such texts might be read together and
coalesce powerfully. So theories about comparative theology do not affect me
much. But still, reading these essays has made me think twice about limits and
hidden pitfalls, and that is good. In the remainder of this response, I point to six
issues that these essays raise.

How Do We Take the Other Seriously?

Bagus Laksana gets us off to a good start, eloquently placing before us the delicate balance that is required if comparative theology is truly to see, respect, and
engage the *other* in a way that is both theologically responsible and fruitful, and
intellectually worthy. Bagus aptly weaves together language that illumines
pilgrimage – matters of identity, imagination, and hospitality – to fashion a compelling account of rich, fully committed learning from the other. The very image
of pilgrimage is interesting, since it nicely combines a risky journey, accomplished at some sacrifice, with a sense of identity and the conviction that there is
a home to return to. He rightly draws in images of the stranger/pilgrim – and
the host – to help us to imagine more richly and holistically the dynamics of

exchange among people of different religions. No otherness is final and static, but rather is always subject to improvization and negotiation – as we take one another seriously, changing in the process. For this reason, deep respect for self and other is required.

Highlighting the work of the imagination at the center of comparative learning is quite apt a reminder of how multi-dimensional good comparative study needs to be. It is a matter of study and usually of reading, to be sure, but it is also a more richly engaging practice that affects us profoundly in what we see and experience in vividly participatory and relational ways. Bagus finally highlights hospitality as a way of understanding this process of respecting and welcoming the other into what remains my home. But he also notes that there are limits to hospitality: ordinarily, we do not want guests to stay on permanently. Pilgrimage is an appropriate image for this journey in interreligious learning, since there is a difference between the pilgrim and the 'vagabond' who wanders without aim, perhaps without a sense of destination or even without home to return to. But it is also true that the pilgrim may be tempted not to finish the round-trip, or may have to invent new reasons, along the way, for completing the journey and making the return: she or he may get tired, dirty, lost, and at times look very much the vagabond.

And there is always the more straightforward fear that the comparative theologian is an invader or colonialist rather than a pilgrim, as she or he approaches others who desire no such attention and do not intend to offer hospitality. All of this may appear vividly, violently, or in a more simple and quiet form when a reader dominates a text which cannot speak back because it is read out of context. But this leads us to the problem of hegemony.

Is Comparative Theology Fair to the Other?

In part due to the panel out of which this volume grew, a key concern of our authors is hegemony – or, as Hugh Nicholson terms it, the 'political, a 'theological hegemonism'. This concern is in part justified due to a postmodern sensitivity to essentialism, the heavy burden of theory, falsely universalized claims. But we also remember the sad histories of our interactions, how in the past comparative learning, including comparative theology, has been self-serving in using the Other for the sake of a predetermined creed or theory.

Hugh contrasts the lineages of the political theological consciousness that restricts and denies the other its freedom, and the liberal rejoinder that seeks to escape that restriction by strategies of universalization. After pluralism, the remedy on the liberal side lies in our new comparativism, which by its particularity and self-consciousness resists the naïve or intentional concealment of bias. But since both the liberal and the political stances self-preserve and self-replicate in new contexts, Hugh's implication seems to be that even the new comparative theology will inevitably fail, fall back into its other, as did the old comparativism and twentieth-century pluralism. The tension of the liberal and political remains, and an implication of Hugh's position is that progress beyond such dichotomies is never definitively possible. This is so even if he appreciates three distinctive features of the new comparative theology: resistance to generalization; the embedding of comparative theology within the communicative and accountable schema of dialogue; and the honest admission of bias. It is ironic or sad that both have 'far others' (the religions) but also more dominant 'near others' (one another). The religions may end up seeming pawns in a European debate about religious meaning.

But I would like also to think, and I believe Hugh agrees, that the dialectic need not lock any particular theological work into the prison of such stereotypical predictions. Even within the dialectic of a politicized exclusivism and the contrasting liberal universalism, we can progress in our self-awareness regarding the limits of what can be accomplished when we venture to learn across religious boundaries. For we do actually study, learn, and engage the other in intellectually substantive ways that break up hegemonic patterns. Perhaps the deeper question is *why* we expend the effort.

Why Engage in Interreligious Study?

That is: if the argument is at some level a dispute between liberals and conservatives in the Christian west, and if the dangers are so real and have played themselves out so many times in history, why take the risk of actually studying another religious tradition? Occasionally I have been told, 'Mind your own business' – leave other religions alone, stick to your own. But I do not think this neat division of religions is tenable, and there are good reasons for *not* minding our own business, even aside from the simple realities of how people's lives increasingly overlap and intermingle, mostly to the good, in today's religiously diverse world. I offer two reasons.

First, there are simple, direct, intellectual grounds. Honest thinking does not stop at boundaries, and our minds are always crossing over established borders. While this crossing over – or transgression – may be justified or criticized in various ways, it nonetheless happens. Curiosity about the wider world may even seem to distinguish a western, Christian religious learning, but this same intellectual dynamic, when pursued with discipline, also provokes serious self-criticism. The desire to know the other will often enough be accompanied by serious skepticism about oneself. I find that this skepticism is operative in my current project on God absent and present: while I might quite nicely reflect on the dynamics of the human–divine relationship just in my own Catholic tradition, there is no *reason* sufficient to discourage inquiry across religious boundaries on the topic. If we are attentive and prudent, we will avoid wild comparisons, but nonetheless still permit the mind to travel where it will. We must keep learning.

Second, we must also admit the role of the faith impulse to see the universal implications of what we believe, and to enact that faith in *understanding* the other, drawing it into a living connection with what we already believe. David Clairmont makes an excellent point: while mission and missionary work have at times been involved in aggression against, and denial of, the Other, we still must make a distinction between hegemony and mission. Not every assertion of truth claims is necessarily an unfair or harmful assertion of power. Life is, in fact, more ambiguous, and as David shows us, the encounter of the Franciscans with the Sri Lankan king shows how difficult it is to get everyone's views on even a small set of issues sufficiently clear that even proper disagreement is possible. It is impossible to find comparative enterprises entirely free of hegemonic impulses, or religious encounters with the other that are nothing but crassly hegemonic. Learning is therefore ambiguous, and we do well to keep thinking in some detail about the history/ies of which we are part, to observe how mission and comparative learning have intersected in various times and places. Mission can in fact generate religious reasons for comparative learning, and even if mission may often enough aim at conversion, an honest intellectual process 'along the way' resists becoming merely an instrument of mission; in fact, learning may also dampen evangelical ardor, problematizing simplistic ambitions.

I find the tension between intellectual and spiritual motivations to be an issue in my own work, as in my new project, *When God is Absent*. While we might be satisfied to reflect on the human–divine relationship in just our own tradition, and while exploration of the theme in Hinduism could lead to a Christian trivialization of unique Hindu insights, it can also be that the desire to understand how God relates unpredictably to the human race is precisely what enables us to honor Hindu insights into what God is like and what God does. As for mission, 'sending' and 'going there' entail a sense of differences and spaces to be negotiated. This spatiality facilitates rather than undercuts serious learning.

We can all admit that *comparison* is fraught with difficulties. But we must also consider the dangers arising from a *theology* that is open and inclusive in some ways but in other ways remains stuck in bad habits that may endure even in otherwise good comparative study. Here we have two issues: the need to reconsider how comparative theology relates to the theology of religions, and the need to reconsider theology more broadly.

Is Comparative Theology Concealing Its Theology of Religions?

Kristin Kiblinger evidences substantial concern about comparative theology's relation to the theology of religions. In her view, not only is it not possible to keep our distance from the theology of religions, but the very idea of such distance, which implies the inadequacy of the theology of religions, is rather dated, since the theology of religions has become more complex and nuanced in recent decades. Like any exclusory practice, a split between the theology of religions and comparative theology is in part made possible by a caricature of one or both. It may be that we comparative theologians have relied on an exaggerated sense of the difference between learning from (in comparative theology) and theologizing about (in the theology of religions), and yet we may also have had to move in this direction, to defend our place in theological circles where it has often been denied that good comparative work can be theological at all.

Does comparative theology really need a theology of religions? It is certainly true that intellectual work always has presuppositions; underlying comparative practice are theological views that enable – and define and energize, constrain and twist – the work being done. Yes, but I think that it is in practice that such implicit influences are exposed. As I have asserted often enough, comparative theology has to be *done*, and that it takes time, and is hard work. Questions about what comparative theology is or what its presuppositions are, are best taken up *after* comparative theological practice and with respect to specific cases. Rather than, 'What is Clooney's theology of religions?' we do better to ask, 'What does Clooney the Christian theologian hope for, in reading together the *Song* and *Tiruvaymoli*, Bernard and Nampillai?'

I also think that the very idea of a clash between comparative theology and the theology of religions has been blown out of proportion, since a simpler point is at stake. I like to think of myself as not constructing a grand theory that in principle entirely excludes the theology of religions; nor do I think Jim Fredericks has meant this either. It would be ironic were we to make a big theoretical point out of this hypothetical clash, such that the difference between the theology of religions and comparative theology would become itself a topic that further delays actual interreligious learning. It is good therefore that Kristin herself turns to the concrete example of Buddhist readings of the Christian, and John Keenan's Christian–Buddhist re-reading of New Testament texts. It becomes easier to understand even her own position once we see the positions she is engaging in the study of Buddhism. Yet in the end, it is not clear how my own work, such as my current exploration of the presence and absence of God in the traditions of the *Song* and *Tiruvaymoli*, would be improved by constructing for it an explicit Christian theology of religions that might then be applied to Srivaisnava Hinduism.

I close this section with several modest observations. With so many scholars engaged in the theology of religions, it is not unreasonable to plead that a few more should instead turn to comparative theology, to bring specific learning about specific other traditions into the conversation. So too, in the long run, we should be able to agree that the theology of religions and comparative theology mirror and imply one another, and even help one another. If comparative theology and the theology of religions are kept proximate to one another – in practice, in expectation – they will uncover and ameliorate each other's hidden flaws. Just as comparative theology has presuppositions, a solitary theology of religions might proceed strangely, in a space where nothing is ever studied in particular, where there is only an unending conversation about the presuppositions of a hypothetical but endlessly deferred actual learning.

Can We Improve the *Theology* in 'Comparative *Theology*'?

But whether the theology we have in mind is *comparative* or a *theology-of*, our idea of 'theology' will always be in need of revision and correction. John Sheveland shows us how a comparative theology can be interreligious and ecumenical at the same time, and thus a richer and deeper theology simply because old habits of separation are broken at home as well as abroad. And then we can go further, since advances in one area of theology may not be taken up in other areas of theology; as we push ahead on one issue, we may miss others. Michelle Voss Roberts points out the danger of perpetuating bad habits even in doing something good, as when a way of theologizing corrects just one fault or blind spot – while letting other bad habits persist uncriticized. A theology may be robustly interreligious, but insensitive to gender issues; a feminist theologian may write as if there are only western Christian theologians.

My solution is usually to admit that shortfalls will always exist, and on that basis then to try to anticipate and mitigate damaging effects by building into my writing an awareness of where theology is going, and also by welcoming critique from theologians with other sensitivities. Or, we might imagine postponing comparative projects until the other theological dangers have been rooted out, but this would be an interminably long process. Better is the suggestion Michelle points to, a co-operative process by which feminist and comparative theologians co-operate in their work, right from the start. I think, moreover, that we can tolerate the ways in which we lag behind. If comparative theologians are often not well attuned to issues of gender and the exclusion of women's voices from established views of what counts religiously and in defining religions, feminist theologians too may fail to take seriously the religions of Asia or rush quickly to judgements that are not founded on solid learning. If we can chasten and challenge one another, we can also be tolerant of the limits of our theologies – while never forgetting that they really are limited. At our best, perhaps we will always be imperfect theologians, insightful in some ways, blinder in others.

Tracy Tiemeier, sharing Michelle's concerns, points even more broadly to the need to move beyond the cultural monolith of white America by making sure that how and where we theologize is also reconsidered in light of new currents in Asian theology. This too is a fine corrective, and we can also welcome the ideal of co-operation among theologians from different cultural and social backgrounds, such that we learn to work together in crafting a comparative theology that is as inclusive and self-critical as possible. But here too we have to make choices about where to try hardest for self-correction, since there is no end to the broadening, corrective process, and we need also to be concerned about race, literacy and orality, economic status, and how different religions need to be treated differently. The list of concerns can become overwhelming, and we will end up focusing on some correctives more than others, while yet admitting that our finite efforts will make our particular theologizing immune to further criticism. Indeed, this volume itself reminds us of the value of co-operative efforts in which the wider range of goals is clear, even as each of us still makes choices about how best to do our own, particular theologizing.

The payoff, of course, has to do with where improved theologies leave us: how is my work 'liberated' by freeing it from constraints and flaws I had not been thinking of, with the result that even what I want to accomplish is now better accomplished? I can imagine, for instance, how a strong feminist sensitivity will free my reading of the *Song* and *Tiruvaymoli* from stereotypes about 'young women in love', the 'beloved', and 'God as lover'.

Which Religions Get Compared in Comparative Theology?

Once we move into the realm where comparative theology is actually practiced, we are not done with interesting issues. We can ask, for instance: which religions get studied in (most) comparative theology? There is no rule, of course, but there is a pattern, and it seems to be that Hinduism and Buddhism receive the most attention. Daniel Joslyn-Siemiatkoski makes a most interesting point, that Judaism is much less likely to be studied by comparative theologians; when it is considered, rarely is the rich breadth of Jewish intellectual history taken into account. Judaism has usually shown up in Christian thinking in a truncated fashion, safely relegated to our past. This tendency may in part be a preference for the less familiar over the more familiar (with respect to Asian religions and Judaism) or conversely, of what we do not take for granted rather than Judaism, which Christians think they understand.

To say that more comparative theologians should study Judaism in particular is not merely to give it a fair place in comparative study. Rather, since Christianity is unthinkable without Judaism, and since the Christian attitude toward Judaism charts the way for attitudes toward other religions, then the Christian attitude to Judaism (*and* the Jewish attitude toward other religions) stands forth as deeply important for how any Christian thinks about any other religion. Ongoing debates about God's covenant/s with Jews and Christians, for instance, seem to me to be fundamental to considerations of how other religions are to be thought about: as Christians treat Judaism differently, so too we will begin to treat other religions differently. Given how important this issue is, we do well also to hope for more advice, particularly from Jewish scholars who will be able to show us how to do comparative theology with respect to Jewish traditions.

Once we start noticing this phenomenon, we can extend the map: much of comparative theology is done with Hinduism and Buddhism, some with Islam and traditions of China, less with Judaism – but yet even less with other religions, such as Native American, or those of Africa. Which religions are studied may have to do with how far 'theology' can be stretched when it comes to traditions less like the great literary traditions of Christianity, and the learning of which requires sociological and anthropological skills that many of us do not have. But perhaps some comparative theological pairings are not a good idea. We need not find theology everywhere, and should not make too much of it if theological exchange seems in the short run impossible. In some cases it may be only in the constructive activity and relationships of dialogue that theology becomes possible. We might also ask: which forms of *Christianity* figure in comparative theological work? It seems that Catholic and liberal Protestant Christianities are disproportionately represented in comparative theology. Is this merely a subdivision of the sociology of western interest in religions, or rather a theologically interesting phenomenon?

One more point may be noted here. It is difficult in a volume like this to actually do comparative theology. But since most issues are clarified and problems alleviated in the doing, I am glad that our authors reaffirm their own commitment to comparative learning: Clairmont through his historical study of the Franciscans and King Bhuvanekabahu VII in Sri Lanka; Kiblinger, in her analysis of Buddhist theologies of religions; Joslyn-Siemiatkoski, in his turn to the rabbis; Tiemeier, in drawing on Antal, and Voss Roberts in using the Hindu Lalla and Christian Mechthilde. Laksana is vivid in bringing together Christian and Muslim insights, drawn from text and from practice too, reflected on next to one another; Sheveland systematically weaves Hindu and Christian insights together, each voice enriching how we hear and understand the other. Laksana aptly reminds us of the role of the imagination in the making of such choices, which cannot be pinned down by any single rational process.

Perhaps we need also to highlight the necessarily autobiographical nature of comparative theology: if the areas of study are chosen and limited, we make sense of this best through admitting the particularities of our own identities as the choosers choosing which religions to compare with one another. This is not to say that we can only construct essentially private rationales, as if history and broad social issues do not matter; but still, making sense of the possibilities before us when we think about undertaking comparative work requires that we make intelligent, personally convincing choices that are rooted in self-knowledge.

Jeffery Long makes a unique contribution by writing from a Hindu perspective, and implicitly confirms my hope that comparative theology need not be a Christian enterprise. Neo-Vedanta is, in his view, a solid base for comparative theology, a testimony to the relatedness of all truths – without falling into a reductive relativism. Of course, the distinction is a fine one, and it may not sway some Christian readers who will not be convinced that an affirmation of all paths and all their truths strengthens rather than debilitates the truth in any of them. Jeffery's essay is also the most notably autobiographical of our essays, as he charts his gradual embrace of Hinduism, out of a Catholic background. Yet it is notable that in this essay Jeffery does not venture far into a (re)consideration of the Catholic tradition from which he came, instead staying focused on his adopted Hindu tradition. Perhaps his personal journey, toward self-identifying as a Hindu, is already so complex and rich that further, intentional interreligious reflection is not desirable? But still, it would be good to see a reverse, return engagement with Catholic theological issues.

What's Next for Comparative Theology?

All the rich insights arising in such studies add up only to a starting point. Every new study that engages seriously the details of another tradition raises more questions than it answers, even as new efforts to theorize multiple instances do help make sense of what is learned, but finish off no conversation. We really are only at the start of a process that will take centuries to come to fruition. In its concreteness and its insistence on the importance of multiple voices, comparative theology cannot be quickly recapitulated in theory. Much more actual work is needed before comparative theology matures.

At this point in my career, my project of reading together the *Song* and *Tiruvaymoli*, Bernard and Nampillai, is a new venture, but my habitual way of crossing religious borders is hardly a novel activity. The essays written here raise all kinds of questions around the boundaries of what I've written elsewhere and even here, and this good, hard interrogation benefits what is still a young field. I readily concede that I have learned how to get my work done in part by worrying about some questions more than others, admitting my weak points, and moving on.

What remains a question for me is how the concerns that these young colleagues have raised will affect their own next projects, new ventures in actual comparative theological reflection. My hope, though, is that my young colleagues will just do their own work, progressing in their own new comparative projects, lavishing time and energy on specific interreligious projects that push them beyond where they have been until now. Only in light of specific research, taken as the substance underlying reflection on comparative theology, will real progress be made in this field. They too will have to keep making choices about what to stress and what to let go of, and the key test will be their ability to make all of it work out in a fruitful way, in further particular examples beyond the work they have already done. How they might read the *Song* and *Tiruvaymoli*, and Bernard and Nampillai, in light of the positions put forward in their essays, is of interest to me. Or conversely, I would be very interested in hearing why they would not want to take up the kind of projects that occupy my attention.

At the end of our reflection we might return to Bagus Laksana's image of the pilgrimage, as if to imagine the goal toward which we still travel. But it is best now to end with John Sheveland's lovely insight, that comparative theology is best conceived of as polyphonic, drawing on multiple melodic lines that, beautiful in themselves, sound all the more lovely when heard together. If individual voices are strong and clear, then the larger whole produces its own lovely effects. That we do this theologically and yet interreligiously, with serious respect for traditions, our own and those of others, is simply something beautiful we can do, together, for God.

Biographical Information

David Clairmont is currently Assistant Professor of Moral Theology at the University of Notre Dame. His research and teaching interests include Catholic moral theology, Franciscan spirituality, comparative religious ethics, and the moral thought of Theravada Buddhism. He has recently completed a book manuscript entitled *Person as Classic: Moral Struggle and Comparative Religious Ethics*, focusing on Christian Trinitarian theology and Theravada Buddhist Abhidhamma as resources for comparative ethics. He is co-editor (with Don Browning) of *American Religions and the Family: How Faith Traditions Cope with Modernization and Democracy* (Columbia University Press, 2007). His current book projects include a co-authored volume (with William Schweiker) entitled *Dimensions of Religious Ethics*, as well as a study of the Franciscan integration of moral exemplarity and symbolic discourse, tentatively entitled *Bonaventure's Hope: The Franciscan Heritage and the Scope of Moral Theology*.

Francis X. Clooney, SJ is Parkman Professor of Theology and Professor of Comparative Theology at Harvard Divinity School. His most recent books are *Beyond Compare: St Francis de Sales and Sri Vedanta Desika on Loving Surrender to God* (Georgetown University Press, 2008); *The Truth, the Way, the Life: Christian Commentary on the Three Holy Mantras of the Srivaisnava Hindus* (Peeters Publishing, 2008); and *Comparative Theology: Deep Learning across Religious Borders* (Wiley-Blackwell, 2010).

James Fredericks, PhD is a faculty member in the Department of Theological Studies at Loyola Marymount University. He is a specialist in interreligious dialogue, especially the dialogue between Buddhism and Christianity, and has lectured internationally in Japan, China, India, Iran, and Europe. He was a Senior Fulbright Research Scholar in Kyoto, Japan, and has held the Numata Chair in Buddhism and Culture at Ryukoku University in Kyoto. For many years he has been a member of the Board of Directors of the Society for

Buddhist–Christian Studies, the Los Angeles Buddhist–Catholic Dialogue Group and the San Francisco Bay Area Zen–Catholic Dialogue Group. In addition to many articles, he is the author of *Faith Among Faiths: Christian Theology and the Non-Christian Religions* (Paulist Press, 1999) and *Buddhists and Christians: Through Comparative Theology to a New Solidarity* (Orbis Books, 2004). His work has been translated into Japanese, Chinese, German, and Spanish.

Daniel Joslyn-Siemiatkoski is Assistant Professor of Church History at the Church Divinity School of the Pacific, a founding member of the Graduate Theological Union, in Berkeley, California. A scholar of pre-modern Jewish–Christian relations and comparative theology, his book *Christian Memories of the Maccabean Martyrs* (Palgrave Macmillan, 2009) analyzes the creation of Christian identity via the lens of veneration of the Maccabean martyrs, Jews who died for the Mosaic Law. He is currently working on a commentary on Mishnah Avot to be published in the series Christian Commentaries on Non-Christian Sacred Texts (Peeters and Eerdmans). He received his PhD from Boston College and is a member of the Episcopal Church.

Kristin Beise Kiblinger lived in Thailand from 1994 to 1996 as a World Teach volunteer. She thereafter earned a PhD in 2002 from the University of Chicago Divinity School, where she studied philosophy of religion and Indian Buddhist thought. A practicing Christian in the Episcopal tradition, currently she is Associate Professor of Religious Studies and co-ordinator of the International Studies minor at Winthrop University in South Carolina. She is the author of *Buddhist Inclusivism: Attitudes Towards Religious Others* (Ashgate, 2005) and a former member of the steering committee for the Comparative Theology group of the American Academy of Religion.

A. Bagus Laksana, SJ is a PhD candidate in comparative theology at Boston College, focusing on Islam and Christianity. He holds a licenciate in systematic theology from the Weston Jesuit School of Theology, Cambridge, MA; and is also on the faculty at the Wedabhakti School of Theology, Sanata Dharma University, Yogyakarta, Indonesia. His research interests include comparative sainthood and theological anthropology, Christian and Muslim pilgrimage, historical Christian–Muslim encounters, comparative mysticism, religious arts, Asian contextual theologies, and inculturation.

Jeffery D. Long is Associate Professor of Religion and Asian Studies and Chair of the Department of Religious Studies at Elizabethtown College in Elizabethtown, Pennsylvania, where he has taught since receiving his doctoral degree at the University of Chicago in 2000. He is also the author of *A Vision for Hinduism: Beyond Hindu Nationalism* and *Jainism: An Introduction*. He is currently serving as Chair of the Steering Committee of DANAM, the Dharma Association of North America, which promotes the constructive study of Indic traditions. He is an active member of the Hindu community in America. He acts regularly as a consultant for the Hindu American Foundation and he and his wife are members of the Hindu American Religious Institute (HARI) Temple, in Harrisburg, Pennsylvania, the Washington DC Kali Temple, and the Ramakrishna Vedanta Society.

Hugh Nicholson is Assistant Professor of Theology at Loyola University, Chicago. A student of Francis Clooney at Boston College (PhD 2001), he specializes in comparative theology with a focus on the Christian and Hindu theological traditions. He has published articles on method in comparative theology and on various aspects of classical Indian philosophy, among other topics. He is currently working on a book manuscript, tentatively entitled *Theology, Comparison, and the Political*, which deals with the problem of reconciling the oppositional nature of religious identity with the ideal of religious tolerance.

Michelle Voss Roberts is Assistant Professor of Religious Studies at Rhodes College in Memphis, Tennessee. A participant in Presbyterian Christianity and a practitioner of yoga, Dr Voss Roberts is the author of several articles in feminist and comparative theology. Her book, *Dualities: A Theology of Difference* (Westminster John Knox, 2010), considers the theologies of Mechthild of Magdeburg and Lalleswari of Kashmir for alternatives to dualistic approaches to divinity, body, and the earth. Her current research reconsiders the Christian tradition of the spiritual senses in conversation with the Hindu theory on *rasa*-s, or aesthetic 'tastes'.

John N. Sheveland, PhD, received his doctoral degree in Systematic and Comparative Theology at Boston College and is currently Assistant Professor of Religious Studies at Gonzaga University, Spokane, WA. His teaching and research interests fall on Christian–Hindu and Christian–Buddhist comparisons, comparative theological anthropologies, and on comparative theological responses to religious militancy.

Tracy Sayuki Tiemeier is Assistant Professor of Theological Studies at Loyola Marymount University in Los Angeles, CA. Completing her PhD in Systematic Theology (minor in Comparative Theology) at Boston College in 2006, Tracy's teaching and research interests bring together Asian and Asian American theologies with comparative theologies. She is also co-chair of the Los Angeles Hindu–Catholic Dialogue.

Name Index

Thematic Index